# LORD
# BEACONSFIELD

*He was a man, take him for all in all,*
*We shall not look upon his like again*

Hamlet, Act 1, Scene 2

# LORD
# BEACONSFIELD

## J. A. FROUDE

NONSUCH

First published 1890
Copyright © in this edition Nonsuch Publishing, 2007

Nonsuch Publishing
Cirencester Road, Chalford, Stroud, Gloucestershire, GL6 8PE
www.nonsuch-publishing.com

Nonsuch Publishing is an imprint of NPI Media Group

British Library Cataloguing in Publication Data.
A catalogue record for this book is available from the British Library.

ISBN 978 1 84588 605 9

Typesetting and origination by NPI Media Group
Printed in Great Britain

# Contents

# Introduction to the Modern Edition

B ENJAMIN DISRAELI (1804–1881) WAS one of the most important political figures of the nineteenth century. During his long and distinguished
career he was an M.P., Leader of the Opposition, Chancellor of the Exchequer
and Prime Minister twice. During his seven years in this last office he initi-
ated a wide range of legislation to improve educational opportunities and the
lives of working people, and as an historical figure he is best remembered for
the lasting impact he had upon British politics.

Disraeli was born into a middle-class London neighbourhood on 21
December 1804. He was the eldest son and second of five children born to
an Italian father, Isaac D'Israeli, and his wife, Maria Besavi. Although the
family was of Jewish descent, his father decided to break with Judaism following quarrels with his synagogue, and his children were instead baptised
into the Church of England. This fortuitous event was to have unforeseen
consequences for Disraeli: without it his political career would never have
happened, as Jews were excluded from serving in Parliament until 1858.
Despite this, Disraeli maintained a broad interest in a variety of different
religions throughout his life—taking much spiritual value from his Jewish
heritage in particular.

He went to school in London until the age of sixteen, and was then educated at home. Here he was surrounded by literary influences: the family
home boasted an extensive library, and his father was a noted author and
critic in his own right. Isaac D'Israeli hoped to encourage his son in an inter-

est in the law, and succeeded in having him articled to a firm of solicitors in the City in 1821. He was later admitted to Lincoln's Inn in 1827, although by this time his ambitions had taken a very different course. Law took a decided back seat, and Disraeli began to show a keen interest in both politics and writing. He made his first attempt at entering the literary world in 1825, when he and publisher John Murray together founded a daily newspaper called *The Representative*. This venture proved unsuccessful, and just a few months later a lack of capital investment dealt it its death blow. However, by 1826 Disraeli had managed to write his first novel, albeit under an assumed name, and upon publication *Vivien Grey* became a bestseller.

The exposure of the book's true origin seemed, initially, to spell disaster for Disraeli. The novel had bitingly satirised John Murray, amongst others, and, despite the fictional names assigned to the characters, it was all too clear to the world who they were intended to depict. He managed to offend many, not only for this but for daring to write so knowingly of the manners of upper-class society, while himself being merely middle class and of Jewish descent, and he faced bitter criticism from figures on the London literary scene. Fortunately, the damage was not permanent, and through his connection with fellow novelist Edward Bulwer-Lytton, as well as his entertainingly flamboyant behaviour, he gained access to that very world which had initially spurned him. He soon published two more successful novels, and was well on his way to establishing his own place in the literary world. In 1830 he gave up law altogether and travelled around Europe and the Near East, always soaking up the places and cultures he discovered for later use in his writing. On his return to England writing formally became his sole profession, while his interest in politics began to strengthen and develop.

Elected to Parliament in 1837, Disraeli gave his maiden speech on 7 December, speaking upon Irish elections. This was something of a disaster— he was shouted down and ridiculed, although he defiantly pronounced that 'the time will come when you will hear me', which was of course true.  In 1839 a significant event occurred in Disraeli's life which involved neither politics nor literature: he got married. His wife, Mary Anne Wyndham Lewis, was the widow of Wyndham Lewis (the author, painter and co-founder of the Vorticist movement) and twelve years his senior. Gossip circulated that he married her for her money, but their long and happy marriage proved there was no doubt of the devotion they had for one another. She was a consistent source of support in both his literary and political careers, and as a reward for Disraeli's services to the nation the Queen made Mary Anne a peeress in her own right, Viscountess Beaconsfield, years before her husband accepted a peerage. In 1841 Sir Robert Peel became Prime Minister, and Disraeli M.P. for Shrewsbury. He wrote to Peel asking for government office but this was refused; he subsequently attached himself to what was known as the 'Young England' group, and soon became it leader. This group sought a new direction for the Tory party—focusing on the preservation of the monarchy and privileged classes, coupled with a great compassion for the poor. Disraeli continued to write novels during this period, all of which reflected the aims and tenets he was pursuing in his political career, as well as demonstrating the biographical nature of his writing. *Coningsby* (1844) was one of a trio of books written in the 1840s that were deeply infused with his political philosophy, with the particular message that the future depended upon the idealism of young politicians, rather than the complacency of the old. It was followed by *Sybil* (1845) and *Tancred* (1847), and it was this series of works that best display the youthful idealism he had at this stage. Later works matured to show more humanitarian ideals, whereas his early works were overwhelmingly influenced by Romanticism. Although Disraeli is less well known for his literary achievements than for his political ones, his novels certainly hold a value of their own. He had a knack for skilfully depicting the aristocratic fashions and mores of the day—despite the fact he himself grew up in a middle-class family—and his books therefore contain an important source of social commentary, as well as displaying elements of stylistic skill.

Although the 'Young England' group disbanded in 1844, Disraeli continued to harbour resentment for Peel for failing to offer him a place in the Cabinet, and also to disagree with him over much of his policy. His feelings were finally given expression in 1845 when Disraeli attacked Peel for disregarding the views of the Conservatives in Parliament who opposed the repeal of the Corn Laws, eventually forcing the resignation of Peel's administration in June 1846. Disraeli finally achieved his place in government in 1852 under the Earl of Derby, as Leader of the House of Commons and Chancellor of the Exchequer. He lost this position when the government resigned and Viscount Palmerston became Prime Minister, marking the opening of parliamentary conflict between the two men. Disraeli regained the office of Chancellor during Derby's second ministry, but this was marked by the failure of a Reform Bill that was defeated by the Liberals, and it was following Disraeli's success in putting the Reform Bill to Parliament for the second time in 1867 that he was asked by the Queen to form his first ministry, at which he remarked, 'I have climbed to the top of the greasy pole'. They soon struck up an unusual rapport thanks to Disraeli's characteristic charm and flattery.

Disraeli had thus achieved his life's ambition, but it was not to last long, as he was defeated by the Liberals at the next election, throwing his position as Conservative leader into jeopardy. The death of his wife soon after was a further blow, as he said at the time, 'I am totally unable to meet the catastrophe'. He did, nevertheless, persevere, and thus began what was Britain's most famous parliamentary rivalry: Disraeli *versus* Gladstone. In the 1874 general election the Tories were victorious and Disraeli formed his second ministry, aged seventy, in which he introduced a large amount of social legislation. This ranged from the 1875 Artisans' & Labourers' Dwellings Improvement Act, which allowed local authorities to destroy slums and provide housing for the poor, to the Public Health Act of the same year, which provided sanitation such as running water and refuse disposal. Disraeli was created Earl of Beaconsfield by Queen Victoria in 1879, and thus governed from the House of Lords. The last few years of his ministry were characterised by foreign affairs, over which he was attacked by Gladstone for his policy of supprting the Ottoman Empire against Russian expansion. In 1880 the general election was lost to the Liberals, and although Disraeli threw himself into the job of opposition, he died on 19 April 1881 from bronchitis.

# I

*Carlyle on Lord Beaconsfield—Judgment of the House of Commons—Family History—The Jews in Spain—Migration to Venice—Benjamin D'Israeli the Elder—Boyhood of Isaac Disraeli*

C ARLYLE, SPEAKING TO ME MANY years ago of parliamentary government as he had observed the working of it in this country, said that under this system not the fittest men were chosen to administer our affairs, but the 'unfittest.' The subject of the present memoir was scornfully mentioned as an illustration; yet Carlyle seldom passed a sweeping censure upon any man without pausing to correct himself. 'Well, well, poor fellow,' he added, 'I dare say if we knew all about him we should have to think differently.' I do not know that he ever did try to think differently. His disposition to a milder judgment, if he entertained such a disposition, was scattered by the Reform Bill of 1867, which Carlyle regarded as the suicide of the English nation. In his 'Shooting Niagara' he recorded his own verdict on that measure and the author of it.

For a generation past it has been growing more and more evident that there was only this issue; but now the issue itself has become imminent, the distance of it to be guessed by years. Traitorous politicians grasping at votes, even votes from the rabble, have brought it on. One cannot but consider them traitorous; and for one's own poor share would rather have been shot than have been concerned in it. And yet, after all my silent indignation and disgust, I cannot pretend to be clearly sorry that such a consummation is expedited. I say to myself, Well, perhaps the sooner such a mass of hypocrisies, universal mismanagements, and brutal platitudes and infidelities ends, if not in some improvement then in death and *finis*, may it not be the better? The sum of our sins increasing steadily day by day will at least be less the sooner the settlement is. Nay, have I not a kind of secret satisfaction of the malicious or even of the judiciary kind (*Schadenfreude,* "mischief joy," the Germans call it, but really it is "justice joy" withal) that he they call Dizzy is to do it; that other jugglers of an unconscious and deeper type, having sold their poor mother's body for a mess of official pottage, this clever, conscious juggler steps in? "Soft, you my honourable friends: *I* will weigh out the corpse of your mother—mother of mine she never was, but only step-mother and milch cow—and you shan't have the pottage—not yours you observe, but mine." This really is a pleasing trait of its sort; other traits there are abundantly ludicrous, but they are too lugubrious even to be momentarily pleasant. A superlative Hebrew conjuror spell-binding all the great lords, great parties, great interests of England to his hand in this manner, and leading them by the nose like helpless mesmerised somnambulist cattle to such issue! Did the world ever see a *flebile ludibrium* of such magnitude before? Lath-sword and scissors of Destiny, Pickle-herring and the three *Parcae* alike busy in it. This too I suppose we had deserved; the end of our poor old England (such an England as we had at last made of it) to be not a fearful tragedy, but an ignominious farce as well.'

The consequences of the precipitation over the cataract not being imme-diate, and Government still continuing, over which a juggler of some kind must necessarily preside, Carlyle, though hope had forsaken him, retained his preference for the conscious over the unconscious. He had a faint pleasure in Disraeli's accession to power in 1874. He was even anxious that I should myself accept a proposal of a seat in Parliament which had been made to me, as a *quasi* follower of Disraeli—not that he trusted him any better, but he thought him preferable to a worse alternative. He was touched with some compunction for what he had written when Disraeli acknowledged Carlyle's supremacy as a man of letters—offered him rank and honours and money, and offered them in terms as flattering as his own proudest estimate of him-self could have dictated. Accept such offers Carlyle could not; but he was affected by the recognition that of all English ministers the Hebrew conjuror should have been the only one who had acknowledged his services to his country, and although he disapproved and denounced Disraeli's policy in the East he did perceive that there might be qualities in the man to which he had not done perfect justice.

However that may be, Disraeli was a child of Parliament. It was Parliament and the confidence of Parliament which gave him his place in the State. For forty years he was in the front of all the battles which were fought in the House of Commons, in opposition or in office, in adversity or in success, in conflict and competition with the most famous debaters of the age. In the teeth of prejudice, without support save in his own force of character, without the advantage of being the representative of any popular cause which appealed to the imagination, he fought his way till the consent of Parliament and country raised him to the Premiership.

Extraordinary qualities of some kind he must have possessed. No horse could win in such a race who had not blood and bone and sinew. Whether he was fit or unfit to govern England, the House of Commons chose him as their best; and if he was the charlatan which in some quarters he is supposed to have been, the Parliament which in so many years failed to detect his unworthiness is itself unfit to be trusted with the nation's welfare. He was not borne into power on the tide of any outside movement. He was not the advocate of any favourite measure with which his name was identified. He rose by his personal qualifications alone, and in studying what those qualifications were we are studying the character of Parliament itself.

The prophets who spoke of the dispersion of the Jews as a penalty for their sins described a phenomenon which probably preceded the Captivity. Through Tyre the Hebrew race had a road open through which they could spread along the shores of the Mediterranean. There was a colony of them in Rome in the time of Cicero. In Carthage they were among a people who spoke their own language. It is likely that they accompanied the Carthaginians in their conquests and commercial enterprises, and were thus introduced into Spain, where a Jewish community undoubtedly existed in St. Paul's time, and where it survived through all changes in the fortunes of the Peninsula. Under the Arabs the Jews of Spain preserved undisturbed their peculiar characteristics. As the crescent waned before the cross they intermarried with Christian families, and conformed outwardly with the established faith while they retained in secret their own ceremonies.

The Jewish people, says Isaac Disraeli in his *Genius of Judaism*, are not a nation, for they consist of many nations. They are Spanish or Portuguese, German or Polish, and, like the chameleon, they reflect the colours of the spot they rest on. The people of Israel are like water running through vast countries, tinged in their course with all varieties of the soil where they deposit themselves. Every native Jew as a political being becomes distinct from other Jews. The Hebrew adopts the hostilities and the alliances of the land where he was born. He calls himself by the name of his country. Under all these political varieties the Jew of the Middle Ages endeavoured to preserve his inward peculiarities. In England, in France, in Germany, in Italy, he enjoyed for the sake of his wealth a fitful toleration, with intervals of furious persecution.

From England he was expelled at the beginning of the fourteenth century, and his property was confiscated to the State. In crusading Spain he had not ventured to practise his creed in the open day, and thus escaped more easily. He was unmolested as long as he professed a nominal Christianity. He was wealthy, he was ingenious, he was enterprising. In his half-transparent disguise he intermarried with the proudest Castilian breeds. He took service under the State, and rose to the highest positions, even in the Church itself. A Jew who had not ceased to be a Jew in secret became Primate of Spain, and when the crowns of Castile and Aragon became united it was reckoned that there was scarcely a noble family in the two realms pure from intermixture of Jewish blood. His prosperity was the cause of his ruin. The kingdom of Granada fell at last before Ferdinand and Isabella, and the Church of Spain addressed itself, in gratitude to Providence, to the purifying of the Peninsula from the unholy presence of the wealthy unbeliever.

The Jews who were willing to break completely with their religious associations remained undisturbed. The Inquisition undertook the clearance of the rest, and set to work with characteristic vigour. Rank was no protection. The highest nobles were among the first who were called for examination before Torquemada's tribunal. Tens of thousands of the 'new Christians' who were convicted of having practised the rites of their own religion after outward conformity with Christianity, were burnt at the stake as 'relapsed.' Those who could escape fled to other countries where a less violent bigotry would allow them a home. Venice was the least intolerant. Venice lived upon its commerce, and the Jews there, as always, were the shrewdest traders in the world. The Venetian aristocrats might treat them as social pariahs, rate them on the Rialto, and spit upon their gabardines, but they had ducats, and their ducats secured them the protection of the law.

Among those who thus sought and found the hospitality of the Adriatic republic at the end of the fifteenth century was a family allied with the house of Lara, and perhaps entitled to bear its name. They preferred, however, to break entirely their connection with the country which had cast them off. They called themselves simply D'Israeli, or Sons of Israel, a name, says Lord Beaconsfield, never borne before or since by any other family, in order that their race might be for ever recognised. At Venice they lived and throve, and made money for two hundred years. Towards the middle of the last century, when Venice was losing her commercial pre-eminence, they began to turn their eyes elsewhere. Very many of their countrymen were already doing well in Holland. England was again open to them. Jews were still under some disabilities there, but they were in no danger of being torn by horses in the streets under charge of eating children at their Passover. They could follow their business and enjoy the fruits of it; and the head of the Venetian house decided that his second son, Benjamin, 'the child of his right hand,' should try his fortune in London. The Disraelis retained something of their Spanish pride, and did not like to be confounded with the lower grades of Hebrews whom they found already established there. The young Benjamin was but eighteen when he came over; he took root and prospered, but he followed a line of his own and never cordially or intimately mixed with the Jewish community, and the tendency to alienation was increased by his marriage.

'My grandfather,' wrote Lord Beaconsfield, 'was a man of ardent character, sanguine, courageous, speculative, and fortunate; with a temper which no disappointment could disturb and a brain full of resources.' He made a fortune, he married a beautiful woman of the same religion as his own and whose family had suffered equally from persecution. The lady was ambitious of social distinction, and she resented upon her unfortunate race the slights and disappointments to which it exposed her. Her husband took it more easily. He was rich. He had a country house at Enfield, where he entertained his friends, played whist, and enjoyed himself, 'notwithstanding a wife who never pardoned him his name.' So successful he had been that he saw his way to founding a house which might have been a power in Europe. But the more splendid his position the more bitter would have been his wife's feelings. He retired therefore early from the field, contented with the wealth which he had acquired. Perhaps his resolution was precipitated by the character of the son who was the only issue of his marriage. Isaac Disraeli was intended for the heir of business, and Isaac showed from the first a determined disinclination for business of any sort or kind. 'Nature had disqualified the child from his cradle for the busy pursuits of men.' 'He grew up beneath a roof of worldly energy and enjoyment, indicating that he was of a different order from those with whom he lived.' Neither his father nor his mother understood him. To one he was 'an enigma,' to the other 'a provocation.' His dreamy, wandering eyes were hopelessly unpractical. His mother was irritated because she could not rouse him into energy. He grew on 'to the mournful period of boyhood, when eccentricities excite attention and command no sympathy.' Mrs Disraeli was exasperated when she ought to have been gentle. Her Isaac was 'the last drop in her cup of bitterness, and only served to swell the aggregate of many humiliating particulars.' She grew so embittered over her grievances that Lord Beaconsfield says 'she lived till eighty without indulging a tender expression;' and must have been an unpleasant figure in her grandson's childish recollections. The father did his best to keep the peace, but had nothing to offer but good-natured common-places. Isaac at last ran away from home, and was brought back after being found lying on a tombstone in Hackney Churchyard. His father 'embraced him, gave him a pony,' and sent him to a day school, where he had temporary peace. But the reproaches and upbraidings recommenced when he returned in the evenings. To crown all, Isaac was delivered of a poem, and for the first time the head of the family was seriously alarmed. Hitherto he had supposed that boys would be boys, and their follies ought not to be too seriously noticed; but a poem was a more dangerous symptom; 'the loss of his argosies could not have filled him with a more blank dismay.'

The too imaginative youth was despatched to a counting-house in Holland. His father went occasionally to see him, but left him for several years to drudge over ledgers without once coming home, in the hope that in this way, if in no other, the evil spirit might be exorcised. Had it been necessary for Isaac Disraeli to earn his own bread the experiment might have succeeded. His nature was gentle and amiable, and though he could not be driven he might have been led. But he knew that he was the only child of a wealthy parent. Why should he do violence to his disposition and make himself unnecessarily miserable? Instead of book-keeping he read Bayle and Voltaire. He was swept into Rousseauism and imagined himself another Emile. When recalled home at last the boy had become a young man. He had pictured to himself a passionate scene in which he was to fly into his mother's arms, and their hearts were to rush together in tears of a recovered affection. 'When he entered, his strange appearance, his gaunt figure, his excited manner, his long hair, and his unfashionable costume only filled her with a sentiment of tender aversion. She broke into derisive laughter, and noticing his intolerable garments reluctantly lent him her cheek.' The result, of course, was a renewal of household misery. His father assured him that his parents desired only to make him happy, and proposed to establish him in business at Bordeaux. He replied that he had written another poem against commerce, 'which was the corruption of man,' and that he meant to publish it. What was to be done with such a lad? 'With a home that ought to have been happy,' says Lord Beaconsfield, 'surrounded with more than comfort, with the most good-natured father in the world and an agreeable man, and with a mother whose strong intellect under ordinary circumstances might have been of great importance to him, my father, though himself of a very sweet disposition, was most unhappy.' To keep him at home was worse than useless. He was sent abroad again, but on his own terms. He went to Paris, made literary acquaintance, studied in libraries, and remained till the eve of the Revolution amidst the intellectual and social excitement which preceded the general convulsion. But his better sense rebelled against the Rousseau enthusiasm. Paris ceasing to be a safe residence, he came home once more, recovered from the dangerous form of his disorder, 'with some knowledge of the world and much of books.'

His aversion to the counting-house was, however, as pronounced as ever. Benjamin Disraeli resigned himself to the inevitable—wound up his affairs and retired, as has been said, upon the fortune which he had realised. Isaac, assured of independence, if not of great wealth, went his own way; published a satire, which the old man over-lived without a catastrophe, and entered the literary world of London. Before he was thirty he brought out his *Curiosities of Literature*, which stepped at once into popularity and gave him a name. He wrote verses which were pretty and graceful, verses which were read and remembered by Sir Walter Scott, and were at least better than his son's. But he was too modest to overrate their value. He knew that poetry, unless it be the best of its kind, is better unproduced, and withdrew within the limits where he was conscious that he could excel. 'The poetical temperament was not thrown away upon him. Because he was a poet he was a popular writer, and made *belles-lettres* charming to the multitude ... His destiny was to give his country a series of works illustrative of its literary and political history, full of new information and new views which time has ratified as just.'

# II

*Family of Isaac Disraeli—Life in London—Birth of his children—Abandons Judaism and joins the Church of England—Education of Benjamin Disraeli—School days—Picture of them in* Vivian Grey *and* Contarini Fleming—*Self-education at home—Early ambition*

I SAAC DISRAELI, HAVING THE ADVANTAGE of a good fortune, escaped the embarrassments which attend a struggling literary career. His circumstances were easy. He became intimate with distinguished men; and his experiences in Paris had widened and liberalised his mind. His creed sate light upon him, but as long as his father lived he remained nominally in the communion in which he was born. He married happily a Jewish lady, Maria, daughter of Mr George Basevi, of Brighton, a gentle, sweet-tempered, affectionate woman. To her he relinquished the management of his worldly affairs, and divided his time between his own splendid library, the shops of book collectors or the British Museum, and the brilliant society of politicians and men of letters. His domestic life was unruffled by the storms which had disturbed his boyhood; a household more affectionately united was scarcely to be found within the four seas. Four children were born to him—the eldest a daughter, Sarah, whose gifts and accomplishments would have raised her, had she been a man, into fame; Benjamin, the Prime Minister that was to be, and two other boys, Ralph and James. They lived in London, but changed their residence more than once. At the outset of their married life they had chambers in the Adelphi. From thence they removed to the King's Road, Gray's Inn, and there, on December 21, 1804, Benjamin was born. He was received into the Jewish Church with the usual rites, the record of the initiation being preserved in the register of the Spanish and Portuguese synagogue Bevis Marks. No soothsayer having foretold his future eminence, he was left to grow up much like other children. He was his mother's darling, and was spoilt. He was unruly, and a noisy boy at home perhaps disturbed his father's serenity. At an early age it was decided that he must go to school, but where it was not easy to decide. English boys were rough and prejudiced, and a Jewish lad would be likely to have a hard time among them. No friend of Isaac Disraeli, who knew what English public schools were then like, would have recommended him to commit his lad to the rude treatment which he would encounter at Eton or Winchester. A private establishment of a smaller kind had to be tried as preliminary.

Disraeli's first introduction to life was at a Mr Poticary s, at Blackheath, where he remained for several years—till he was too old to be left there, and till a very considerable change took place in the circumstances of the family. In 1817 the grandfather died. Isaac Disraeli succeeded to his fortune, removed from Gray's Inn Road, and took a larger house—No 6 Bloomsbury Square, then a favourite situation for leading lawyers and men of business. A more important step was his formal withdrawal from the Jewish congregation. The reasons for it, as given by himself in his *Genius of Judaism*, were the narrowness of the system, the insistence that the Law was of perpetual obligation, while circumstances changed and laws failed of their objects. 'The inventions,' he says, 'of the Talmudical doctors, incorporated in their ceremonies, have bound them hand and foot, and cast them into the caverns of the lone and sullen genius of rabbinical Judaism, cutting them off from the great family of mankind and perpetuating their sorrow and their shame.' The explanation is sufficient, but the resolution was probably of older date. The coincidence between the date of his father's death and his own secession points to a connection between the two events. His mother's impatience of her Jewish fetters must naturally have left a mark on his mind, and having no belief himself in the system, he must have wished to relieve his children of the disabilities and inconveniences which attached to them as members of the synagogue. At all events at this period he followed the example of his Spanish ancestors in merging himself and them in the general population of his adopted country. The entire household became members of the Church of England. The children read their Prayer Books and learned their catechisms. On July 31 in that year Benjamin Disraeli was baptised at St. Andrew's Church, Holborn, having for his godfather his father's intimate friend the distinguished Sharon Turner.

The education problem was thus simplified, but not entirely solved. The instruction at Mr Poticary's was indifferent. 'Ben' had learnt little there. The

Latin and Greek were all behindhand, and of grammar, which in those days was taught tolerably effectively in good English schools, he had brought away next to nothing. But he was quick, clever, impetuous. At home he was surrounded with books, and had read for himself with miscellaneous voracity. In general knowledge and thought he was far beyond his age. His father's wish was to give him the best education possible—to send him to Eton, and then to a university. His mother believed that a public school was a place where boys were roasted alive. 'Ben' was strong and daring, and might be trusted to take care of himself. The objections, however, notwithstanding the removal of the religious difficulty, were still considerable. The character of a public school is more determined by the boys than by the masters. There were no institutions where prejudice had freer play at the beginning of the present century. The rationality of a Disraeli could neither be concealed nor forgotten, and though he might be called a Christian, and though he might be ready to return blow for blow if he was insulted or ill-used, it is not likely that at either one of our great public foundations he would have met with any tolerable reception. He would himself have willingly run the risk, and regretted afterwards, perhaps, that he had no share in the bright Eton life which he describes so vividly in *Coningsby*. It was decided otherwise. The school chosen for him was at Walthamstow. The master was a Dr Cogan, a Unitarian. There were many boys there, sons most of them of rich parents; but the society at a Unitarian school seventy years ago could not have been distinguished for birth or good breeding. Neither *Vivian Grey* nor *Contarini Fleming* can be trusted literally for autobiographical details; but Disraeli has identified himself with Contarini in assigning many of his own personal experiences, and Vivian has always been acknowledged as a portrait sketched from a lookingglass. In both these novels there are pictures of the hero's school days, so like in their general features that they may be taken as a fair account of Disraeli's own recollections. He was fifteen when he went to Walthamstow and was then beyond the age when most boys begin their school career.

'For the first time in my life,' says Contarini, 'I was surrounded by struggling and excited beings. Joy, hope, sorrow, ambition, craft, dullness, courage, cowardice, beneficence, awkwardness, grace, avarice, generosity, wealth, poverty, beauty, hideousness, tyranny, suffering, hypocrisy, tricks, love, hatred, energy, inertness, they were all there and sounded and moved and acted about me. Light laughs and bitter cries and deep imprecations, and the deeds of the friendly, the prodigal, and the tyrant, the exploits of the brave, the graceful, and the gay, and the flying words of native wit and the pompous sentences of acquired knowledge, how new, how exciting, how wonderful!'

Contarini is Disraeli thus launched into a school epitome of the world after the Unitarian pattern. It was a poor substitute for Eton. The young Disraeli soon asserted his superiority. He made enemies, he made friends, at all events he distinguished himself from his comrades. School work did not interest him, and he paid but slight attention to it. He wanted ideas, and he was given what seemed to him to be but words. He lost the opportunity of becoming an exact scholar. On the other hand in thought, in imagination, in general attainments, he was superior to everyone about him, masters included. Superiority begets jealousy. Boys never pardon a comrade who is unlike themselves. He was taunted with his birth, as it was inevitable that he would be. As inevitably he resented the insult. Contarini Fleming and Vivian Grey both fight and thrash the biggest boy in their school. The incident in the novels is evidently taken from the writer's experience. Disraeli was a fighter from his youth, with his fist first, as with his tongue afterwards. It was characteristic of him that he had studied the art of self-defence, and was easily able to protect himself. But both his heroes were unpopular, and it may be inferred that he was not popular any more than they. The school experiment was not a success and came to an abrupt end. Vivian Grey was expelled; Contarini left of his own accord, because he learnt nothing which he thought would be of use to him, and because he 'detested school more than he ever abhorred the world in the darkest moment of experienced manhood.' The precise circumstances under which Disraeli himself made his exit are not known to me, but his stay at Walthamstow was a brief one, and he left to complete his education at home. His father, recollecting the troubles of his own youth, abstained from rebukes or reproaches, left him to himself, helped him when he could, and now and then, if we may identify him with Vivian, gave him shrewd and useful advice. Disraeli wanted no spurring. He worked for twelve hours a day, conscious that he had singular powers and passionately ambitious to make use of them.He was absolutely free from the loose habits so common in the years between boyhood and youth; his father had no fault to find with his conduct, which he admitted had been absolutely correct. The anxiety was of another kind. He did not wish to interfere with his son's direction of himself, warned him, very wisely, 'not to consider himself a peculiar boy.' 'Take the advice,' said Mr Grey to Vivian, 'of one who has committed as many—aye, more—follies than yourself. Try to ascertain what may be the chief objects of our existence in this world. I want you to take no theological dogmas for granted, nor to satisfy your doubts by ceasing to think; but whether we are in this world in a state of probation for another, or whether at death we cease altogether, human feelings tell me that we have some duties to perform to our fellow-creatures, to our friends, and to ourselves.'

Disraeli's conception of himself was that he had it in him to be a great man, and that the end of his existence was to make himself a great man. With his father's example before him literature appeared the readiest road. Contarini when a boy wrote romances and threw them into the river, and composed pages of satire or sentiment 'and grew intoxicated with his own eloquence.' He pondered over the music of language, studied the cultivation of sweet words, and constructed elaborate sentences in lonely walks, and passed his days in constant struggle to qualify himself for the part which he was determined to play in the game of life. Boyish pursuits and amusements had no interest for him. In athletic games he excelled if he chose to exert himself, but he rarely did choose unless it was in the science of self-defence. He rode well and hard, for the motion stimulated his spirits; but in galloping across the country he was charging in imagination the brooks and fences in the way of his more ambitious career.

This was one side of him in those early years; another was equally remarkable. He intended to excel among his fellow-creatures, and to understand what men and women were like was as important to him as to understand books. The reputation of Vivian Grey's father—in other words, his own father—had always made him an honoured guest in the great world. For this reason he had been anxious that his son should be as little at home as possible, for he feared for a youth the fascination of London society. This particular Society was what Disraeli was most anxious to study, and was in less danger from it than his father fancied. He was handsome, audacious, and readily made his way into the circle of the family acquaintance 'Contarini was a graceful, lively lad, with enough of dandyism to prevent him from committing *gaucheries*, and with a devil of a tongue.' 'He was never at a loss for a compliment or a repartee,' and 'was absolutely unchecked by foolish modesty.' 'The nervous vapidity of my first rattle,' says the *alter ego* Vivian, 'soon subsided into a continuous flow of easy nonsense. Impertinent and flippant, I was universally hailed as an original and a wit. I became one of the most affected, conceited, and intolerable atoms that ever peopled the sunbeam of Society.' The purpose which lay behind Disraeli's frivolous outside was as little suspected by those who saw him in the world as the energy with which he was always working in his laborious hours. The stripling of seventeen was the same person as the statesman of seventy, with this difference only, that the affectation which was natural in the boy was itself affected in the matured politician, whom it served well as a mask or as a suit of impenetrable armour.

# III

In the neighbourhood of the square in which the Disraelis now resided there lived a family named Austen, with whom the young Benjamin became closely intimate. Mr Austen was a solicitor in large practice; his wife was the daughter of a Northamptonshire country gentleman—still beautiful, though she had been for some years married, a brilliant conversationalist, a fine musician, and an amateur artist of considerable power. The house of this lady was the gathering-place of the young men of talent of the age. She early recognised the unusual character of her friend's boy. She invited him to her salons, talked to him, advised and helped him. A writer in the *Quarterly Review* (January 1889), apparently a connection of the Austens, remembers having been taken by them as a child to call on the Disraelis. 'Ben,' then perhaps a school-boy returned for the holidays, was sent for, and appeared in his shirt-sleeves with 'boxing gloves.' His future destination was still uncertain. Isaac Disraeli, who had no great belief in youthful genius, disencouraged his literary ambition, and was anxious to see him travelling along one of the beaten roads. Mr Austen was probably of the same opinion. 'Ben's' own views on this momentous subject are not likely to have been much caricatured in the meditations of Vivian Grey.

'The Bar!—pooh! Law and bad jokes till we are forty, and then with the most brilliant success the prospect of gout and a coronet. Besides, to succeed as an advocate I must be a great lawyer, and to be a great lawyer I must give up my chances of being a great man. The "services" in war time are fit only for desperadoes (and that truly am I), and in peace are fit only for fools. The Church is more rational. I should certainly like to act Wolsey, but the thousand and one chances are against me, and my destiny should not be a chance.' Practical always Disraeli was, bent simply on making his way, and his way to a great position. No *ignes fatui* were likely to mislead him into spiritual morasses, no love-sick dreams to send him wandering after imaginary Paradises. He was as shrewd as he was ambitious, and he took an early measure of his special capabilities. 'Beware,' his father had said to him, 'of trying to be a great man in a hurry.' His weakness was impatience. He could not bear to wait. Byron had blazed like a new star at five-and-twenty; why not he? Pitt had been Prime Minister at a still earlier age, and of all young Disraeli's studies political history had been the most interesting to him. But to rise in politics he must get into Parliament, and the aristocrats who condescended to dine in Bloomsbury Square, and to laugh at his impertinence, were not likely to promise him a pocket borough. His father could not afford to buy him one, nor would have consented to squander money on so wild a prospect. He saw that to advance he must depend upon himself and must make his way into some financially inde-pendent position. While chafing at the necessity he rationally folded his wings, and on November 18, 1821, when just seventeen he was introduced into a solicitor's office in Old Jewry. Mr Maples, a member of the firm, was an old friend of Isaac Disraeli, and to Mr Maples's department 'Ben' was attached. Distasteful as the occupation must have been to him, he attached himself zealously to his work. He remained at his desk for three years, and Mr Maples described him as 'most assiduous in his attention to business, as showing great ability in the transaction of it,' and as likely, if allowed to go to the Bar, to attain to eminence there.

If the project had been carried out the anticipation would probably have been verified. The qualities which enabled Disraeli to rise in the House of Commons would have lifted him as surely, and perhaps as rapidly, into the high places of the profession. He might have entered Parliament with greater facility and with firmer ground under his feet. He acquiesced in his father's wishes; he was entered at Lincoln's Inn, and apparently intended to pursue a legal career; but the Fates or his own adventurousness ordered his fortunes otherwise. His work in the office had not interfered with his social engagements. He met distinguished people at his father's table—Wilson Croker, then Secretary to the Admiralty; Samuel Rogers; John Murray, the proprietor of the *Quarterly Review*, and others of Murray's brilliant contributors. The Catholic question was stirring. There were rumours of Reform, and the political atmosphere was growing hot. Disraeli observed, listened, took the measure of these men, and thought he was as good as any of them. He began to write in the newspapers. The experienced Mr Murray took notice of him as a person of whom something considerable might be made. These acquaintances enabled him to extend his knowledge of the world, which began to shape itself into form and figure. To understand the serious side of things requires a matured faculty. The ridiculous is caught more easily. With Mrs Austen for an adviser, and perhaps with her assistance, he composed a book which, however absurd in its plot and glaring in its affectation, revealed at once that, a new writer had started into being, who would make his mark on men and things. That a solicitor's clerk of twenty should be able to produce *Vivian Grey* is not, perhaps, more astonishing than that Dickens, at little more than the same age, should have written *Pickwick*. All depends on the eye. Most of us encounter every day materials for a comedy if we could only see them. But genius is wanted for it, and the thing, when accomplished, proves that genius has been at work.

The motto of Vivian Grey was sufficiently impudent:

Why, then, the world's mine oyster,
Which with my sword I'll open.

The central figure is the author himself caricaturing his own impertinence and bringing on his head deserved retribution; but the sarcasm, the strength of hand, the audacious personalities caught the attention of the public, and gave him at once the notoriety which he desired. *Vivian* was the book of the season; everyone read it, everyone talked about it, and keys were published of the characters who were satirised. Disraeli, like Byron, went to sleep a nameless youth of twenty-one and woke to find himself famous.

A successful novel may be gratifying to vanity, but it is a bad introduction to a learned profession. Attorneys prefer barristers who stick to business and do not expatiate into literature. A single fault might be overlooked, and *Vivian Grey* be forgotten before its author could put on his wig, but a more serious cause interrupted his legal progress. He was overtaken by a singular disorder, which disabled him from serious work. He had fits of giddiness, which he described as like a consciousness of the earth's rotation. Once he fell into a trance, from which he did not completely recover for a week. He was recommended to travel, and the Austens took him abroad with them for a summer tour. They went to Paris, to Switzerland, to Milan, Venice, Florence, Geneva, and back over Mont Cenis into France. His health became better, but was not re-established, and he returned to his family still an invalid.

The 'law' was postponed, but not yet abandoned. In a letter to his father, written in 1832, he spoke of his illness as having robbed him of five years of life; as if this, and this alone, had prevented him from going on with his profession. Meanwhile there was a complete change in the outward circumstances of the Disraeli household. Isaac Disraeli, who had the confirmed habits of a Londoner, whose days had been spent in libraries and his evenings in literary society, for some reason or other chose to alter the entire character of his existence. Like Ferrars in 'Endymion,' though not for the same cause, he tore himself away from all his associations and withdrew with his wife and children to an old manor house in Buckinghamshire, two miles from High Wycombe. Bradenham, their new home, is exactly described in the account which Disraeli gives of the Ferrars's place of retirement; and perhaps their first arrival there and their gipsy-like encampment in the old hall, the sense, half-realised, that they were being taken away from all their interests and associations, may equally have been drawn from memory. The Disraelis, however, contrived happily enough to fit themselves to their new existence. Disraeli all through his life delighted in the country and country scenes. The dilapidated manor house was large and picturesque. The land round it was open down, or covered thinly with scrub and woods. They had horses and could gallop where they pleased. They had their dogs and their farmyard; they made new friends among the tenantry and the labourers. Disraeli's head continued to trouble him, but the air and the hills gave him his best chance of recovery. His father, contented with an occasional lecture, left him to himself. He was devoted to his mother and passionately attached to his sister. Altogether nothing could be calmer, nothing more affectionately peaceful than the two or three years which he passed at Bradenham after this migration. Though he could not study in London chambers, he could read and he could write, and over his writing he worked indefatigably, if not with great success. He added a second part to *Vivian Grey*. Clever it could not help being, but it had not the flavour of the first. He wrote the *Young Duke*, a flashy picture of high society which might have passed muster as the ephemeral production of an ordinary novelist. Neither of these, however, indicated any literary advance, nor did he himself attach any value to them. In a happier interval, perhaps, when he had a respite from his headaches, he threw off three light satires, which, with one exception, are the most brilliant of all his productions. *Ixion in Heaven* is taken from the story of the King of Thessaly who was carried to Olympus and fell in love with the queen of the gods. Disraeli's classical knowledge probably went no farther than *Lemprière's Dictionary*, but Lemprière gave him all that he wanted. The form and tone are like Lucian's, and the execution almost as good. No characters in real life are more vivid than those which he draws of the high-bred divinities at the court of the Father of the gods, while the Father himself is George IV, Apollo Byron, and the ladies well-known ornaments of the circles of the Olympians of May Fair.

Equally good is the *Infernal Marriage*, the rape of Proserpine and her adventures in her dominions below. The wit which we never miss in Disraeli rises here into humour which is rare with him, and a deeper current of thought can be traced when the Queen of Hell pays a visit to Elysium, finding there the few thousand families who spend their time in the splendid luxury of absolute idleness; high-born, graceful beings without a duty to perform, supported by the toil of a million gnomes, and after exhausting every form of amusement ready to perish of ennui.

The third fragment, written in these years, which Lord Beaconsfield included in his collected works (he probably wrote others which are lost in the quick-sands of keepsakes and annuals) was *Popanilla*, a satire on the English Constitution. He has changed his manner from Lucian's to Swift's. *Popanilla* might have been another venture of Mr Lemuel Gulliver if there had been malice in it. The satire of Swift is inspired by hatred and scorn of his race. The satire of Disraeli is pleasant, laughing, and good humoured. In all his life he never hated anybody or anything, never bore a grudge or remembered a libel against himself. Popanilla is a native of an unknown island in an unknown part of the Pacific, an island where modern civilisation had never penetrated and life was a round of ignorant and innocent enjoyment. In an evil hour a strange ship is wrecked upon the shore. A box of books is flung up upon the sands, books of useful knowledge intended for the amelioration of mankind, spiritual, social, moral, and political. Popanilla finds it, opens it, and with the help of these moral lights sets to work to regenerate his countrymen. He makes himself a nuisance, and is sent floating in a canoe which carries him to Vray Bleusia, or modern England. Being a novelty, he is enthusiastically welcomed, becomes a lion, and is introduced to the charms and wonders of complicated artificial society. The interest is in the light which is thrown on Disraeli's studies of English politics. The chapter on 'Fruit' is a humorously correct sketch of the

Anglican Church. Mr Flummery Flum represents political economy, and the picture of him betrays Disraeli's contempt for that once celebrated science, now relegated to the exterior planets. *Popanilla* can be still read with pleasure as a mere work of fancy. It has more serious value to the student of Disraeli's character. As a man of letters he shows at his best in writings of this kind. His interest in the life which he describes in his early novels was only superficial, and he could not give to others what he did not feel. In *Ixion*, in the *Infernal Marriage*, in *Popanilla* we have his real mind, and matter, style, and manner are equally admirable.

His future was still undetermined. His father continued eager to see him at the Bar, but his health remained delicate and his disinclination more and more decided; There was a thought of buying an estate for him and setting him up as a country gentleman. But to be a small squire was a poor object of ambition. He wished to travel, travel especially in the East, to which his semi-Asiatic temperament gave him a feeling of affinity. The Holy Land, as the seat of his own race, affected his imagination. He had a romantic side in his mind in a passion for Jerusalem. His intellect had been moulded by the sceptical philosophy of his fathers; but, let sceptics say what they would, a force which had gone out from Jerusalem had governed the fate of the modern world.

His desire, when he first made it known, was not encouraged. 'My wishes,' he said, 'were knocked on the head in a calmer manner than I could have expected from my somewhat rapid but too indulgent sire.' He lingered on at Bradenham till even his literary work had to end. He could not 'write a line without effort,' and he wandered aimlessly about the woods; 'solitude and silence' not making his existence easy, but at least tolerable.

The objection to his travelling had been perhaps financial. If this was the difficulty it was removed by his friends the Austens, who, we are briefly told, came to his assistance and enabled him to carry out his purpose. He found a companion ready to go with him in Mr William Meredith, a young man of talent and good fortune who was engaged to be married to his sister. They started in June 1830, and their adventures are related in a series of brilliant and charming letters to his family, letters which show the young Disraeli no longer in the mythological drapery of 'Grey' and 'Contarini Fleming,' but under his own hand as he actually was. Spain was their first object. The Disraelis retained their pride in their Spanish descent in a dim and distant fashion, and had not forgotten that in right of blood they were still Spanish nobles. Steam navigation was in its infancy, but small paddle-wheeled vessels ran from London to Cork and Dublin, touching at Falmouth, from which outward-bound ships took their departure. They reached Falmouth with no worse adventure than a rough passage, and Disraeli was flattered to find that the family fame had so far preceded him. He met a Dr Cornish there, who was full of admiration for *Vivian Grey*, 'knows my father's works by heart and thinks our revered sire the greatest man that ever lived.' From Gibraltar on July 1 he wrote to his father himself:

> The rock is a wonderful place, with a population infinitely diversified—Moors with costumes radiant as a rainbow in an Eastern melodrama, Jews with gabardines and skull caps, Genoese highlanders and Spaniards whose dress is as picturesque as those of the sons of Ivor … In the garrison are all your works, in the merchants' library the greater part. Each possesses the copy of another book supposed to be written by a member of our family which is looked upon at Gibraltar as one of the masterpieces of the nineteenth century. At first I apologised and talked of youthful blunders and all that, really being ashamed, but finding them, to my astonishment, sincere, and fearing they were stupid enough to adopt my last opinion, I shifted my position just in time, looked very grand, and passed myself off for a child of the sun, like the Spaniards in Peru.

Government House opened its hospitalities. Sir George D——, a proud, aristocratic, but vigorous old man, was not a person likely to find such a pair of travellers particularly welcome to him. Disraeli's affectations of dress and manner approached vulgarity, and Meredith, though a superior person, was equally absurd in this respect. But Disraeli, at any rate where he cared to please, never failed to make himself liked. Sir George was polite, Lady D. more than polite. Though she was old and infirm, 'her eyes were so brilliant and so full of *moquerie* that you forgot her wrinkles.' Of course they were welcome guests in the regimental mess rooms, clever young civilians who could talk and were men of the world being an agreeable change in the professional monotony, though perhaps the visitors mistook to some extent the impression which they produced.

'Tell my mother,' Disraeli wrote, 'that as it is the fashion among the dandies of this place (that is, the officers, for there are no others) not to wear waistcoats in the morning, her new studs come into fine play and maintain my reputation for being a great judge of costume, to the admiration and envy of many subalterns. I have also the fame of being the first who ever passed the Straits with two canes, a morning and an evening cane. I change my cane on the gun-fire and hope to carry them both on to Cairo.

It is wonderful the effect those magical wands produce. I owe to them even more attention than to being the supposed author of—what is it? I forget.'

With Gibraltar for head-quarters they made excursions into the Spanish territory; the first through the Sierra Nevada, on a route arranged for them by the governor. Travelling was dangerous, and accommodation no better than at Don Quixote's enchanted castle. The banditti were everywhere. Two Englishmen had just arrived from Cadiz whom José Maria had stopped and rifled on the way. The danger was exciting. They set out in the long hot days of July, taking a model valet with them. Brunet had been all over the world and spoke all languages except English. Their baggage was of the slightest, not to tempt José Maria, Disraeli confining himself to 'the red bag' which his mother had made for his pistols.

'We were picturesque enough in our appearance,' he wrote. 'Imagine M. and myself on two little Andalusian mountain horses with long tails and jennet necks, followed by a large beast of burden, with Brunet in white hat and slippers, lively, shrivelled, and noisy as a pea dancing upon tin; our Spanish guide, tall and with a dress excessively *brodé* and covered with brilliant buttons, walking by the side. The air of the mountains, the rising sun, the rising appetite, the variety of picturesque persons and things we met, and the impending danger made a delightful life, and had it not been for the great enemy I should have given myself up entirely to the magic of the life. But that spoiled all. It is not worse. Sometimes I think it lighter about the head, but the palpitation about the heart greatly increases; otherwise my health is wonderful. Never have I been better. But what use is this when the end of all existence is debarred me? I say no more upon this melancholy subject, by which I am ever and infinitely depressed, and often most so when the world least imagines it. To complain is useless and to endure almost impossible.'

José Maria was in everyone's mouth, but the travellers did not fall in with him. After a week they were again enjoying the hospitalities of Gibraltar. The climate, the exercise, the novelty were all delightful. Disraeli was a child of the sun, as he often said of himself. His health mended and his spirits rose. He wore his hair in long curls. The women, he said, mistook it for a wig, and 'I was obliged to let them pull it to satisfy their curiosity.' The Judge Advocate buttonholed him. 'I found him a bore and vulgar. Consequently I gave him a lecture upon canes, which made him stare, and he has avoided me ever since.' But everyone liked Disraeli. 'Wherever I go,' he said, 'I find plenty of friends and plenty of attention.' He had not come to Spain to linger in a garrison town. The two friends were soon off again for a ride through Andalusia. Cadiz was enchanting with its white houses and green *jalousies* sparkling in the sun; 'Figaro in every street and Rosina in every balcony.' He saw a bull-fight; he was introduced to the Spanish authorities, and conducted himself with Vivian Grey-like impudence. 'Fleuriz, the governor of Cadiz,' he wrote, 'is a singular brute. The English complain that when they are presented to him he bows and says nothing. The consul announced me to him as the son of the greatest author in England; the usual reception, however, only greeted me. But I, being prepared for the savage, was by no means silent, and made him stare for half an hour in a most extraordinary manner. He was sitting over some prints just arrived from England—a view of Algiers and the fashions for June. The question was whether the place was Algiers, for it had no title. I ventured to inform his Excellency that it was, and that a group of gentlemen displaying their extraordinary coats and countenances were personages no less eminent than the Dey and his principal councillors of State. The dull Fleuriz, after due examination, insinuated scepticism, whereupon I offered renewed arguments to prove the dress to be Moorish. Fleuriz calls a young lady to translate the inscription, which proves only that they are fashions for June. I add at Algiers. Fleuriz, unable to comprehend badinage, gives a Mashallah look of pious resignation, and has bowed to the ground every night since that he has met me.'

After Cadiz Seville, and then Malaga. Brigands everywhere, but not caring to meddle with travellers who had so little with them worth plundering. Once only there was alarm. 'We saved ourselves by a moonlight scamper and a change of road.' An adventure, however, they had at Malaga which recalls Washington Irving's story of the inn at Terracina, with this difference, that Disraeli and his companion did not show the gallantry of Irving's English hero.

'I was invited,' he says, 'by a grand lady of Madrid to join her escort to Granada, twenty foot-soldiers armed, and *tirailleurs* in the shape of a dozen muleteers. We refused, for reasons too long to detail, and set off alone two hours before, expecting an assault. I should tell you we dined previously with her and her husband, having agreed to meet to discuss matters. It was a truly Gil Blas scene. My lord, in an undress uniform, slightly imposing in appearance, greeted us with dignity; the *señora* young and really very pretty, with infinite vivacity and grace. A French valet leant on his chair, and a *dueña* such as Staphenaff would draw, broad and supercilious, with jet eyes, mahogany complexion, and a cocked up nose, stood by my lady bearing a large fan. She was most complaisant, as she evidently had more confidence in two thick-headed Englishmen with their Purdeys and Mantons than in her specimens of the once famous Spanish infantry. She did not know that we were cowards upon principle. I could screw up my courage to a duel in a battle—but—'

In short, in spite of the lady's charms and their united eloquence, Disraeli and Meredith determined to start alone. They had learnt that a strong band of brigands were lying in wait for the noble pair. They took a cross road, lost their way, and slept with pack-saddles for pillows, but reached Granada without an interview with José. A fine description of Granada and Saracenic architecture was sent home from the spot. In return Disraeli requires his sister to 'tell him all about Bradenham—about dogs and horses, orchards, gardens; who calls, where you go, who my father sees in London, what is said.' 'This is what I want,' he writes; 'never mind public news. There is no place like Bradenham, and each moment I feel better I want to come back.'

Affectation, light-heartedness, and warm home feelings are strangely mixed in all this; and no one of his changing moods is what might be expected in a pilgrim to Jerusalem in search of spiritual light. But this was Disraeli—a character genuine and affectionate, whose fine gifts were veiled in foppery which itself was more than half assumed. His real serious feeling comes out prettily in a passage in which he sums up his Peninsular experiences. 'Spain is the country for adventure. A weak government resolves society into its original elements, and robbery becomes more honourable than war, inasmuch as the robber is paid and the soldier is in arrears. A wonderful ecclesiastical establishment covers the land with a privileged class … I say nothing of their costume. You are wakened from your slumbers by the *rosario*, the singing procession by which the peasantry congregate to their labours. It is most effective, full of noble chants and melodious responses, that break upon the still fresh air and your ever fresher feelings in a manner truly magical. Oh, wonderful Spain! I thought enthusiasm was dead within me and nothing could be new. I have hit, perhaps, upon the only country which could have upset my theory, a country of which I have read little and thought nothing.'

Health was really mending. 'This last fortnight,' he says, 'I have made regular progress, or rather felt, perhaps, the progress which I had already made. It is all the sun—not society or change of scene. This, however agreeable, is too much for me and ever turns me back. It is when I am alone and still that I feel the difference of my system, that I miss the old aches and am conscious of the increased activity and vitality and expansion of the blood.'

After Spain Malta was the next halting-place; Malta, with its garrison and military society, was Gibraltar over again, with only this difference, that Disraeli fell in with a London acquaintance there in James Clay, afterwards member for Hull and a figure in the House of Commons.

The arrival of a notoriety was an incident in the uniformity of Maltese existence. 'They have been long expecting your worship's offspring,' he tells his father, 'so I was received with branches of palm.' He accepted his honours with easy superiority. 'To govern men,' he said, 'you must either excel them in their accomplishments or despise them. Clay does one, I do the other, and we are both equally popular. Affectation here tells better than wit. Yesterday at the racket court, sitting in the gallery among strangers, the ball entered and lightly struck me and fell at my feet. I picked it up, and observing a young rifle man excessively stiff, I humbly requested him to forward its passage into the court, as I really had never thrown a ball in my life ... I called on the Governor and he was fortunately at home. I flatter myself that he passed through the most extraordinary quarter of an hour of his existence. I gave him no quarter and at last made our nonchalant Governor roll on the sofa from his risible convulsions. Clay confesses my triumph is complete and unrivalled.'

'I continue much the same,' he reported of himself—still infirm but no longer destitute of hope. I wander in pursuit of health like the immortal exile in pursuit of that lost shore which is now almost glittering in my sight. Five years of my life have been already wasted, and sometimes I think my pilgrimage may be as long as that of Ulysses.' Like the Greek he was exposed to temptations from the Circes and the Sirens, but he understood the symptoms and knew where to look for safety. 'There is a Mrs —— here in Malta,' he writes to Ralph Disraeli, 'with a pretty daughter, *cum multis aliis*; I am sorry to say, among them a beauty very dangerous to the peace of your unhappy brother. But no more of that. In a few weeks I shall be bounding, and perhaps sea-sick, upon the Egean, and then all will be over. Nothing like an emetic in these cases.'

James Clay was rich, and had provided a yacht in which, with the Byronic fever on him, he professed to intend to turn corsair. He invited Disraeli and Meredith to join him, and they sailed for Corfu in October equipped for enterprise. 'You should see me,' he said, 'in the costume of a Greek pirate—a blood-red shirt with silver studs as big as shillings, an immense scarf for girdle, full of pistols and daggers, red cap, red slippers, broad blue-striped jacket and trowsers.' 'Adventures are to the adventurous;' so Ixion had written in Athene's album. Albania was in insurrection. Unlike Byron, whom he was supposed to imitate, Disraeli preferred the Turks to the Greeks whom he despised, and thought for a moment of joining Redshid's army as a volunteer, to see what war was like. When they reached Corfu the rebellion was already crushed, but Redshid was still at Yanina, the Albanian capital, and he decided at least to pay the Grand Vizier a visit. The yacht took them to Salora. There they landed, and proceeded through the mountains with a handful of horse for an escort. They halted the first night at Arta, 'a beautiful town now in ruins.' 'Here,' he said, 'for the first time I reposed upon a divan, and for the first time heard a muezzin from a minaret.' In the morning they waited on the Turkish governor. 'I cannot describe to you,' he wrote in a humorous description of his interview, 'the awe with which I first entered the divan of a great Turk, and the curious feeling with which I found myself squatting on the right hand of a bey, smoking an amber-mouthed chibouque, drinking coffee, and paying him compliments through an interpreter.'

The Turks had been kind to his own race at a time when Jews had no other friends, and from the first Disraeli had an evident liking for them. They set out again after a few hours. 'We journeyed over a wild mountain pass,' the diary continues, 'a range of ancient Pindus, and before sunset we found ourselves at a vast but dilapidated khan as big as a Gothic castle, situated on a high range, built as a sort of half-way house for travellers by Ali Pasha, now turned into a military post.' They were received by a bey, who provided quarters for them. They were ravenously hungry; but the bey could not understand their language, nor they his. He offered them wine; they produced brandy, and communication was thus established. 'The bey drank all the brandy; the room turned round; the wild attendants who sat at our feet seemed dancing in strange and fantastic whirls. The bey shook hands with me; he shouted English, I Greek. "Very good," he had caught up from us. "Kalo, kalo," was my rejoinder. He roared; I smacked him on the back. I remember no more. In the middle of the night I woke, found a flagon of water, and drank a gallon at a draught. I looked at the wood fire and thought of the blazing blocks in the hall at Bradenham; asked myself whether I was indeed in the mountain fortress of an Albanian chief, and shrugging my shoulders went to bed and woke without a headache. We left our jolly host with regret. I gave him my pipe as a memorial of our having got tipsy together.'

At Yanina they found the Turkish army quartered in the ruins of the town. The Grand Vizier occupied the castle with the double dignity of a prince and a general. He was surrounded with state, and they were made to wait ten minutes before they could be admitted to his presence.

'Suddenly we are summoned to the awful presence of the pillar of the Turkish Empire, the renowned Redshid; an approved warrior, a consummate politician, unrivalled as a dissembler in a country where dissimulation is part of the moral culture … The hall was vast, covered with gilding and arabesques … Here, squatted up in a corner of a large divan, I bowed with all the nonchalance of St. James's Street to a little ferocious-looking, shriv-elled, careworn man, plainly dressed, with a brow covered with wrinkles and a countenance clouded with anxiety and thought … I seated myself on the divan of the Grand Vizier, who, the Austrian consul observed, "had destroyed in the course of the last three months, not in war, upwards of 4,000 of my acquaintance," with the self-possession of a morning call. Some compliments passed between us. Pipes and coffee were brought. Then his Highness waved his hand, and in an instant the chambers were cleared. Our conversation I need not repeat. We congratulated him on the pacification of Albania. He rejoined that the peace of the world was his only object and the happiness of mankind his only wish. This went on for the usual time. He asked us no questions about ourselves or our country, as the other Turks did, but seemed quite overwhelmed with business, moody and anxious. While we were with him three separate Tartars arrived with despatches. What a life! … I forgot to tell you that with the united assist-ance of my English, Spanish, and fancy wardrobe I sported a costume in Yanina which produced a most extraordinary effect on that costume-lov-ing people. A great many Turks called on purpose to see it. "*Questo vestito Inglese, o di fantasia?*" asked a little Greek physician. I oracularly replied, "*Inglese e fantastico.*"

Had the Greek physician enquired not about the *vestito,* but about the wearer of it, the answer might have been the same.

The account of this visit to Yanina was composed after the return of the party to the yacht. Here is a description in Disraeli's other manner:

> I write you this from that Ambracian gulf where the soft triumvir gained more glory by defeat than attends the victory of harsher warriors. The site is not unworthy of the beauty of Cleopatra. From the summit of the land the gulf appears like a vast lake walled in on all sides by mountains more or less distant. The dying glory of a Grecian eve bathes with warm light promontories and gentle bays and infinite modulation of purple outline. Before me is Olympus, whose austere peak glitters yet in the sun. A bend in the land alone hides from me the islands of Ulysses and Sappho. When I gaze upon this scene, and remember the barbaric splendour and turbulent existence which I have just quitted with disgust, I recur to the feelings in the indulgence of which I can alone find happiness and from which an inexorable destiny seems resolved to shut me out.

In a sketch like the present the tour cannot be followed minutely. Athens is finely painted, but Disraeli's classical education had been too imperfect to enable him to fill with figures and incidents the scenes which he was looking upon. The golden city was more after his heart. 'It is near sun set,' he wrote on November 20, 'and Constantinople is in full sight. It baffles description, though so often described. I feel an excitement which I thought dead.' He did describe, however, and drew magnificent pictures of the towns and palaces, and the motley-coloured crowd which thronged the bazaars. Lytton Bulwer was one of his London acquaintances. To him he wrote from Constantinople:

> I confess to you that my Turkish prejudices are very much confirmed by my residence in Turkey. The life of this people greatly accords with my taste. To repose on voluptuous divans and smoke superb pipes, daily to indulge in the luxury of a bath which requires half a dozen attendants for its perfection, to court the air in a carved *caique* by shores which are a perpetual scene, and to find no exertion greater than a canter on a barb, this I think a more sensible life than the bustle of clubs, the boring of drawing-rooms, and the coarse vulgarity of our political controversies.

Disraeli's English contemporaries who were aspiring to Parliamentary fame, and with whom in a few years he was to cross swords, were already learning the ways of the House of Commons, or training in subordinate official harness. Little would any of those who saw him lounging on divans, with a turban on his head and smoking cherry sticks longer than himself, have dreamt that here was the man who was to rise above them all and be Prime Minister of England. He too was forming himself for something, though as yet he could not tell for what. Ambitious visions haunted his imagination, even grander than he was ever to realise. On their way back thro the Dardanelles the party paused for a sight of the Plain of Troy. As Disraeli stood on the sacred soil and gazed on the grass mound which was called the tomb of Patroclus, the thought passed through him that as the heroic age had produced its Homer, the Augustan era its Virgil, the Renaissance its Dante, the Reformation its Milton, why should not the revolutionary epoch produce its representative poet? Why should not that poet be himself? Why not but for two reasons? that the modern European revolution is disintegration and not growth, the product of man's feeble-ness, not of his greatness, and therefore no subject for a poem; and again because Disraeli could never learn to detach himself from his work and forget the fame with which success was to reward him; and therefore to be a poet was not among the gifts which the Fates had in store for him. It was well for him, however, to indulge the dream. No man ever rises to greatness in this world who does not aim at objects beyond his powers.

Cyprus followed, and then Jaffa, and from Jaffa they crossed the mountains to Jerusalem. Disraeli was not given to veneration, but if he venerated anything it was the genius and destiny of his own race. Even the Holy City could not transport him out of himself, but it affected him more than anything which he had ever seen in his life. The elaborate but artificial account of his impressions, which is to be read in *Tancred,* is a recollection of what he wrote to his sister about twenty years before:

> From Jaffa a party of six, well mounted and armed, we departed for Jerusalem, and crossed the plain of Ramle, vast and fertile. Ramle—the ancient Arimathea—is the model of one's idea of a beautiful Syrian village—all the houses isolated and each surrounded by palm trees; the meadows and the exterior of the village covered with olive trees, or divided by rich plantations of Indian fig … Next day, at length, after crossing a vast hill, we saw the Holy City. I will describe it to you from the Mount of Olives. This is a high hill, still partially covered with the tree which gives it its name. Jerusalem is situated upon an opposite height which descends as a steep ravine and forms, with the assistance of the Mount of Olives, the narrow valley of Jehoshaphat. Jerusalem is entirely surrounded by an old feudal wall, with towers and gates of the time of the crusaders, and in perfect preservation. As the town is built upon a hill you can from the opposite height discern the roof of almost every house. In the front is the magnificent mosque built upon the site of the Temple. A variety of domes and towers rise in all directions. The houses are of bright stone. I was thunderstruck. I saw before me apparently a gorgeous city. Nothing can be conceived more wild and terrible and barren than the surrounding scenery, dark, strong, and severe; but the ground is thrown about in such picturesque undulation that the mind [being] full of the sublime, not the beautiful, rich and waving woods and sparkling cultivation would be misplaced.
>
> Except Athens I never saw anything more essentially striking, no city except that whose sight was so pre-eminently impressive. I will not place it below the city of Minerva. Athens and Jerusalem in their glory must have been the first representatives of the beautiful and the sublime. Jerusalem in its present state would make a wonderful subject for Martin, and a picture from him could alone give you an idea of it.

This week has been the most delightful of all our travels. We dined every day on the roof of a house by moonlight; visited the Holy Sepulchre of course, though avoided the other *coglionerie*. The House of Loretto is probability to them. But the Easterns will believe anything. Tombs of the Kings very fine. Weather delicious; mild summer heat. Made an immense sensation. Received visits from the Vicar-General of the Pope, two Spanish priors, &c ... Mr Briggs, the great Egyptian merchant, has written from England to say that great attention is to be paid me, because I am the son of the celebrated author.

The extracts must be cut short. The visit to Jerusalem was in February 1831. In April Disraeli was in Egypt, and ascended the Nile to Thebes. 'Conceive a feverish and tumultuous dream full of triumphal gates, processions of paintings, interminable walls of heroic sculpture, granite colossi of gods and kings, prodigious obelisks, avenues of sphinxes, and halls of a thousand columns thirty feet in girth and of proportionate height. My eyes and mind yet ache with a grandeur so little in unison with our own littleness. The landscape was quite characteristic; mountains of burning sand, vegetation unnaturally vivid, groves of cocoa trees, groups of crocodiles, and an ebony population in a state of nudity armed with spears of reeds.'

Far in the future lay the Suez Canal and the influence which the young visitor was one day to exercise over the fortunes of Egypt. The tour was over. His health was recovered. He was to return to England and take to work again, uncertain as yet whether he was not to go back to his Coke and Blackstone. His thoughts for the present were turned on Bradenham and its inmates. A chest of Eastern armour, pipes, and other curiosities was ready-packed at the end of May, to accompany him home for the decoration of the hall. On May 28 he wrote in high spirits of his approaching return: 'I am delighted with my father's progress. How I long to be with him, dearest of men, flashing our quills together, standing together in our chivalry as we will do, now that I have got the use of my brain for the first time in my life.'

These letters from abroad, and the pictures which Disraeli draws of himself and of his adventures in them, show him as he really was, making no effort to produce an effect, in the easy undress of family confidence, not without innocent vanities, but light-hearted and gay at one moment, at another deeply impressionable with anything which was interesting or beautiful. The affectations which so strongly characterised his public appearances were but a dress deliberately assumed, to be thrown off when he left the stage like a theatrical wardrobe.

The expedition, which had remained so bright to the end, unhappily had a tragic close. On the eve of departure William Meredith caught the small-pox at Alexandria, and died after a few days' illness. His marriage with Sarah Disraeli was to have taken place immediately after their arrival in England. The loss to her was too deep for reparation; she remained single to her own life's close. To Disraeli himself the shock gave 'inexpressible sorrow, and 'cast a gloom over him for many years.'

# IV

The law had not been finally abandoned—perhaps in deference to Isaac Disraeli's continued anxiety on the subject. Schemes and projects, however, which had shaped themselves in Disraeli's own mind during his travels had to be executed first. He brought home with him a brain restored to energy, though with saddened spirits. There was the 'Revolutionary Epic' to be written, and an Eastern story which was brought out afterwards as the tale of *Alroy*. Before undertaking either of them, however, he drew a second portrait of himself in *Contarini Fleming*. Vivian Grey was a clever, independent youth, with the world before him, with no purpose save to make himself conspicuous. Disraeli now hoped to be a poet, and in *Contarini* his aim, he said, was to trace the development and function of the poetic character. The flippancy of *Vivian* is gone. The tone is calm, tender, and at times morbid. The hero is taken through a series of adventures. He tries politics, but politics do not interest him. He falls in love. The lady of his affections dies and leaves him in despair. Contarini revives to find a desire, and perhaps a capacity—for he cannot be confident that he is not deceiving himself—to become the poet which Disraeli was then aspiring to make himself. The outward characteristics of that character could at least be assumed. Contarini becomes a wanderer like Byron, and visits the same scenes from which Disraeli had just returned. The book contains passages of striking beauty, so striking that Goethe sent praises and compliments, and Milman, who reviewed it, said it was a work in no way inferior to 'Childe Harold,' and equally calculated to arrest public attention. Yet the story ends in nothing. The river loses itself in the sands. Contarini is but Disraeli himself in the sick period of undetermined energies. He meditates on the great problems of life, and arrives at the conclusions adopted almost universally by intellectual men before they have learnt to strike out their course and to control circumstances and their own nature.

'I believe in that destiny before which the ancients bowed. Modern philosophy has infused into the breast of man a spirit of scepticism, but I think that ere long science will become again imaginative, and that as we become more profound we may also become more credulous. Destiny is our will, and our will is nature. The son who inherits the organisation of the father will be doomed to the same fortunes as his sire, and again the mysterious matter in which his ancestors were moulded may in other forms, by a necessary attraction, act upon his fate. All is mystery; but he is a slave who will not struggle to penetrate the mystery.'

Such passages as this were not ominous of much success in the high functions to which Contarini was aspiring. Much more interesting, because more natural, is a dialogue which was probably an exact reproduction of a conversation between Disraeli and his father. The father of Contarini entirely objects to his son's proposed destination of himself.

'A poet!' exclaims the old man. 'What were the great poets in their lifetime? The most miserable of their species—depressed, doubtful, obscure, or involved in petty quarrels and petty persecutions; often unappreciated, utterly uninfluential, beggars, flatterers of men, unworthy even of their recognition. What a train of disgustful incidents! what a record of degrading circumstances is the life of a great poet! A man of great energies aspires that they should be felt in his lifetime; that his existence should be rendered more intensely vital by the constant consciousness of his multiplied and multiplying powers. Is posthumous fame a substitute for all this? Try the greatest by this test, and what is the result? Would you rather have been Homer, or Julius Caesar, Shakespeare or Napoleon? No one doubts. We are active beings, and our sympathy, above all other sympathies, is with great actions. Remember that all this time I am taking for granted you may be a Homer. Let us now recollect that it is perhaps the most impossible incident that can occur. The high poetic talent, as if to prove that the poet is only at the best a wild, although beautiful, error of nature, is the rarest in creation. What you have felt is what I have felt myself. Mix in society and I will answer for it that you lose your poetic feeling; for in you, as in the majority, it is not a matter of faculty originating in a peculiar organisation, but simply the consequence of nervous susceptibility that is common to us all.'

Contarini admits the truth of what his father said, but answers that his ambition is great, as if he must find some means to satisfy it. He did not think he would find life tolerable unless he was in an eminent position, and was conscious that he deserved it. Fame, and not posthumous fame, was necessary to his felicity. Such a feeling might lead to exertion, and on some roads might lead to success; but poetry is a jealous mistress and must be pursued for her own sake if her favours are ever to be won. Disraeli would not part with his hope till the experiment had been tried. He destroyed a tragedy which he had already composed; but he was better satisfied with his 'Revolutionary Epic.' Three cantos were written, and fifty copies were printed. These he resolved to submit to the judgment of his friends. If the verdict was unfavourable he would burn his lyre.

The recitation was at a party at Mrs Austen's, and a scene is thus described which 'was never to be forgotten' by those who witnessed it. 'There was something irresistibly comic in the young man dressed in the fantastic cox-combical costume that he then affected—velvet coat thrown wide open, ruffles on the sleeves, shirt collars turned down in Byronic fashion, an elab-orate embroidered waistcoat from which issued voluminous folds of frill, shoes adorned with red rosettes, his black hair pomatumed and elaborately curled, and his person redolent with perfume. Standing with his back to the fire, he explained the purpose of his poem. It was to be to the revolution-ary age what the 'Iliad,' the 'Æneid,' and 'Paradise Lost' had been to their respective epochs. 'He had imagined the genius of feudalism and the gen-ius of federation appearing before the almighty throne and pleading their respective and antagonistic causes.'[1]

With this prelude he recited his first canto. It was not without passages sonorous and even grand, but the subject itself was hopeless. Disraeli had not yet discerned that modern revolution had nothing grand about it, that it was merely the resolution of society into its component atoms, that cen-turies would have to pass before any new arrangement possessing worth or dignity would rise out of the ruin. The audience was favourably disposed, but when the poet left the room a gentleman present declaimed an impromptu burlesque of the opening lines, which caused infinite merriment to those present. Disraeli said afterwards of himself that in his life he had tried many things, and though he had at first failed he succeeded at last. This was true; but poetry was not one of these many things. He was wise enough to accept the unfavourable verdict, and to recognise that, although his ambition was feverish as ever, on this road there were no triumphs before him. The dream that he could become a great poet was broken.

His prose writings deserved better and fared better. *Contarini Fleming* and the tale of *Alroy* were well received. Milman, as was said above, compared *Contarini* to 'Childe Harold.' Beckford found Alroy wildly original, full of intense thought, awakening, delightful. Both these eminent critics were too lavish of their praise, but they expressed the general opinion. The fame of *Vivian Grey* was revived. The literary world acknowledged that a new star had appeared, and Disraeli became a London lion. The saloons of the great were thrown open to him. Bulwer he knew already. At Bulwer's house he was introduced to Count d'Orsay, Lady Morgan, Mrs Norton, Mrs Gore, and other notabilities. Lady Blessington welcomed him at Kensington. Flying higher he made acquaintance with Lord Mulgrave, Lord William Lennox, and Tom Moore. He frequented the fashionable smoking-rooms, sporting his Eastern acquirements. A distinguished colonel, supposing that he meant to push his good fortune, gave him a friendly warning. 'Take care, my good fellow. I lost the most beautiful woman in the world by smoking; it has prevented more liaisons than the dread of a duel or Doctors' Commons.' 'You have proved it a very moral habit,' replied Disraeli. His ambition did not run in the line which the colonel suspected. Success as a novelist might gratify vanity, but could never meet Disraeli's aspirations. He met public men, and studied the ways of them, dimly feeling that theirs was the sphere where he could best distinguish himself. At a dinner at Lord Eliot's he sat next to Peel. 'Peel most gracious,' he reported to his sister next day.[2] 'He is a very great man indeed, and they all seem afraid of him. I observed that he attacked his turbot almost entirely with his knife. I could conceive that he could be very disagreeable; but yet he was in a most condescending humour, and unbent with becoming haughtiness. I reminded him by my dignified familiarity both that he was an ex-Minister and I a present Radical.' He went to the gallery of the House of Commons, 'heard Macaulay's best speech, Sheil, and Charles Grant. Macaulay admirable, but between ourselves I could floor them all. This *entre nous*. I was never more confident of anything than that I could carry everything before me in that House.' In that House, perhaps. He knew that he had a devil of a tongue, that he was clever, ready, without fear, and, however vain, without the foolish form of vanity which is called modesty. He had studied politics all his life, and having no interests at stake with either of the great parties, and, as being half a foreigner, lying outside them both, he could take a position of his own. In that House; but, again, how was he to get there? Young men of genius may be invited to dinners in the great world, but seats in Parliament will be only found for them if they will put on harness and be docile in the shafts. Disraeli had shown no qualities which promised official usefulness; he called himself a Radical, but he was a Radical in his own sense of the word. He did not talk democratic platitudes, and insisted that if he entered Parliament he would enter it independent of party ties. Notoriety as a novelist even in these more advanced days is no recommendation to a constituency, unless backed by money or connection, and of these Disraeli had none.

One chance only seemed to offer. There was a possibility of a vacancy at High Wycombe, close to his father's house. There he was personally known, and there, if the opportunity were offered, he intended to try. Meantime he extended his London acquaintance, and one friend he acquired the importance of whom to his future career he little dreamt of. He was introduced by Lytton Bulwer, 'at particular desire,' to Mrs Wyndham Lewis, 'a pretty little woman,' he says, 'a flirt and a rattle—indeed, gifted with a volubility, I should think, unequalled. She told me she liked silent, melancholy men. I answered that I had no doubt of it.'

The intimacy with Mrs Wyndham Lewis was matured, and was extended to her husband, a gentleman of large fortune and member for Maidstone. Meantime his chief associates in London were the set who gathered about Lady Blessington, young men of fashion and questionable reputation, who were useful to him perhaps as 'studies' for his novels, but otherwise of a value to him less than zero. Although he never raced, never gambled, or gave way to any kind of dissipation, his habits of life were expensive, and his books, though they sold well, brought him money in insufficient quantity. His fashionable impecunious friends who wanted loans induced him to introduce them to men in the City who knew him, or who knew his connections. These persons were ready to make advances if Disraeli would give his own name as an additional security. The bills, when due, were not paid. Disraeli had to borrow for himself to meet them,[3] and to borrow afterwards on his own account. When he was once involved the second step was easy, and this was the beginning of difficulties which at one time brought him to the edge of ruin. He was careless, however, careless in such matters even to the end of his life. His extraordinary confidence in his own powers never allowed him to doubt.

Several sketches of him have been preserved as he appeared in these years in the London world. N.P. Willis, the American, met him at a party at Lady Blessington's.

> He was sitting in a window looking on Hyde Park, the last rays of sunlight reflected from the gorgeous gold flowers of a splendidly embroidered waistcoat. Patent leather pumps, a white stick with a black cord and tassel, and a quantity of chains about his neck and pockets, served to make him a conspicuous object. He has one of the most remarkable faces I ever saw. He is lividly pale, and but for the energy of his action and the strength of his lungs would seem to be a victim of consumption. His eye is black as Erebus, and has the most mocking, lying-in wait sort of expression conceivable. His mouth is alive with a kind of working and impatient nervousness; and when he has burst forth, as he does constantly, with a particularly successful cataract of expression, it assumes a curl of triumphant scorn that would be worthy of Mephistopheles. His hair is as extraordinary as his taste in waistcoats. A thick, heavy mass of jet black ringlets falls on his left cheek almost to his collarless stock, which on the right temple is parted and put away with the smooth carefulness of a girl. The conversation turned on Beckford. I might as well attempt to gather up the foam of the sea as to convey an idea of the extraordinary language in which he clothed his description. He talked like a racehorse approaching the winning post, every muscle in action.

His dress was purposed affectation. It led the listener to look for only folly from him, and when a brilliant flash broke out it was the more startling as being so utterly unlooked for from such a figure. Perhaps he overacted his extravagance. Lady Dufferin told Mr Motley that when she first met him at a dinner party he wore a black velvet coat lined with satin, purple trousers with a gold band running down the outside seam, a scarlet waistcoat, long lace ruffles falling down to the tips of his fingers, white gloves with several brilliant rings outside them, and long black ringlets rippling down upon his shoulders. She told him that he made a fool of himself by appearing in such fantastic shape, never guessing for what reason it had been adopted.

Here is another picture from Mr Madden's memoirs of Lady Blessington:

> I frequently met Disraeli at her house. Though in general society he was usually silent and reserved, he was closely observant. It required generally a subject of more than common interest to animate and stimulate him into

the exercise of his marvellous powers of conversation. When duly excited, however, his command of language was truly wonderful, his powers of sarcasm unsurpassed. The readiness of his wit, the quickness of his perception, the grasp of his mind, that enabled him to seize all the points of any subject under discussion, persons would only call in question who had never been in his company at the period I refer to.

Such was Disraeli when, in the summer of 1832, he offered himself as a candidate to the electors of High Wycombe. The expected vacancy had occurred. It was the last election under the unreformed constituency. The voters were only some forty or fifty in number. One seat in the borough had been a family property of the Whig Carringtons; the other was under the influence of Sir Thomas Baring, whose interest went with the Government. Disraeli started as a Radical. He desired generally to go into Parliament as a profession, as other men go to the Bar, to make his way to consequence and to fortune. But he did not mean to take any brief which might be offered him. He was infected to some extent by the general Reform enthusiasm. Lord Grey's measure had taken half their power from the aristocracy and the landed interest, and had given it to the middle classes. There the Whigs desired to stop and to put off the hungry multitude (who expected to be better clothed and fed and housed) with flash notes on the Bank of Liberty. Ardent young men of ability had small belief in the virtues of the middle classes. They were thinking of a Reform which was to make an end of injustice and misery, a remodelling of the world. Carlyle, in the Dumfriesshire Highlands, caught the infection, and believed for a time in the coming of a new era. Disraeli conceived that 'Toryism was worn out, and he could not condescend to be a Whig.' He started against the Carringtons on the line of the enthusiasts, advocating the ballot and triennial Parliaments. For cant of all kinds he had the natural hatred which belongs to real ability. The rights of man to what was called liberty he never meddled with. He desired practical results. His dislike of the Whigs recommended him to their enemies, and half his friends in the borough were Tories. The local newspapers supported him as an independent. But help was welcome from any quarter but the Whigs. Bulwer, who worked hard for him, procured commendatory letters from O'Connell, Burdett, and Hume, and these letters were placarded ostentatiously in the Wycombe market-place.

The Government was in alarm for Sir T. Baring's seat; Colonel Grey, Lord Grey's son, was brought down as their candidate. Isaac Disraeli seems to have stood aloof and to have left his son to his own resources. Disraeli himself did not mean to lose for want of displaying himself. He drove into

Wycombe in an open carriage and four, dressed with his usual extravagance—laced shirt, coat with pink lining, and the morning cane which
had so impressed the Gibraltar subalterns. Colonel Grey had arrived on his
first visit to the borough, and Disraeli seized the opportunity of his appearance for an impromptu address. 'All Wycombe was assembled,' he wrote,
describing the scene. 'Feeling it was the crisis, I jumped upon the portico of
the "Red Lion" and gave it them for an hour and a quarter. I can give you
no idea of the effect. I made them all mad. A great many absolutely cried. I
never made so many friends in my life, and converted so many enemies. All
the women are on my side, and wear my colours—pink and white.' Colonel
Grey told Bulwer that he never heard a finer command of words. Wycombe
was prouder than ever of its brilliant neighbour; but of course he failed.
Hume had shaken the Radicals by withdrawing his support before the election; Government influence and the Carringtons did the rest. Disraeli,
however, had made a beginning and never let himself be disheartened.

This election was in June. On August 16 Parliament was dissolved, and he
offered himself a second time to the new constituency. He invited them, in his
address, to have done with 'political jargon,' to 'make an end of the factious
slang of Whig and Tory, two names with one meaning, and only to delude the
people,' and to 'unite in forming a great national party.' 'I come before you,' he
said, 'to oppose this disgusting system of factions; I come forward wearing the
badge of no party and the livery of no faction. I seek your suffrages as an independent neighbour ... I will withhold my support from every Ministry which
will not originate some great measure to ameliorate the condition of the lower
orders.' This too was not to serve him. Party government may be theoretically
absurd when the rivalry is extended from measures to men. When the functions
of an Opposition are not merely to resist what it disapproves, but to dethrone
the other side, that they may step into its place, we have a civil war in the midst
of us, and a civil war which can never end because the strength of the combat-
ants is periodically renewed at the hustings. Lord Lyndhurst and the Duke of
Wellington were by this time interested in Disraeli.

'The Duke and the Chancellor are besetting old Carrington in my favour,'
he wrote. 'They say he must yield. I am not sanguine, but was recommended
to issue the address. The Duke wrote a strong letter to the chairman of the
election committee, saying if Wycombe was not ensured something else must
be done for Disraeli, as a man of his acquirements and reputation must not be
thrown away. L. showed me the letter, but it is impossible to say how things
will go. It is impossible for anyone to be warmer than the Duke or Lyndhurst,
and I ought to say the same of Chandos.'

The Carrington family would not yield; Disraeli was defeated again, and it became clear that he must look elsewhere than to Wycombe. More than one seat might have been secured for him if he would have committed himself to a side, but he still insisted that if he entered Parliament he would enter it unfettered by pledges. There was an expected chance at Marylebone. When he proposed himself as a candidate he was asked on what he intended to stand. 'On my head,' he answered. Lyndhurst wished him to stand at Lynn as a friend of Lord Chandos. Lord Durham offered to return him as a Radical. 'He must be a mighty independent personage,' observed Charles Greville, when he persisted in the same reply. He realised by degrees that he was making himself impossible, but he would not yield without a further effort. There was curiosity about him, which he perhaps overrated, for he published a pamphlet as a self-advertisement, with the title 'What is He?' of the same ambitiously neutral tint. His object now was to make himself notorious, and the pamphlet he said, 'was as much a favourite with the Tories as with the Rads.'

In society he was everywhere, dining with Lyndhurst, dining with O'Connell, or at least invited to dine with him, at fêtes and water parties, at balls and suppers. D'Orsay painted his picture. The world would have spoilt him with vanity if his self-confidence had not been already so great that it would admit of no increase. His debts were growing. He had again borrowed for his election expenses. It was hinted to him that he might mend his fortune by marriage. 'Would you like Lady —— for a sister-in-law?' he says in a letter to Miss Disraeli. 'Very clever, £25,000, and domestic.' 'As for love,' he added, 'all my friends who married for love and beauty either beat their wives or live apart from them. This is literally the case. I may commit many follies in life, but I never intend to marry for love, which I am sure is a guarantee for infelicity.'

Whatever might be his faults he was no paltry fortune-hunter. He trusted to himself, and only himself. He did not sit down upon his disappointments. The press at any rate was open to him. He wrote incessantly, 'passing days in constant composition.' In the season he was always in London; in the winter either at Bradenham or at some quiet place by himself, riding for health and 'living solely on snipes.' Determined to be distinguished, he even made a show, and not a bad one, in the hunting field. Writing from Southend in 1834, he says, 'Hunted the other day with Sir H. Smythe's hounds, and though not in pink was the best mounted man in the field, riding an Arabian mare, which I nearly killed—a run of thirty mile; and I stopped at nothing.'

It was as a politician that he was desiring to keep himself before men's eyes, if not in Parliament yet as a political writer; his pen was busy with a

'Vindication of the British Constitution,' but he meant also to be known for the manly qualities which Englishmen respect.

Public events meantime hastened on. In England after each rush in the direction of Liberalism there is always a reaction. Within two years of the passing of the Reform Bill Lord Grey and his friends had disgusted the Radicals in Parliament. The working men, finding that they had been fed with chaff instead of corn, had turned to Chartism. The Tories closed up their broken ranks. The king dismissed the Ministers, and sent to Rome for Peel to take the helm. The step itself may have been premature; but Sir Robert was able to take a commanding position before the country, and form a party strong enough to hold the Whigs in check if too weak to prevent their returning to office. Disraeli, though he never much liked Peel, had found by this time that there was no place in Parliament for a man who had a position to make for himself unless he joined one party or the other. He swallowed his pride, probably on the advice of Lyndhurst, with whom he was now on intimate terms. The cant of Radicalism was distasteful to him. The Whigs were odious. He made up his mind to enlist under Peel. In the spring of 1835 Lord Melbourne came back in alliance with O'Connell, while the world was ringing with the Rathcormack massacre. Thirteen lives had been lost, and 'something was to be done' for the pacification of Ireland. 'O'Connell is so powerful,' wrote Disraeli, 'that he says he will be in the Cabinet. How can the Whigs submit to this? It is the Irish Catholic party that has done all this mischief.' O'Connell was not taken into the Cabinet, but under the new arrangement would be more powerful than if restrained by office. Disraeli, who had shown in *Popanilla* what he thought about the English administration of that unfortunate island, had said openly that large changes were needed there, but it was another thing to truckle to anarchy and threats of rebellion.

Mr Labouchere, the member for Taunton, was in the new Ministry. Custom required that he should resign his seat and be re-elected. Disraeli, supported by the Carlton Club, went down to oppose him in the Tory interest. He was late in the field. He soon saw that for the present occasion at least he must again fail but he found supporters enough to make it worth his while to fight and keep himself conspicuous. 'As to Taunton itself,' he wrote in the heat of the conflict,[4] 'the enthusiasm of Wycombe is a miniature to it, and I believe in point of energy, eloquence, and effect I have far exceeded my former efforts.' He was beaten, though two-thirds of the electors promised him their votes on the next opportunity. The Taunton election went by, and would have been forgotten like a thousand others but for an incident which grew out of it. Disraeli desired notoriety, and notoriety he was to have. The Irish alliance was not popular in England. Irish alliances never are popular when the meaning of them is to purchase the support of a disloyal faction, to turn the scale in a struggle for power between English parties. Such an alliance had been last tried by Strafford and Charles I, with unpleasant consequences both to them and to Ireland. Now the Whigs were trying the same game—the Whigs, who were the heirs of the Long Parliament. The combination of English Liberals and Irish Papists was in itself a monstrous anomaly. Disraeli had no personal dislike of O'Connell, and had been grateful for his support at Wycombe; but he was now retained on the Tory side, and he used the weapons which were readiest to his hand. In one of the speeches which he thought so successful he had called O'Connell an incendiary, and spoke of the Whigs as 'grasping his bloody hand.' The Protestant Somersetshire yeomen no doubt cheered him to his heart's content. The speech, being exceptionally smart, was reported at length and fell under O'Connell's eyes. O'Connell was good-natured, but he knew Disraeli only as a young politician whom he had asked to dinner and had endeavoured to serve. Disraeli had gone out of his way to call him bad names, he might well have thought ungraciously and ungratefully. He was himself the unrivalled master of personal abuse. He saw an opening for a bitter joke, and very naturally used it. At a public meeting in Dublin he mentioned the part which he had taken at Wycombe; he had been repaid, he said by an atrocity of the foulest description.

> The miscreant had the audacity to style me an incendiary. I was a greater incendiary in 1831 than I am at present, if ever I was one, and he is doubly so for having employed me. He calls me a traitor; my answer to this is, he is a liar. His life is a living lie. He is the most degraded of his species and kind, and England is degraded in tolerating and having on the face of her society a miscreant of his abominable, foul, and atrocious nature. His name shows that he is by descent a Jew. They were once the chosen people of God. There were miscreants amongst them, however, also, and it must certainly have been from one of those that Disraeli descended. He possesses just the qualities of the impenitent thief that died upon the cross, whose name I verily believe must have been Disraeli. For aught I know the present Disraeli is descended from him, and with the impression that he is I now forgive the heir at law of the blasphemous thief that died upon the cross.

All the world shouted with laughter. The hit was good, and the provocation, it was generally felt, had been on Disraeli's side. But there are limits

to license of tongue even in political recrimination, and it was felt also that
O'Connell had transgressed those limits. An insult so keen and bitter could
be met in one way only. Disraeli had already been spattered by the mud which
flies so freely in English political contests. He had found that 'the only way to
secure future ease was to take up a proper position early in life, and to show
that he would not be insulted with impunity.' He put himself into the hands
of Count d'Orsay. D'Orsay considered that a foreigner should not interfere
in a political duel, and found Disraeli another friend; but he undertook himself the management of the affair. O'Connell having once killed an antagonist
on an occasion of this kind, had 'registered a vow in heaven' that he would
never fight again. But Morgan O'Connell had recently fought Lord Alvanley
in his father's behalf, and was now invited to answer for the Dublin speech. If
he was to meet every person who had suffered from his father's tongue his life
would have been a short one. He replied that he had fought Lord Alvanley
because Lord Alvanley had insulted his father; he was not accountable for
what his father might say of other people. Disraeli undertook to obviate this
difficulty. He addressed O'Connell in a letter published in the *Times*, which,
if less pungent, at least met Morgan O'Connell's objection. 'Although,' he
said, 'you have placed yourself out of the pale of civilisation I am one who will
not be insulted even by a yahoo without chastising it ... I admire your scur-
rilous allusion to my origin; it is clear the hereditary bondsman has already
forgotten the clank of his fetters ... I had nothing to appeal to but the good
sense of the people. No threatening skeleton canvassed for me. A death's-head
and cross-bones were not blazoned on my banners; my pecuniary resources
too were limited. I am not one of those public beggars that we see swarming
with their obtrusive boxes in the chapels of your creed, nor am I in possession
of a princely revenue from a starving race of fanatical slaves.'

He expected, he said in conclusion, to be a representative of the people
before the repeal of the Union. 'We shall meet at Philippi.'

Disraeli waited at home till the night of the day on which the letter
appeared for the effect of his missive. No notice being taken of it, 'he
dressed and went to the opera.' When Peel had challenged O'Connell
some years before, the police interfered; on this occasion the same thing
had happened. 'As I was lying in bed this morning,' Disraeli wrote on May
9 to his sister, 'the police officers from Marylebone rushed into my cham-
ber and took me into custody. I am now bound to keep the peace in £500
sureties—a most unnecessary precaution as if all the O'Connells were to
challenge me I could not think of meeting them now. The general effect is
the thing, and that is that all men agree I have shown pluck.'

If Disraeli gained nothing by this encounter he at least lost nothing. He was more than ever talked about, and he had won approval from a high authority at any rate. 'You have no idea,' said Lord Strangford to him, 'of the sensation produced at Strathfieldsaye. The Duke said at dinner it was the most manly thing done yet.' On one side only his outlook was unfavourable. The Taunton election had been a fresh expense. He had again to borrow, and his creditors became pressing. Judgments were out against him for more debts than he could meet. About this time—the date cannot be fixed exactly, but the fact is certain—a sheriff's officer appeared at Wycombe on the way to Bradenham to arrest him. Dr Rose,[5] a medical man in the town, heard of the arrival, and sent on an express with a warning 'to hide Ben in the well.' Affairs were again smoothed over for the moment. 'Ben,' undaunted as ever, worked on upon his own lines. He completed his 'Vindication of the British Constitution'— vindication rather of Democratic Toryism—amidst the harassing of duns. It was dedicated to Lyndhurst, and Lyndhurst paid him a visit at his father's house. He had a smart quarrel with the *Globe* over a revival of the O'Connell business. In the spring of 1836 appeared the Runnymede letters in the *Times*, philippics against the Whig leaders after the manner of Junius. He was elected at the Canton Club, to his great satisfaction, and when the newspapers abused him he quoted a saying of Swift, 'that the appearance of a man of genius in the world may be always known by the virulence of dunces.' To assist his finances a proposal was made to him to edit the *Arabian Nights* 'with notes and an additional tale by the author of *Vivian Grey*.' He described it as 'a job which would not take up more than a month of his time' and by which he might make 'twelve or fifteen hundred pounds.' Happily for his literary repu-tation this adventure was not prosecuted. Some one in the City introduced him to a speculation connected with a Dutch loan, which took him twice to the Hague and taught him the mysteries of finance. More legitimately in the midst of embarrassments and platform speeches he wrote *Henrietta Temple* and *Venetia*, the first a pretty love-story which offered no opportunities for his peculiar gifts, the second an attempt to exhibit in a novel the characters of Byron and Shelley. They would have made a reputation for an ordinary writer. They sustained the public interest in Disraeli. Of his speeches there was one at Wycombe in which he said that there would be no tranquillity in Ireland 'till the Irish people enjoyed the right to which the people of all countries were entitled, to be maintained by the soil which they cultivated with their labour.' In another there is a prophetic passage. 'I cannot force from my mind the conviction that a House of Commons concentrating in itself the whole powers of the State might—I should say would—constitute a despotism of the most formidable and dangerous description.' A third was the celebrated Ducrow speech—the Whig Premier as Ducrow first riding six horses at once, and as they foundered one by one left at last riding a jackass, which showed what Disraeli could do as a mob orator when he chose to condescend to it.

Bulwer said of one of these speeches that it was the finest in the world, and of one of the novels that it was the very worst. The criticism was smartly worded, and on both sides exaggerated; but it was true that, if Disraeli had been undistinguished as a speaker, his early novels would have been as the 'flowers of the field,' charming for the day that was passing over them and then forgotten. His political apprenticeship was at last over; the object of his ambition, the so deeply coveted seat in the House of Commons, was within his reach, and he was to pass into his proper sphere—to pass into it too while still young, for after all that he had done and experienced he was still only thirty-three. Few men, with the odds so heavy against them, had risen so high in so short a time

1. *Quarterly Review*, January 1889, p. 30.
2. May 24, 1832
3. This is authentic, though I cannot give my authority.—J. A. F.
4. April 27, 1835.
5. Father of Sir Philip Rose, who was afterwards Disraeli's executor.

# V

*Returned to Parliament for Maidstone—Takes his place behind Sir R. Peel—Maiden speech—Silenced by violence—Peel's opinion of it—Advice of Shiel—Second speech on copyright completely successful—State of politics— England in a state of change—Break-up of ancient institutions—Land and its duties—Political economy and Free Trade—Struggle on the Corn Laws*

THE ACQUAINTANCE WITH MR AND Mrs Wyndham Lewis had grown into a close friendship. Mr Lewis, as has been said, was member for Maidstone, and had large local influence in the borough. The death of William IV, in the summer of 1837, dissolved Parliament; and Disraeli, being adopted by Mr Lewis as his colleague, was returned by an easy majority. The election again gave the Whigs a majority, but not a large one. The tide was fast ebbing, and the time was near when the Conservatives, as the Tories now called themselves, were to see the balance turn in their favour. Lord Melbourne meanwhile remained Minister, but a Minister who desired to be able to do nothing. Ministers with a powerful party behind them are driven occasionally into measures which they would have preferred to avoid. The electors who have given them power require them to use it. Whigs and Tories alike know that their time will be short unless by some sensational policy they can gratify public expectation. Nothing was expected of Lord Melbourne, and persons who dreaded change of any kind, from whichever side it might come, were satisfied that it should be so. I remember Bishop Phillpotts rubbing his hands over the situation, and saying that he hoped never more to see a strong Government.

It was a time of 'slack water;' nevertheless Disraeli was supremely happy. He had now a career open before him, and a career in which he was certain that he could distinguish himself. His delight was boyish. He said, 'It makes a difference in public opinion of me.' The election was in July, and Parliament met in November. He took his seat on the second bench behind Peel, a place which he intended, if possible, to secure for himself. Peel's character had rallied the Conservative party, and to Peel personally they looked for guidance. Yarde Buller being asked his opinion on some question, replied that Peel had not made up his mind; Old Toryism was gone with Lord Eldon; the Reform Bill, once passed, was to be the law of the land. Disraeli had no personal interest in any of the great questions which divided English opinion. He owned no land; he was unconnected with trade; he had none of the hereditary prepossessions of a native Englishman. He was merely a volunteer on the side with which, as a man of intellect, he had most natural sympathy. He took a brief from the Conservatives, without remuneration in money, but trusting to win fame, if not fortune, in an occupation for which he knew that he was qualified. He began in the ranks, and Peel was his leader; and his leader, till he had made a place for himself, he loyally prepared to serve.

'Peel welcomed me very warmly,' he reported to Bradenham, 'and all noticed his cordial demeanour. He looks very well, and asked me to join a swell dinner at the Carlton on Thursday—a House of Commons dinner purely,' he said. 'By that time we shall know something of the temper of the House.' A fortnight later he mentioned, with evident pride, that he had met Peel again, and Peel took wine with him.

Success to Disraeli in the House of Commons was the alternative of a financial catastrophe. His debts were large; money had been necessary to him for the position to which he aspired. He had no securities to offer, and never entangled friends in his pecuniary dealings. He had gone frankly to the professional money-lenders, who had made advances to him in a speculation upon his success. There was no deception on either side—Disraeli was running his talents against the chance of failure. If he succeeded the loans would be paid. If he did not succeed, the usurers had played for a high stake and had lost it, that was all. At worst he was but following the example of Burke and the younger Pitt. As his bills fell due, they had been renewed at 8 and 10 per cent and even more, and when he commenced his political life would have been formidable to anyone but himself. They were all eventually paid, and he was never charged, even in thought, with having abused afterwards the opportunities of power to relieve himself. But it was with this weight upon his back that he began his Parliamentary career. He had started on his own merits, for he had nothing else to recommend him, and he had challenged fate by the pretensions which he had put forward for himself. His birth was a reproach to be got over. He had no great constituency at his back, no popular cause to represent. He was without the academic reputation which so often smooths the entrance to public life, and the Tory gentlemen, among whom he had taken his place, looked upon him with dubious eyes. 'Had I been a political adventurer,' he said at Wycombe, 'I had nothing to do but join the Whigs.' The Radicals would have welcomed him into their ranks; but the Radicals looked on him as an apostate, as a mischievous insect to be crushed on the first opportunity. The *Globe* had assailed him brutally, and he had replied in kind. 'The Whig Samson should never silence him with the jaw of an ass. He would show the world what a miserable poltroon, what a craven dullard, what a literary scarecrow, what a mere thing stuffed with straw and rubbish was the *soi-disant* director of public opinion and official organ of Whig politics.' A first speech in the House of Commons is usually treated with indulgence. The notoriety which Disraeli had brought on himself by these encounters was to make him a solitary exception. He had told O'Connell that they would meet at Philippi. Three weeks after Disraeli had taken his seat there was a debate upon some election manoeuvres in Ireland. Hard blows had been exchanged. Sir F. Burdett had called O'Connell a paid patriot. O'Connell had replied that he had sacrificed a splendid professional income to defend his country's rights. 'Was he for this to be vilified and traduced by an old renegade?' Immediately after O'Connell Disraeli rose. His appearance was theatrical, as usual. He was dressed in a bottle-green frock coat, with a white waistcoat, collarless, and with needless display of gold chain. His face was lividly pale, his voice and manner peculiar. He began naturally and sensibly, keeping to the point of the debate. He was cheered by his own side, and might have got through tolerably enough; but the gentlemen below the gangway had determined that his Philippi should not end with a victory. Of course he did not yet know the House of Commons. Affected expressions, which would have been welcomed at Wycombe or Taunton, were received with scornful laughter. He bore it for a time good-humouredly, and begged them to hear him out. He was answered with fresh peals of mockery. He had to speak of the alliance between the Whigs and the Irish Catholics. With a flourish of rhetoric he described Melbourne as flourishing in one hand the keys, of St. Peter, in the other, he was going to say, 'the cap of Liberty,' but the close of the sentence was drowned in derisive shouts. The word had gone out that he was to be put down. Each time that he tried to proceed the storm burst out, and the Speaker could not silence it. Peel cheered him repeatedly. The Tory party cheered, but to no purpose. At last, finding it useless to persist, he said he was not surprised at the reception which he had experienced. He had begun several times many things and had succeeded at last. Then pausing and looking indignantly across the House, he exclaimed in a loud and remarkable tone, which startled even the noisy hounds who were barking loudest, 'I will sit down now, but the time will come when you will hear me.'

No one suffers long through injustice. His ill-wishers had tried to embarrass him and make him break down. They had not succeeded, and probably even O'Connell himself felt that he had been unfairly dealt with. People watched him curiously the rest of the evening to see how he bore his treatment. He was said to have sat with his arms folded, looking gloomily on the floor. His own account shows that he was not depressed at all, and that indeed the experience was not entirely new.

'I made my maiden speech last night,' he tells his sister, 'rising very late after O'Connell, but at the request of my party and with the full sanction of Sir Robert Peel. I state at once that my *début* was a failure—not by my breaking down or incompetency on my part, but from the physical power of my adversaries. It was like my first *début* at Aylesbury, and perhaps in that sense may be auspicious of ultimate triumph in the same scene. I fought through all with undaunted pluck and unruffled temper, made occasionally good isolated hits when there was silence, and finished with spirit when I found a formal display was ineffectual. My party backed me well, and no one with more zeal and kindness than Peel, cheering me repeatedly, which is not his custom. The uproar was all organised by the Rads and the Repealers. In the lobby, at the division, Chandos, who was not near me in speaking, came up and congratulated me. I replied I thought there was no cause for congratulation, and muttered "Failure!" "No such thing," said Chandos; "you are quite wrong. I have just seen Peel, and I said to him, 'Now tell me exactly what you think of Disraeli.' Peel replied, 'Some of my party were disappointed and talk of failure; I say just the reverse. He did all that he could under the circumstances; I say anything but failure: he must make his way.'" The Attorney-General (Campbell), to whom I never spoke in my life, came up to me in the lobby and spoke to me with great cordiality. He said, "Now, Mr Disraeli, could you just tell me how you finished one sentence in your speech? We are anxious to know. 'In one hand the keys of St. Peter and in the other——'" "In the other the cap of Liberty, Sir John." He smiled and said, "A good picture." I replied, "But your friends would not allow me to finish my picture." "I assure you," he said, "there was the liveliest desire to hear you from us. It was a party at the bar, over whom we have no control; but you have nothing to be afraid of." Now I have told you all.—Yours, D., in very good spirits.'

Disraeli's collapse was the next day's delight at the clubs. Sheil, though an Irish leader, declined to join in it. 'I have heard what you say,' he answered to the wits who appealed to him, 'and what is more, I heard this same speech of Mr Disraeli; and I tell you this: If ever the spirit of oratory was in a man it is that man. Nothing can prevent him from being one of the first speakers of the House of Commons.'

The speech, however, might have been a failure Sheil admitted, if Disraeli had been allowed to go on. The manner was unusual; the House of Commons had not grown accustomed to it. 'Get rid of your genius for a session,' he said to Disraeli himself. 'Speak often, for you must not show yourself cowed, but speak shortly. Be very quiet; try to be dull; only argue and reason imperfectly. Astonish them by speaking on subjects of detail; quote figures, dates, and calculations. In a short time the House will sigh for the wit and eloquence they know are in you. They will encourage you to pour them forth, and thus you will have the ear of the House and be a favourite.'

Disraeli's sense was stronger than his vanity. His whole fate was at stake, and he knew it. He took Sheil's advice. A week after he had been howled down he spoke again on the Copyright Bill, a subject which he perfectly understood. Again when he rose he was observed with curious attention. It was thought that he would allude to his first misadventure; he made not the least reference to it. His voice, naturally impressive, was in good condition. What he said was exactly to the purpose. His conclusion, if simple, was excellent.

> I am glad to hear from her Majesty's Government that the interests of literature have at length engaged their attention. It has been the boast of the Whig party, and a boast not without foundation, that in many brilliant periods of our literary annals they have been the patrons of letters. As for myself, I trust that the age of literary patronage has passed; and it will be honourable to the present Government if under its auspices it is succeeded by that of literary protection.

The House was willing to be pleased. Lord John Russell cheered the allusion to his Liberal predecessors. The Radicals approved of the independence which he claimed for the future of his own profession. Peel loudly applauded, and never after had Disraeli to complain that he was not listened to with respect. The cabal which would have silenced him had, in fact, made his reputation. His colleague and his Maidstone constituents were delighted. In the remainder of the session he was frequently on his feet, but only to say a few sensible sentences and never putting himself forward on great occasions.

Notwithstanding all that has been said and continues to be said about the outset of his Parliamentary career, he had made solid progress in the estimation of the House, and, far more to the purpose, his quick apprehension had learnt the temper and disposition of the House itself.

Before proceeding further a brief sketch must be given of the state of public affairs when Disraeli's political life commenced. The British Islands were
covered with the shells of institutions which no longer answered the purpose
for which they were intended. The privileges remained. The duties attaching
to them were either unperformed or, from change of circumstances, incapable of performance. Down to the Reformation of the sixteenth century the
beliefs and habits of the English nation were formed by the Catholic Church.
Men and women of all ranks were brought up on the hypothesis that their
business in this world was not to grow rich, but to do their duties in the state
of life to which they had been called. Their time on earth was short. In the
eternity which lay beyond their condition would wholly depend on the way
in which it had been spent. On this principle society was constructed, and
the conduct, public and private, of the great body of the people was governed
by the supposition that the principle was literally true.

History takes note of the exception of the foolish or tyrannical king, the
oppressive baron, the profligate Churchman, the occasional expressions of
popular discontent. Irregularities in human life are like the river cataracts
and waterfalls which attract the landscape painter. The historian dwells upon
them because they are dramatically interesting, but the broad features of
those ages must be looked for in the commonplace character of everyday
existence, which attracts little notice and can be traced only in the effects
which it has produced. It was thus that the soil of this island was cleared and
fenced and divided into fields as by a pencil. It was then that in every parish
there arose a church, on which piety lavished every ornament which skill
could command, and then and thus was formed the English nation, which
was to exercise so vast an influence on the fortunes of mankind. They were
proud of their liberty. A race never lived more sternly resolute to keep the soil
of their sea-girt island untrodden by the foot of the invader. Liberty in the
modern sense, liberty where the rights of man take the place of the duties of
a man—such a liberty they neither sought nor desired. As in an army, each
man had had his own position under a graduated scale of authority, and the
work was hardest where the rank was highest. The baron was maintained in
his castle on the produce of the estate. But the baron had the hardest knocks
in the field of battle. In dangerous times he was happy if he escaped the
scaffold. He maintained his state in the outward splendour which belonged
to his station, but in private he lived as frugally as his tenants, sleeping on
a hard bed, eating hard, plain food, with luxury unheard of and undreamt
of. The rule was loyalty—loyalty of the lord to the king, loyalty of lord to
peasant and of peasant to lord. So deeply rooted was the mutual feeling that

for long gene rations after the relation had lost its meaning, and one of the parties had forgotten that it ever had a meaning, reverence and respect to the owner of the land lingered on and is hardly extinct to-day.

In the towns the trades were organised under the guilds. The price of food, the rate of wages from household servant to field labourer and artisan, were ordered by statute on principles of equity. For each trade there was a council, and false measure and bad quality of goods were sharply looked to. The miller could not adulterate his flour. The price of wheat varied with the harvest, but the speculator who bought up grain to sell again at famine price found himself in the hands of the constable. For the children of the poor there was an education under the apprentice system, to which the most finished school-board training was as copper to gold. Boys and girls alike were all taught some useful occupation by which they could afterwards honestly maintain themselves. If there were hardships they were not confined to a single class, but were borne equally by the great and the humble. A nation in a healthy state is an organism like the human body. If the finger says to the hand, 'I have no need of thee; I will go my way, touch what pleases me, and let alone what I do not care to meddle with,' the owner of the hand will be in a bad way. A commonwealth, or common weal, demands that each kind shall do the work which belongs to him or her. When he or she, when individuals generally begin to think and act for themselves, to seek their rights and their enjoyments, and forget their duties, the work of dissolution has already set in.

The fear of God made England, and no great nation was ever made by any other fear. When the Catholic Church broke down it survived under Protestant forms, till Protestantism too dwindled into opinion and ceased to be a rule of life. We still read our Bibles and went to church; we were zealous for the purity of our faith, and established our societies to propagate it; but the faith itself became consistent with the active sense that pleasure was pleasant and wealth was power, and while our faith would make things right in the next world we might ourselves make something out of the present. From the Restoration downwards the owners of land began to surround themselves with luxuries, and the employers of labour to buy it at the cheapest rate. Selfishness became first a practice and then developed boldly into a theory. Life was a race in which the strongest had a right to win. Every man was to be set free and do the best which he could for himself. The Institutions remained. Dukes and earls and minor dignitaries still wore their coronets and owned the soil. Bishops were the spiritual lords of their dioceses, and the rector represented the Church in his parish. The commercial companies survived in outward magnificence. But in aiming at wealth they all alike forfeited their power. Competition became the sole rule of trade; a new philosophy was invented to gild the change; artisans and labourers were taught to believe that they would gain as largely as the capitalists. They had been bondsmen; they were now free, and all would benefit alike. Yet somehow *all* did not benefit alike. The houses of the upper classes grew into palaces, and the owners of them lived apart as a separate caste; but the village labourer did not find his lot more easy because he belonged to nobody. As population increased his wages sank to the lowest point at which he could keep his family alive. The 'hands' in the towns fared no better. If wages rose the cost of living rose along with them. The compulsory apprentice system was dropped, and the children were dragged up in squalor upon the streets. Discontent broke out in ugly forms: ricks were burnt in the country, and in the northern cities there was riot and disorder. They were told that they must keep the peace and help themselves. Their labour was an article which they had to sell, and the value of it was fixed by the relations between supply and demand. Man could not alter the laws of nature, which political economy had finally discovered. Political economy has since been banished to the exterior planets ; but fifty years ago to doubt was heresy, to deny was a crime to be censured in all the newspapers. Carlyle might talk scornfully of the 'Dismal Science.' Disraeli might heap ridicule on Mr Flummery Flum. But Mr Flummery Flum was a prophet in his day and led the believers into strange places. The race for wealth went on at railroad speed. Vast fortunes were accumulated as the world's markets opened wider. The working classes ought to have shared the profits, and they were diligently instructed that they had gained as much as their employers. But their practical condition remained unaltered, and they looked with strange eyes upon the progress in which, for one cause or another, they did not find that they participated. The remedy of the economists was to heat the furnace still hotter, to abolish every lingering remnant of restraint, and stifle complaint by admitting the working men to political power. The enlightened among the rich were not afraid, for they were entrenched, as they believed, behind their law of nature. In its contracts with labour capital must always have the advantage; for capital could wait and hungry stomachs could not wait. In the meantime let the Corn Laws go. Let all taxes on articles of consumption go. Trade would then expand indefinitely, and all would be well. 'The wealth of the nation,' the Free-Traders of Manchester said, depends on its commerce. The commerce of England is shackled by a network of duties. The consumer pays dear for the necessaries of life, which he might buy cheap but for artificial interference. The raw materials of our industry are burdened with restrictions. But for these we might multiply our mills, expand our connections, provide work and food for the millions who are now hungry. With your Corn Laws you are starving multitudes to maintain the rents of a few thousand Elysians, who neither toil nor spin, who might be blotted off the surface of the soil to-morrow and none would miss them; who consume the labours of the poor on a splendour of living unheard of since the Roman Empire, and extort the means of this extravagance by an arbitrary law. You say you must have a revenue to maintain your fleets and armies, and that it cannot be raised except by customs duties. Your fleets and armies are not needed. Take away your commercial fetters, allow the nations of the earth a free exchange of commodities with us, and you need not fear that they will quarrel with us: wars will be heard of no more, and the complaints of the poor that they are famished to supply the luxuries of the rich will no longer cry to Heaven.

The Free-Traders might have been over-sanguine, but on the Corn Laws it was hard to answer them. The duties attaching to the ownership of land had fallen to shadows. The defence of the country had passed to the army. Internal peace was maintained by the police. Unless they volun-teered to serve as magistrates the landlords had but to receive their rents and do as they pleased with their own. An aristocracy whose achievements, as recorded in newspapers, were the slaughter of unheard-of multitudes of pheasants, an aristocracy to one of whose distinguished members a granite column was recently erected on a spot where he had slain fifty brace of grouse in half an hour, were scarcely in a position to demand that the poor man's loaf should be reduced in size, for fear their incomes should suffer diminution. Carlyle said that he had never heard an argument for the Corn Laws which might not make angels weep. If the fear of suffering in their pockets had been the only motive which influenced the landed interest in its opposition to free trade, there would have been nothing to be said for it; but if that had been all, Corn Laws in such a country as England could never have existed at all. Protection for native industry had been established for centuries. It had prevailed and still prevails in spite of the arguments of Free-Traders all the world over, and under all forms of government. The principle of it has been and is that no country is in a sound or safe condition which cannot feed its own population independent of the foreigner. Peace could not be counted on with an empire so extended as ours. Occasions of quarrel might arise which no prudence could avert. The world had seen many a commercial commonwealth rise to temporary splendour, but all had gone the same road, and a country which depended on its imports for daily bread would be living at the mercy of its rivals. Christianity had failed to extinguish war. It was not likely that commerce would succeed better, and the accidents of a single campaign, the successful blockade of our ports even for a month or a fortnight, might degrade us into a shameful submission. British agriculture was the creation of protection. Under the duties which kept out foreign corn waste lands had been reclaimed, capital had been invested in the soil, and with such success and energy that double the wheat was raised per acre in England as was produced in any country in the world. The farmer prospered, the labourer at least existed, and the country population was maintained. Take protection away and wheat would cease to be grown. The plough would rust in the shed; the peasantry of the villages would dwindle away. They would drift into the towns in festering masses, living precariously from day to day, ever pressing on the means of employment with decaying physique and growing discontent. Cobden said the cost of carriage would partially protect the farmer. His own industry must do the rest. The ocean steamers have made short work of the cost of carriage; the soil could yield no more than it was bearing already. Cobden's more daring followers said that if the country districts returned to waste and forest the nation itself would be no poorer. In the defence of protection and in the denunciation of it there was alike a base element. The landlords were alarmed for their private interests. The manufacturer did expect that if the loaf was cheaper labour would be cheaper, for by orthodox doctrine labour adjusted itself to the cost of living. But to statesmen, whose business it was to look beyond the day that was passing over them, there was reason to pause before rushing into a course from which there could be no return, and which in another century might prove to have been a wild experiment. The price of food might-be gradually reduced without immediate revolution, and the opportunity might be used to attach the colonies more closely to the mother country. The colonies and India, with the encouragement of an advantage in the home market, could supply corn without limit, and their connection with us would be cemented by interest; while if they were placed on the same level as foreigners they would perhaps take us at our word and become foreigners. The traders insisted that if we opened our ports all the world would follow our example. But prophecies did not always prove correct, and, if the world did not follow our example, to fight prohibitive duties with free imports might prove a losing bargain.

# VI

INTO THIS MAELSTROM DISRAELI WAS plunged when he entered Parliament. He had his own views. He knew the condition of the poor both in England and Ireland. He had declared that no Government should have his support which did not introduce some large measure to improve that condition. He had chosen the Conservative side because he had no belief in the promises of the political economists, or in the blessed results to follow from cutting the strings and leaving everyone to find his level. He held to the old conception of the commonwealth that all orders must work faithfully together; that trade was to be extended not by cheapness and free markets, but by good workmanship and superior merit; and that the object which statesmen ought to set before themselves was the maintenance of the character of the people, not the piling up in enormous heaps of what wealth had now come to mean. The people themselves were groping, in their trades unions, after an organisation which would revive in other forms the functions of the Guilds; and the exact science of political economy would cease to be a science at all, whenever motives superior to personal interest began to be acted upon. Science was knowledge of facts; the facts most important to be known were the facts of human nature and human responsibilities; and the interpretation of those facts which had been revealed to his own race, Disraeli actually believed to be deeper and truer than any modern speculations. Though calling himself a

Christian, he was a Jew in his heart. He regarded Christianity as only Judaism developed, and, if not completely true, yet as immeasurably nearer to truth than the mushroom philosophies of the present age. He had studied Carlyle, and in some of his writings had imitated him. Carlyle did not thank him for this. Carlyle detested Jews, and looked on Disraeli as an adventurer fishing for fortune in Parliamentary waters. His novels he despised. His chains and velvets and affected airs he looked on as the tawdry love of vulgar ornament characteristic of Houndsditch. Nevertheless, Disraeli had taken his teaching to heart, and in his own way meant to act upon it. He regarded the aristocracy, like Carlyle also, in spite of the double barrels, as the least corrupted part of the community; and to them, in alliance with the people, he looked for a return of the English nation to the lines of true progress. The Church was moving at Oxford. A wave of political Conservatism was sweeping over the country. He thought that in both these movements he saw signs of a genuine reaction, and Peel, he still believed, would give effect to his hopes.

These were his theoretic convictions, while outwardly he amused himself in the high circles which his Parliamentary notoriety had opened to him. His letters are full of dukes and princes and beautiful women, and balls and dinners; he ventured liberties, even in the presence of the great Premier, and escaped unpunished. In the spring of 1839 he notes a dinner in Whitehall Gardens. 'I came late,' he says, 'having mistaken the hour. I found some twenty-five gentlemen grubbing in solemn silence. I threw a shot over the table and set them going, and in time they became noisy. Peel, I think, was pleased that I broke the awful stillness, as he talked to me a good deal, though we were far removed.' But though he enjoyed these honours and magnificences perhaps more than he need have done, he kept an independence of his own. It was supposed that he was looking for office, and that Peel's neglect of him in 1841 was the cause of his subsequent revolt. Peel did make some advances to him through a third person, and said afterwards in the House that Disraeli had been ready to serve under him; but if office was really his object, never did any man take a worse way of recommending himself. In the summer of the same year (1839) the monster Chartist petition was brought down to the House of Commons in the name of the working people of England, and the general disposition was to treat it as an absurdity and an insult. Disraeli, when his turn came to speak, was not ashamed to say that, though he disapproved of the Charter, he sympathised with the Chartists. They were right, he thought, in desiring a fairer share in the profits of their labour, and that fairer share they were unlikely to obtain from the commercial constituencies whom the Reform Bill had enfranchised. Great duties could alone confer great station, and the new class which had been invested with political station had not been bound up with the mass of the people by the exercise of corresponding obligations. Those who possessed power without discharging its conditions and duties, were naturally anxious to put themselves to the least possible expense and trouble. Having gained their own object, they wished to keep it without appeal to their pockets, or cost of their time. The true friends of the people ought to be the aristocracy, and in very significant words he added that 'the English nation would concede any degree of political power to a class making simultaneous advances in the exercise of great social duties.'

The aristocracy had lost their power because their duties had been neglected. They might have wealth or they might have power; but not both together. It was not too late to reconsider the alternative. The Chartists, finding themselves scoffed out of the House of Commons, took to violence. There were riots in Birmingham, and a Chartist convention sat in London threatening revolution. Lord John Russell appealed for an increase of the police. Disraeli was one of a minority of five who dared to say that it was unnecessary, and that other measures ought to be tried. When the leaders were seized, he supported his friend, Tom Duncombe, in a protest against the harshness of their treatment. The Chancellor of the Exchequer rebuked him. Fox Maule, a junior member of the Government, charged him with being 'an advocate of riot and disorder.' In later times Disraeli never struck at small game. When he meant fight, he went for the leading stag of the herd. On this occasion he briefly touched his two slight antagonists. 'Under- Secretaries,' he said, 'were sometimes vulgar and ill-bred. From a Chancellor of the Exchequer to an Under-Secretary of State was a descent from the sublime to the ridiculous, though the sublime was on this occasion rather ridiculous, and the ridiculous rather trashy!'

It is scarcely conceivable that if Disraeli was then aspiring to harness under Sir Robert, he would have committed himself with such reckless audacity; and his action was the more creditable to him as the profession which he had chosen brought him no emoluments. His financial embarrassments were thickening round him so seriously, that without office it might soon become impossible to continue his Parliamentary career. Like Bassanio,

> When he had lost one shaft,
> He shot his fellow of the self-same flight
> The self-same way with more advised watch
> To find the other forth, and by adventuring both
> He oft found both.

But one shaft had disappeared after another till he had reached the last in his quiver. He had not been personally extravagant. He had moved in the high circles to which he had been admitted rather as an assured spectator than as an imitator of their costly habits. But his resources were limited to the profits of his writings, and to such sums as he could raise on his own credit. His position was critical in the extreme, and Disraeli's star might then have set like a planet which becomes visible at twilight on the western horizon, and shows out in its splendour only to set into the sea. The temptation to sell oneself under such circumstances would have been too much for common Parliamentary virtue. But Disraeli was a colt who was not to be driven in a team by a master. Lord Melbourne had asked him once what he wished for. He had answered coolly that he wished to be Prime Minister. The insanity of presumption was in fact the insanity of second sight; but 'vaulting ambition' would have 'fallen on the other side' if a divinity had not come to his assistance.

The heroes of his political novels are usually made to owe their first success to wealthy marriages. Coningsby, Egremont, Endymion, though they deserve their good fortune, yet receive it from a woman's hand. Mr Wyndham Lewis, who had brought Disraeli into Parliament, died unexpectedly the year after. His widow, the clever rattling flirt, as he had described her on first acquaintance, after a year's mourning, became Disraeli's wife. She was childless. She was left the sole possessor of a house at Grosvenor Gate, and a life income of several thousands a year. She was not beautiful. Disraeli was thirty-five, and she was approaching fifty. But she was a heroine if ever woman deserved the name. She devoted herself to Disraeli with a completeness which left no room in her mind for any other thought. As to him, he had said that he would never marry for love. But if love, in the common sense of the word, did not exist between these two, there was an affection which stood the trials of thirty years, and deepened only as they both declined into age. She was his helpmate, his confidante, his adviser; from the first he felt the extent of his obligations to her, but the sense of obligation, if at first felt as a duty, became a bond of friendship perpetually renewed. The hours spent with his wife in retirement were the happiest that he knew. In defeat or victory he hurried home from the House of Commons to share his vexation or his triumph with his companion, who never believed that he could fail. The moment in his whole life which perhaps gave him greatest delight was that at which he was able to decorate her with a peerage. To her he dedicated *Sybil*. 'I,' he says, 'would inscribe this work to one whose noble spirit and gentle nature ever prompt her to sympathise with the suffering; to one whose sweet voice has often encouraged, and whose taste and judgment have ever, guided its pages, the most severe of critics, but a "perfect wife." The experience of his own married life he describes in *Coningsby* as the solitary personal gift which nature had not bestowed upon a special favourite of fortune. 'The lot most precious to man and which a beneficent Providence has made not the least common—to find in another heart a perfect and profound sympathy, to unite his existence with one who could share all his joys, soften all his sorrows, aid him in all his projects, respond to all his fancies, counsel him in his cares and support him, in his perils, make life charming by her charms, interesting by her intelligence, and sweet by the vigilant variety of her tenderness—to find your life blessed by such an influence, and to feel that your influence can bless such a life; the lot the most divine of divine gifts, so perfect that power and even fame can never rival its delights—all this nature had denied to Sidonia.' It had not been denied to Disraeli himself.

The carriage incident is well known. On an anxious House of Commons night, Mrs Disraeli drove down with her husband to Palace Yard. Her finger had been caught and crushed in the carriage-door. She did not let him know what had happened, for fear of disturbing him, and was not released from her torture till he had left her. That is perfectly authentic, and there are other stories like it. A husband capable of inspiring and maintaining such an attachment most certainly never ceased to deserve it. Savagely as he was afterwards attacked, his most indignant enemy never ventured to touch his name with scandal. A party of young men once ventured a foolish jest or two at Mrs Disraeli's age and appearance, and rallied him on the motives of his marriage. 'Gentlemen,' said Disraeli, as he rose and left the room, 'do none of you know what gratitude means?' This was the only known instance in which he ever spoke with genuine anger.

'Gratitude,' indeed, if deeply felt, was as deeply deserved. His marriage made him what he became. Though never himself a rich man, or endeavouring to make himself such, he was thenceforward superior to fortune. His difficulties were gradually disposed of. He had no longer election agents' bills to worry him, or debts to usurers running up in compound ratio. More important to him, he was free to take his own line in politics, relieved from the temptation of seeking office.

# VII

THE DISCOVERY OF THE STEAM-ENGINE had revolutionised the relations of mankind, and during the decline of the Melbourne Ministry was revolutionising the imagination the English nation. The railroads were annihilating distances between town and town. Roads were opening across the ocean, bringing the remotest sea-coasts in the world within sure and easy reach. Possibilities of an expansion of commerce practically boundless inflated hopes and stimulated energies. In past generations England had colonised half the new world; she had become sovereign of the sea; she had preserved the liberties of Europe, and had made her name feared and honoured in every part of the globe; but this was nothing compared to the prospect, which was now unfolding itself, of becoming the world's great workshop. She had invented steam; she had coal and iron in a combination and quantity which no other nation could rival; she had a population ingenious and vigorous, and capable, if employment could be found for them, of indefinite multiplication. The enthusiasm of progress seized the popular imagination. No word was tolerated which implied a doubt, and the prophets of evil, like Carlyle, were listened to with pity and amusement. The stars in their courses were fighting for the Free Traders. The gold-discoveries stimulated the circulation in the national veins, and prosperity advanced with leaps and bounds.

The tide has slackened now; other nations have rejected our example, have nursed their own industries, and supply their own wants. The volume of English trade continues to roll on, but the profits diminish. The crowds who throng our towns refuse to submit to a lowering of wages, and perplex economists and politicians with uneasy visions: we are thus better able to consider with fairness the objections of a few far-seeing statesmen forty and fifty years ago.

As far as the thoughts of an ambitious youth who had taken Pistol's 'The world's mine oyster' as the motto of his first book, and perhaps as the rule of his life—of a gaudy coxcomb who astonished drawing-rooms with his satin waistcoats, and was the chosen friend of Count D'Orsay—as far as the thoughts of such a person as this could have any affinity with those of the stern ascetic who, in the midst of accumulating splendour, was denouncing woe and desolation, so far, at the outset of his Parliamentary life, the opinions of Benjamin Disraeli, if we take *Sybil* for their exponent, were the opinions of the author of *Past and Present*. Carlyle thought of him as a fantastic ape. The interval between them was so vast that the comparison provokes a smile. Disraeli was to fight against the Repeal of the Corn Laws: Carlyle said that of all strange demands, the strangest was that the trade of owning land should be asking for higher wages; and yet the Hebrew conjuror, though at a humble distance, and not without an eye open to his own advancement, was nearer to him all along than Carlyle imagined. Disraeli did not believe any more than he that the greatness of a nation depended on the abundance of its possessions. He did not believe in a progress which meant the abolition of the traditionary habits of the people, the destruction of village industries, and the accumulation of the population into enormous cities, where their character and their physical qualities would be changed and would probably degenerate. The only progress which he could acknowledge was moral progress, and he considered that all legislation which proposed any other object to itself would produce, in the end, the effects which the prophets of his own race had uniformly and truly foretold.

Under the old organisation of England, the different orders of men were bound together under reciprocal obligations of duty. The economists and their political followers held that duty had nothing to do with it. Food, wages, and all else had their market value, which could be interfered with only to the general injury. The employer was to hire his labourers or his hands at the lowest rate at which they could be induced to work. If he ceased to need them, or if they would not work on terms which would remunerate him, he was at liberty to turn them off. The labourers, in return, might make the best of their own opportunity, and sell their services to the best advantage which competition allowed. The capitalists found the arrangement satisfactory to them. The people found it less satisfactory, and they replied by Chartism and rick-burnings. The economists said that the causes of discontent were the Corn Laws and the other taxes on food. Farmers and land-owners exclaimed that if the Corn Laws were repealed, the land must go out of cultivation. The Chartists were not satisfied with the remedy, because they believed that, with cheap food, wages would fall, and they would be no better off than they were. It was then slack water in the political tides. Public feeling was at a stand, uncertain which way to turn. The Reform Bill of 1832 had left to property the preponderance of political power, and everyone who had anything to lose began to be alarmed for himself. The Conservative reaction became more and more evident. The faith of the country was in Sir Robert Peel. He had been opposed to the Reform Bill, but when it was passed he had accepted it as the law of the land, and had reconstituted his party out of the confidence of the new constituencies. He had been a declared Protectionist. He had defended the Corn Laws, and had spoken and voted for them. He had resisted the proposal by the Whigs of a fixed eight-shilling duty, and had accepted and gloried in the position of being the leader of the gentlemen of England. But he had refused to initiate any policy of his own. He was known to be cautious, prudent, and a master of finance. He was no believer in novel theories or enthusiastic visions, but he had shown by his conduct on the Catholic question that he could consider and allow for the practical necessities of things. He was, however, above all things an avowed Conservative, and as a Conservative the country looked to him to steer the ship through the cataracts.

Another phenomenon had started up carrying a Conservative colour. Puseyism had appeared at Oxford, and was rapidly spreading. The Church of England, long paralysed by Erastianism and worldliness, was awaking out of its sleep, and claiming to speak again as the Divinely-appointed ruler of English souls. Political economy had undertaken to manage things on the hypothesis that men had no souls, or that their souls, if they possessed such entities, had nothing to do with their commercial relations to one another. The Church of England, as long as it remained silent or sleeping, had seemed to acquiesce in the new revelation, but it was beginning to claim a voice again in the practical affairs of the world, and the response, loud and strong, indicated that there still remained among us a power of latent conviction which might revive the force of noble and disinterested motive. A Church of England renovated and alive again might, some thought, become an

influence of incalculable consequence. Carlyle's keen, clear eyes refused to
be deceived. 'Galvanic Puseyism,' he called it, and 'dancings of the sheeted
dead.' A politician like Disraeli looking out into the phenomena in which
he was to play his part, and thinking more of what was going on among
the people than of the immediate condition of Parliamentary parties, conceived that he saw in the new movement, not only an effort of Conservative
energy, but an indication of a genuine recoil from moral and spiritual anarchy towards the Hebrew principle in which he really believed. Two forces he
saw still surviving in England which had been overlooked, or supposed to
be dead—respect for the Church, and the voluntary loyalty (which, though
waning, might equally be recovered) of the people towards the aristocracy.
Perhaps he overrated both because he had been himself born and bred outside their influence, and thus looked at them without the insight which he
gained afterwards on more intimate acquaintance. To some extent, however,
they were realities, and were legitimate subjects of calculation. Extracts from
his writings will show how his mind was working: He had been studying
the action of the Reform Bill of 1832. No one pretended, he said, that it had
improved the character of Parliament itself.

> But had it exercised a beneficial influence in the country? Had it elevated the
> tone of the public mind? Had it cultivated the popular sensibilities to noble
> and ennobling ends? Had it proposed to the people of England a higher test
> of national respect and confidence? ... If a spirit of rapacious covetousness,
> desecrating all the humanities of life, has been the besetting sin of England
> for the last century and a half, since the passing of the Reform Act the altar of
> Mammon has blazed with a triple worship. To acquire, to accumulate, to plun-
> der each other by virtue of philosophic phrases—to propose a Utopia to consist
> only of Wealth and Toil—this has been the business of enfranchised England
> for the last twelve years, until we are startled from our voracious strife by the
> wail of intolerable serfage.[1]

Again:

> Born in a library, and trained from early childhood by learned men who did
> not share the passions and the prejudices of our political and social life, I had
> imbibed on some subjects conclusions different from those which generally
> prevail, and especially with reference to the history of our own country. How
> an oligarchy had been substituted for a kingdom, and a narrow-minded and
> bigoted fanaticism flourished in the name of religious liberty, were problems

long to me insoluble, but which early interested me. But what most attracted my musing, even as a boy, were the elements of our political parties, and the strange mystification by which that which was national in our Constitution had become odious, and that which was exclusive was presented as popular.

What has mainly led to this confusion is our carelessness in not distinguishing between the excellence of a principle and its injurious or obsolete application. The feudal system may have worn out; but its main principle—that the tenure of property should be the fulfilment of duty—is the essence of good government. The divine right of kings may have been a plea for feeble tyrants; but the divine right of government is the key of human progress, and without it governments sink into a police, and a nation is degraded into a mob ... National institutions were the ramparts of a multitude against large estates, exercising political power, derived from a limited class. The Church was in theory, and once it had been in practice, the spiritual and intellectual trainer of the people. The privileges of the multitude and the prerogative of the sovereign had grown up together, and together they had waned. Under the plea of Liberalism, all the institutions which were the bulwark of the multitude had been sapped and weakened, and nothing had been substituted for them. The people were without education, and relatively to the advance of science and the comfort of the superior classes, their condition had deteriorated and their physical quality as a race was threatened.

To change back the oligarchy into a generous aristocracy round a real throne; to infuse life and vigour into the Church as the trainer of the nation by the revival of Convocation, then dumb, on a wise basis; to establish a commercial code on the principles successfully negotiated by Lord Bolingbroke at Utrecht, and which, though baffled at the time by a Whig Parliament, were subsequently and triumphantly vindicated by his pupil and political heir, Mr Pitt; to govern Ireland according to the policy of Charles I, and not of Oliver Cromwell; to emancipate the political constituency of 1832 from its sectarian bondage and contracted sympathies; to elevate the physical as well as the moral condition of the people by establishing that labour required regulation as much as property—and all this rather by the use of ancient forms and the restoration of the past, than by political revolutions founded on abstract ideas—appeared to be the course which the circumstances of the country required, and which, practically speaking, could only, with all their faults and backslidings, be undertaken and accomplished by a reconstructed Tory party.

When I attempted to enter public life, I expressed these views, long meditated, to my countrymen ... I incurred the accustomed penalty of being looked on as a visionary ... Ten years afterwards, affairs had changed. I had been some time in Parliament, and had friends who had entered public life with myself, who listened always with interest, and sometimes with sympathy … The writer, and those who acted with him, looked then upon the Anglican Church as a main machinery by which these results might be realised. There were few great things left in England, and the Church was one. Nor do I doubt that if a quarter of a century ago there had arisen a Churchman equal to the occasion, the position of ecclesiastical affairs in this country would have been very different from that which they now occupy. But these great matters fell into the hands of monks and schoolmen. The secession of Dr Newman dealt a blow to the Church under which it still reels. That extraordinary event has been "apologised" for, but it has never been explained. The tradition of the Anglican Church was powerful. Resting on the Church of Jerusalem modified by the Divine school of Galilee, it would have found that rock of truth which Providence, by the instrumentality of the Semitic race, had promised to St. Peter. Instead of that, the seceders sought refuge in mediaeval superstitions which are generally only the embodiments of Pagan ceremonies and creeds.[2]

Writing after the experience of thirty years of Parliamentary life, Disraeli thus described the impressions and the hopes with which he commenced his public career. He was disappointed by causes which he partly indicates, and by the nature of things which he then imperfectly realised. But, carefully considered, they explain the whole of his action down to the time when he found his expectation incapable of realisation. His Church views were somewhat hazy, though he was right enough about the Pagan ceremonies.

After their marriage, the Disraelis spent two months on the Continent. They went to Baden, Munich, Frankfort, Ratisbon, Nuremburg, seeing galleries and other curiosities. In November they returned to England, to the house in Grosvenor Gate which was thenceforward their London home, and Disraeli took his place on an equal footing as an established member of the great world. He was introduced to the Duke of Wellington, who had hitherto known him only by reputation. He received Peel's congratulations on his marriage with admitted pride and pleasure, and began to give dinners on his own account to leading members of his party. The impecunious adventurer had acquired the social standing without which the most brilliant gifts are regarded with a certain suspicion.

At the general election in 1841, Sir Robert Peel was borne into power, with a majority returned on Protectionist principles, larger than the most sanguine enthusiast had dared to hope for, Disraeli himself being returned for Shrewsbury—his connection with Maidstone having been probably broken by his late colleague's death. When the new Parliament settled to work,

Peel took the reins, and settled the finances by an income-tax—then called a temporary expedient, but in fact a necessary condition of the policy which at once he proceeded to follow. Duties were reduced in all directions, but there was no word of commercial treaties. Free Trade principles were visibly to be adopted, so far as the state of parties would allow, and the indications grew daily stronger that no such policy as Disraeli desired had come near the Premier's mind. The middle classes had confidence in Peel. It seemed that Peel had confidence in them, and Disraeli had none at all. Still, Peel was his political chief, and Disraeli continued to serve him, and to serve effectively and zealously. More and more he displayed his peculiar powers. When he chose he was the hardest hitter in the House of Commons; and as he never struck in malice, and selected always an antlered stag for an adversary, the House was amused at his audacity. Palmerston on some occasion regretted that the honourable member had been made an exception to the rule that political adherents ought to be rewarded by appointments. He trusted that before the end of the Session the Government would overlook the slight want of industry for the sake of the talent. Disraeli 'thanked the noble viscount for his courteous aspirations for his political promotion. The noble viscount was a master of the subject. If the noble viscount would only impart to him the secret by which he had himself contrived to retain office during so many successive administrations, the present debate would not be without a result.' Such a passage at arms may have been the more entertaining because Disraeli was supposed to have resented the neglect of his claims when Peel was form-ing his Administration. It is probable that Peel had studied the superficial aspects of his character, had underrated his ability, had discerned that he might not be sufficiently docile, or had suspected and resented his advocacy of the Chartists. Disraeli may have thought that the offer ought to have been made to him, but it is evident that on other grounds the differences between them would tend to widen. The Tariff of 1842 was the first note of alarm to the Conservative party—Disraeli defended it, but not with an entire heart. 'Peel,' he said in a letter to his sister,[3] 'seems to have pleased no party, but I suppose the necessity of things will force his measure through: affairs may yet simmer up into foam and bubble, and there may be a row.' The Conservatives had been trusted by the county with an opportunity of trying their principles which, if allowed to pass, might never be renewed. Their leader was not yet openly betraying them, but everyone but himself began to perceive that the Conservatism of the Government was only to be Liberalism in disguise.

Disraeli individually had the satisfaction of feeling that he was becoming a person of consequence. He ran across to Paris, and dined privately with

Louis Philippe. In London he was presented to the King of Hanover, 'the second king who has shaken hands with me in six months.' Public affairs he found 'uncertain and unsatisfactory,' Peel 'frigid and feeble,' and 'general grumbling.' He continued to speak, and speak often and successfully; but the mutual distrust between him and his chief was growing.

Peel among his magnificent qualities had not the art of conciliating the rack-and-file of his supporters. He regarded them too much as his own creatures, entitled to no consideration. Disraeli, taking the whole field of politics for his province, met with rebuke after rebuke. He had seen by this time that for his own theories there was no hope of countenance from the present chief. He had formed a small party among the younger Tory members—men of rank and talent, with a high-bred enthusiasm which had been kindled by the Church revival. A party including Lord John Manners, George Smyth, Henry Hope, and Baillie Cochrane was not to be despised; and thus reinforced and encouraged, he ventured to take a line of his own.

Among the articles of faith was the belief that Ireland ought to be treated on the principles of Charles I, and not on the principles of Cromwell. O'Connell in 1843 was setting Ireland in a flame again, and Peel, better acquainted with Ireland than Disraeli, and hopeless of other remedy, had introduced one of the periodic Coercion Bills. The Young Englanders, as he and his friends were now called, had Catholic sympathies, and they imagined that religion was at the bottom of these perpetual disturbances. Coercion answered only for the moment. A more conciliatory attitude towards the ancient creed might touch the secret of the disease. Disraeli perhaps wished to show that he bore no malice against O'Connell or against his tail. He thought that he could persuade the Irish that they had more to hope for from Cavalier Tories than from Roundhead Whigs. Of Irish history he knew as little as the rest of the House of Commons. He had heard, perhaps, of the Glamorgan Articles and Charles I's negotiations with the Kilkenny Parliament. Peel, when in opposition, had talked about conciliation. In office he had nothing to propose but force. Disraeli, when the Bill came before the House, gave the first sign of revolt; he said that it was one of those measures which to introduce was degrading, and to oppose disgraceful. He would neither vote for it nor against it; but as Peel had departed from the policy which he had led his party to hope that he meant to pursue before he came into power, he (Disraeli), speaking for himself and his friends, declared that they were now free from the bonds of party on this subject of Ireland, for the right hon. gentleman himself had broken them. They had now a right to fall back on their own opinions.

Something still more significant was to follow. A few days later (August. 1843) the Eastern question came up. Disraeli, whose friendship for the Turks was of old standing, asked a question relating to Russian interference in Servia. Peel gave an abrupt answer to end the matter. Palmerston, however, taking it up, Disraeli had a further opportunity of speaking. He complained that Turkey had been stabbed in the back by the diplomacy of Europe; that the integrity and independence of the Turkish dominions were of vital consequence, &c. But the point of his speech was in the sting with which it concluded. Winding up in the slow, deliberate manner which he made afterwards so peculiarly effective, he reminded the House of his own previous question, 'couched, he believed, in Parliamentary language, and made with all that respect which he felt for the right hon. gentleman.' 'To this inquiry,' he said, 'the right hon. gentleman replied with all that explicitness of which he was a master, and all that courtesy which he reserved only for his supporters.'

The House of Commons had much of the generous temper of an English public school. Boys like a little fellow who has the courage to stand up to a big one, and refuses to be bullied. The Whigs were amused at the mutiny of a Tory subordinate. The Tory rank-and-file had so often smarted under Peel's contempt that the blow told, and Disraeli had increased his consequence in the House by another step. Those who judge of motive by events, and assure themselves that when the actions of a man lead up to particular effects, those effects must have been contemplated by himself from the outset of his career, see indication in these speeches of a deliberate intention on Disraeli's part to supersede Sir Robert Peel in the leadership of the Conservative party. The vanity of such a purpose, had it been really entertained, would have been exceeded by the folly of his next movement. In the following year O'Connell's monster meetings had become a danger to the State. Peer had again to apply to the House of Commons, with a general sense on both sides that the authority of the Crown must be supported. Disraeli, almost alone among the English members, took the same daring attitude which he had assumed on the Chartist petition. Being in reality a stranger in the country of his adoption, he was able to regard the problems with which it was engaged in the light in which they appeared to other nations. The long mismanagement of Ireland, its chronic discontent and miserable state, were regarded everywhere as the blot upon the English escutcheon, and the cause of it was the mutual jealousy and suspicion of parties at Westminster. If a remedy was ever to be found, party ties must be thrown to the winds. What, he asked, did this eternal Irish question mean? One said it was a physical question, another a spiritual question. Now it was the absence of an aristocracy, then the absence of railroads. It was the Pope one day, potatoes the next. Let the House consider Ireland as they would any other country similarly situated, in their closets. They would see a teeming population denser to the square mile than that of China, created solely by agriculture, with none of those sources of wealth which are developed by civilisation, and sustained upon the lowest conceivable diet. That dense population in extreme distress inhabited an island where there was an Established Church which was not their Church, and a territorial aristocracy the richest of whom lived in distant capitals. They had a starving population, an absentee aristocracy, and an alien Church, and, in addition, the weakest executive in the world. That was the Irish question. Well, then, what would honourable gentlemen say if they were reading of a country in that position? They would say at once 'the remedy was revolution.' But Ireland could not have a revolution; and why? Because Ireland was connected with another and more powerful country. Then what was the consequence? The connection with England became the cause of the present state of Ireland. If the connection with England prevented a revolution, and a revolution was the only remedy, England logically was in the odious position of being the cause of all the misery in Ireland. What, then, was the duty of an English Minister? To effect by his policy all those changes which a revolution would do by force. That was the Irish question in its integrity ... If the noble lord (Lord John Russell) or any other honourable member came forward with a comprehensive plan, which would certainly settle the question of Ireland, no matter what the sacrifice might be, he would support it, though he might afterwards feel it necessary to retire from Parliament or to place his seat at the disposal of his constituency (*Life of Lord Beaconsfield*, T.P. O'Connor, 6th edition, p. 255, &c.).

Truer words had not been spoken in Parliament on the subject of Ireland for half a century, nor words more fatal to the immediate ambition of the speaker, if ambition he then entertained beyond a patriotic one; and many a session, and many a century perhaps, would have to pass before a party could be formed in England strong enough to carry on the government on unadulterated principles of patriotism.

1. *Sybil.*
2. Preface to *Lothair.*
3. February 2, 1842.

# VIII

A CCORDING TO DISRAELI'S THEORY OF government, the natural rulers of England were the aristocracy, supported by the people. The owners of the soil were the stable element in the Constitution. Capitalists grew like mushrooms, and disappeared as rapidly; the owners of the land remained. Tenants and labourers looked up to them with a feeling of allegiance; and that allegiance might revive into a living principle if the aristocracy would deserve it by reverting to the habits of their forefathers. That ancient forces could he awakened out of their sleep seemed proved by the success of the Tractarian movement at Oxford. The bold motto of the 'Lyra Apostolica' proclaimed that Achilles was in the field again, and that Liberalism was to find its master. The Oxford leaders might look doubtfully on so strange an ally as a half-converted Israelite. But Disraeli and the Young Englanders had caught the note, and were endeavouring to organise a political party on analogous lines. It was a dream. No such regeneration, spiritual or social, was really possible. Times were changed, and men had changed along with them. The Oxford movement was already undermined, though Disraeli knew it not. The English upper classes were not to be persuaded to alter habits which had become a second nature to them, or the people to be led back into social dependence by enthusiasm and eloquence. Had any such resurrection of the past been on the cards, Disraeli was not the necromancer who could have bid the dead live again. No one had a keener sense of the indications in others than he had. Fuller self-knowledge would have told him that the friend of D'Orsay and Lady Blessington, of Tom Duncombe and Lytton Bulwer, was an absurd associate in an ecclesiastical and social revival. He seemed to think that if Newman had paid more attention to *Coningsby*, the course of things might have been different. Saints had worked with secular politicians at many periods of Christian history; why not the Tractarian with him? Yet the juxtaposition of Newman and Disraeli cannot be thought of without an involuntary smile. It would be wrong to say that Disraeli had no sincere religious convictions. He was a Hebrew to the heart of him. He accepted the Hebrew tradition as a true account of the world, and of man's place in it. He was nominally a member of the Church of England; but his Christianity was something of his own, and his creed, as sketched in his *Life of Lord George Bentinck*, would scarcely find acceptance in any Christian community.

I have mentioned *Coningsby*. It is time to see what *Coningsby* was. Disraeli's novels had been brilliant, but he had touched nowhere the deeper chords of enduring feeling, His characters had been smart, but trivial; and his higher flights, as in the 'Revolutionary Epic,' or his attempts to paint more delicate emotion, as in *Henrietta Temple* or in *Venetia*, if not failures, were not successes of a distinguished kind. He had shown no perception of what was simple, or true, or tender, or admirable. He had been at his best when mocking at conventional humbug. But his talent as a writer was great, and, with a subject on which he was really in earnest, might produce a powerful effect. To impress the views of the Young Englanders upon the public, something more was needed than speeches in Parliament or on platforms. Henry Hope, son of the author of *Anastasius*, collected them in a party at his house at Deepdene, and there first 'urged the expediency of Disraeli's treating in a literary form those views and subjects which were the matter of their frequent conversations.' The result was *Coningsby* and *Sybil*.

*Coningsby; or, the New Generation* carried its meaning in its title. If England was to be saved by its aristocracy, the aristocracy must alter their ways. The existing representatives of the order had grown up in self-indulgence and social exclusiveness; some excellent, a few vicious, but all isolated from the inferior ranks, and all too old to mend. The hope, if hope there was, had to be looked for in their sons.

As a tale, *Coningsby* is nothing; but it is put together with extreme skill to give opportunities for typical sketches of character, and for the expression of opinions on social and political subjects. We have pictures of fashionable society, gay and giddy, such as no writer ever described better; peers, young, middle-aged, and old, good, bad, and indifferent, the central figure a profligate old noble of immense fortune, whose person was easily recognised, and whose portrait was also preserved by Thackeray. Besides these intriguing or fascinating ladies, political hacks, country gentlemen, mill-owners, and occasional wise outsiders, looking on upon the chaos and delivering oracular interpretations or prophecies. Into the middle of such a world the hero is launched, being the grandson and possible heir of the wicked peer. Lord Monmouth is a specimen of the order which was making aristocratic government impossible. To tax corn to support Lord Monmouth was plainly impossible. The story opens at Eton, which Disraeli describes with an insight astonishing in a writer who had no experience of English public school life, and with a fondness which confesses how much he had lost in the substitutes to which he had been himself condemned. There Coningsby makes acquaintance with the high-born youths who are to be his companions in the great world which is to follow, then in the enjoyment of a delightful present, and brimming with enthusiastic ambitions. They accompany each other to their fathers' castles, and schemes are meditated and begun for their future careers; Disraeli letting fall, as he goes on, his own political opinions, and betraying his evident disbelief in existing Conservatism, and in its then all-powerful leader. He finds Peel constructing a party without principles, with a basis therefore necessarily latitudinarian, and driving into political infidelity. There were shouts about Conservatism; but the question, What was to be conserved? was left unanswered. The Crown was to keep its prerogatives provided they were not exercised; the House of Lords might keep its independence if it was never asserted; the ecclesiastical estate if it was regulated by a commission of laymen. Everything, in short, that was established might remain as long as it was a phrase and not a fact. The Conservatism of Sir Robert 'offered no redress for the present, and made no preparations for the future. On the arrival of one of those critical conjunctures which would periodically occur in all States, the power of resistance would be wanting; the bar curse of political infidelity would paralyse all action, and the conservative Constitution would be discovered to be a *caput mortuum*.

'Coningsby found that he was born in an age of infidelity in all things, and his heart assured him that a want of faith was a want of nature. He asked himself why governments were hated and religions despised, why loyalty was dead and reverence only a galvanised corpse. He had found age perplexed and desponding, manhood callous and desperate. Some thought that systems would last their time, others that something would turn up. His deep and pious spirit recoiled with disgust and horror from lax chance medley maxims that would, in their consequence, reduce men to the level of brutes.'

He falls in with all varieties of men bred in the confusion of the old and the new. An enthusiastic Catholic landlord tries to revive the customs of his ancestors, supported by his faith, but perplexed by the aspect of a world no longer apparently under supernatural guidance. 'I enter life,' says Mr Lyle, 'in the midst of a convulsion in which the very principles of our political and social system are called in question. I cannot unite myself with the party of destruction. It is an operative cause alien to my being. What, then, offers itself? The duke talks to me of Conservative principles, but he does not inform me what they are. I observe, indeed, a party in the State whose rule it is to consent to no change until it is clamorously called for, and then instantly to yield: but those are concessionary, not Conservative, principles. This party treats our institutions as we do our pheasants. They preserve only to destroy them. But is there a statesman among these Conservatives who offers us a dogma for a guide, or defines any great political truth which we should aspire to establish? It seems to me a barren thing, this Conservatism; an unhappy cross-breed, the mule of politics, that engenders nothing.'

Coningsby had saved the life of a son of a Northern mill-owner at Eton. They became attached friends, though they were of opposite creeds. Coningsby's study of the social problem carries him to Manchester, where he hears from Millbank the views entertained in the industrial circles of the English aristocracy. Mr Millbank dislikes feudal manners as out of date and degenerate.

'I do not understand,' he says, 'how an aristocracy can exist, unless it is distinguished by some quality which no other class of the community possesses. Distinction is the basis of aristocracy. If you permit only one class of the population, for example, to bear arms, they are an aristocracy: not much to my taste, but still a great fact. That, however, is not the characteristic of the English peerage. I have yet to learn that they are richer than we are, better informed, or more distinguished for public or private virtue. Ancient lineage! I never heard of a peer with an ancient lineage. The real old families of the country are to be found among the peasantry. The gentry, too, may lay claim to old blood: I know of some Norman gentlemen whose fathers undoubtedly came in with the Conqueror. But a peer with an ancient lineage is to me quite a novelty. The thirty years' Wars of the Roses freed us from these gentlemen, I take it. After the battle of Tewkesbury a Norman baron was almost as rare a being as a wolf ... We owe the English peerage to three sources—the spoliation of the Church, the open and flagrant sale of its honours by the elder Stuarts, and the borough-mongering of our own times. These are the three main sources of the existing peerages of England, and in my opinion disgraceful ones.'

'And where will you find your natural aristocracy?' asked Coningsby. 'Among those,' Millbank answers, 'whom a nation recognises as the most eminent for virtue, talents, and property, and, if you will, birth and standing in this land. They guide opinions, and therefore they govern. I am no leveller; I look upon an artificial equality as equally pernicious with a factitious aristocracy, both depressing the energies and checking the enterprise of a nation. I am sanguine. I am the disciple of progress, but I have cause for my faith. I have witnessed advance. My father often told me that in his early days the displeasure of a peer of England was like a sentence of death.'

A more remarkable figure is Sidonia, the Hebrew financier, who is represented very much in the position of Disraeli himself, half a foreigner, and impartial onlooker, with a keen interest in the stability of English institutions, but with the insight possible only to an outsider, who observes without inherited prepossessions. Sidonia, the original of whom is as easily recognised, is, like Disraeli, of Spanish descent. His father staked all that he was worth on the Waterloo Loan, became the greatest capitalist in Europe, and bequeathed his business and his fortune to his son.

The young Sidonia 'obtained, at an early age, that experience of refined and luxurious society which is a necessary part of a finished education.

'It gives the last polish to the manners. It teaches us something of the powers of the passions, early developed in the hotbed of self-indulgence. It instils into us that indefinable tact seldom obtained in later life, which prevents us from saying the wrong thing, and often impels us to do the right. He was admired by women, idolised by artists, received in all circles with great distinction, and appreciated for his intellect by the very few to whom he at all opened himself; for, though affable and generous; it was impossible to penetrate him: though unreserved in his manners, his frankness was limited to the surface. He observed everything, thought ever, but avoided serious discussion. If you pressed him for an opinion, he took refuge in raillery, and threw out some grave paradox with which it was not easy to cop ... He looked on life with a glance rather of curiosity than contempt. His religion walled him out from the pursuits of a citizen. His riches deprived him of the stimulating anxieties of a man. He perceived himself a lone being without cares and without duties. He might have discovered a spring of happiness in the sensibilities of the heart; but this was a sealed fountain to Sidonia. In his organisation there was a peculiarity, perhaps a great deficiency: he was a man without affection. It would be harsh to say that he had no heart, for he was susceptible of deep emotions; but not for individuals—woman was to him a toy, man a machine.'

Though Sidonia is chiefly drawn from another person, Disraeli himself can be traced in this description. The hand is the hand of Esau; the voice is the voice of Jacob. 'The secret history of the world was Sidonia's pastime.' 'His great pleasure was to contrast the hidden motive with the public pretext of transactions.' This was Disraeli himself, and through Sidonia's mouth Disraeli explains to Coningsby the political condition of England. The Constitution professed to rest on the representation of the people. Coningsby asks him what a representative system means. He replies: 'It is a principle of which only a limited definition is current in this country. People may be represented without periodic elections of neighbours who are incapable to maintain their interests, and strangers who are unwilling ... You will observe one curious trait in the history of this country. The depositary of power is always unpopular: all combine against it: it always falls. Power was deposited in the great barons; the Church, using the king for its instrument, crushed the great barons. Power was deposited in the Church; the king, bribing the Parliament, plundered the Church. Power was deposited in the king; the Parliament, using the people, beheaded the king, expelled the king, changed the king, and finally for a king substituted an administrative officer. For a hundred and fifty years Power has been deposited in Parliament, and for the last sixty or seventy years it has been becoming more and more unpopular. In 1832, it endeavoured by a reconstruction to regain the popular affection; but, in truth, as the Parliament then only made itself more powerful, it has only become more odious. As we see that the barons, the Church, the king, have in turn devoured each other, and that the Parliament, the last devourer, remains, it is impossible to resist the impression that this body also is doomed to be devoured; and he is a sagacious statesman who may detect in what form and in what quarter the great consumer will arise.'

'Whence, then,' Coningsby asks, 'is hope to be looked for?' Sidonia replies 'In what is more powerful than laws and institutions, and without which the best laws and the most skilful institutions may be a dead letter or the very means of tyranny: in the national character. It is not in the increased feebleness of its institutions that I see the peril of England. It is in the decline of its character as a community. In this country, since the peace there has been an attempt to advocate a reconstruction of society on a purely rational basis. The principle of utility has been powerfully developed. I speak not with lightness of the disciples of that school: I bow to intellect in every form: and we should be grateful to any school of philosophers, even if we disagree with them: doubly grateful in this country where for so long a period our statesmen were in so pitiable an arrear of public intelligence. There has been an attempt to reconstruct society on a basis of material motives and calculations. It has failed. It must ultimately have failed under any circumstances. Its failure in an ancient and densely-peopled kingdom was inevitable. How limited is human reason the profoundest engineers are most conscious. We are not indebted to the reason of man for any of the great achievements which are the landmarks of human action and human progress. It was not reason that besieged Troy. It was not reason that sent forth the Saracen from the desert to conquer the world, that inspired the Crusader, that instituted the monastic orders. It was not reason that created the French revolution. Man is only truly great when he acts from the passions, never irresistible but when he appeals to the imagination. Even Mormon counts more votaries than Bentham. The tendency of advanced civilisation is, in truth, to pure monarchy. Monarchy is indeed a government which requires a high degree of civilisation for its full development. It needs the support of free laws and manners, and of a widely-diffused intelligence. Political compromises are not to be tolerated except at periods of rude transition. An educated nation recoils from the imperfect vicariate of what is called representative government. Your House of Commons, that has absorbed all other powers in the State, will in all probability fall more rapidly than it rose. Public opinion has a more direct, a more comprehensive, a more efficient organ for its utterance than a body of men sectionally chosen. The printing-press absorbs the duties of the sovereign, the priest, the Parliament. It controls, it educates, it discusses.

No attempt can be made here to analyse *Coningsby*. The object of these extracts is merely to illustrate Disraeli's private opinions. Space must be made for one more—a conversation between Coningsby and the younger Millbank. 'Tell me, Coningsby,' Millbank says, 'exactly what you conceive to be the state of parties in this country.' Coningsby answers, 'The principle of the exclusive Constitution of England having been conceded by the Acts of 1827–1832, a party has arisen in the State who demand that the principle of political Liberalism shall consequently be carried to its full extent, which it appears to them is impossible without getting rid of the fragments of the old Constitution which remain. This is the destructive party, a party with distinct and intelligible principles. They are resisted by another party who, having given up exclusion, would only embrace as much Liberalism as is necessary for the moment—who, without any embarrassing promulgation of principles, wish to keep things as they find them as long as they can; and these will manage them as they find them, as well as they can: but, as a party must have the semblance of principles, they take the names, of the things they have destroyed. Thus, they are devoted to the prerogatives of the Crown, although in truth the Crown has been stripped of every one of its prerogatives. They affect a great veneration for the Constitution in Church and State, though everyone knows it no longer exists. Whenever public opinion, which this party never attempts to form, to educate, or to lead, falls into some perplexity, passion, or caprice, this party yields without a struggle to the impulse, and, when the storm has passed, attempts to obstruct and obviate the logical and ultimately inevitable results of the measures they have themselves originated, or to which they have consented. This is the Conservative party.

'As to the first school, I have no faith in the remedial qualities of a government carried on by a neglected democracy who for three centuries have received no education. What prospect does it offer us of those high principles of conduct with which we have fed our imaginations and strengthened our wills? I perceive none of the elements of government that should secure the happiness of a people and the greatness of a realm. But if democracy be combated only by Conservatism, democracy must triumph and at no distant date. The man who enters political life at this epoch has to choose between political infidelity and a destructive creed.'

'Do you declare against Parliamentary government?'

'Far from it: I look upon political change as the greatest of evils, for it comprehends all. But if we have no faith in the permanence of the existing settlement ... we ought to prepare ourselves for the change which we deem impending ... I would accustom the public mind to the contemplation of an existing though torpid power in the Constitution capable of removing our social grievances, were we to transfer to it those prerogatives which the Parliament has gradually usurped, and used in a manner which has produced the present material and moral disorganisation. The House of Commons is the house of a few: the sovereign is the sovereign of all. The proper leader of the people is the individual who sits upon the throne.'

'Then you abjure the representative principle?'

'Why so? Representation is not necessarily, or even in a principal sense, Parliamentary. Parliament is not sitting at this moment: and yet the nation is represented. in its highest as well as in its most minute interests. Not a grievance escapes notice and redress. I see in the newspapers this morning that a pedagogue has brutally chastised his pupil. It is a fact known over all England— opinion is now supreme, and opinion speaks in print. The representation of the Press is far more complete than the representation of Parliament. Parliamentary representation was the happy device of a ruder age, to which it was admirably adapted. But it exhibits many symptoms of desuetude. It is controlled by a system of representation more vigorous and comprehensive, which absorbs its duties and fulfils them more efficiently ... Before a royal authority, supported by such a national opinion, the sectional anomalies of our country would disappear. Under such a system even statesmen would be educated. We should have no more diplomatists who could not speak French, no more bishops ignorant of theology, no more generals-in-chief who never saw a field. There is a polity adapted to our laws, our institutions, our feelings, our manners, our traditions: a polity capable of great ends, and appealing to high sentiments: a polity which, in my opinion, would render government an object of national affection, would terminate sectional anomalies, and extinguish Chartism.'

Disraeli was singularly regardless of the common arts of party popularity. He had spoken in defence of the Chartists when he was supposed to be bidding for a place under Sir Robert Peel; he had used language about Ireland, sweeping, peremptory, going to the heart of the problem, which Whig and Tory must have alike resented; and he had risked his seat by his daring. He was now telling the country, in language as plain as Carlyle's, that Parliament was an effete institution—and the House of Commons which he treated so disdainfully was in a few years to choose him for its leader. The anomalies in Disraeli's life grow more astonishing the deeper we look into them.

*Sybil*, published the next year, is more remarkable than even *Coningsby*. *Sybil; or, the Two Nations*, the two nations being the Rich and the Poor. Disraeli had personally studied human life in the manufacturing towns. He had seen the workman, when trade was brisk and wages high, enjoying himself in his Temple of the Muses; he had seen him, when demand grew slack, starving with his family in the garret, with none to help him. He had observed the insolent frauds of the truckmaster. He had seen the inner side of our magnificent industries which legislation was struggling to extend: he had found there hatred, anarchy, and incendiarism, and he was not afraid to draw the lurid picture in the unrelieved colours of truth.

The first scene opens on the eve of the Derby, when, in a splendid clubroom, the languid aristocrats, weary of the rolling hours, are making up their betting-books—they the choicest and most finished flowers of this planet, to whom the Derby is the event of the year. They are naturally high-spirited young men, made for better things, but spoilt by their education and surroundings.

From the youth we pass to the mature specimens of the breed who are in possession of their estates and their titles. Lord Marney's peerage dates from the suppression of the monasteries, in which his ancestor had been a useful instrument.

The secretary of Henry VIII's vicar-general had been rewarded by the lands of a northern abbey. The property had grown in value with the progress of the country. The family for the three centuries of its existence had never produced a single person who had contributed any good thing to the service of the commonwealth. But their consequence had grown with their wealth, and the Lord Marney of *Sybil* was aspiring to a dukedom. He is represented (being doubtless drawn from life) as the harshest of landlords, exacting the utmost penny of rent, leaving his peasantry to squalor and disease, or driving them off his estates to escape the burden of the poor-rate, and astonished to find Swing and his bonfires starting up about him as his natural reward. The second great peer of the story, Lord Mowbray, of a yet baser origin and character, owns the land on which has grown a mushroom city of mills and mill-hands. The ground-rents have made him fabulously rich, while, innocent of a suspicion that his wealth has brought obligations along with it, he lives in vulgar luxury in his adjoining castle.

On both estates the wretchedness is equal, though the character of it is different. Lord Marney rules in a country district. A clergyman asks him how a peasant can rear his family on eight shillings a week. 'Oh, as for that,' said Lord Marney, 'I have generally found the higher the wages, the worse the workmen. They only spend their money in the beer-shops. They are the curse of the country.' The ruins of the monastery give an opportunity for a contrast between the old England and the new, by a picture of the time when the monks were the gentlest of landlords, when exactions and evictions were unknown, and when churches were raised to the service of God in the same spots where now rise the brick chimneys and factories as the spires and temples of the modern Mammon-worship.

In Mowbray, the town from which the earl of that name drew his revenue, the inhabitants were losing the elementary virtues of humanity. Factory-girls deserted their parents, and left them to starve, preferring an independence of vice and folly; mothers farmed out their children at threepence a week to be got rid of in a month or two by laudanum and treacle. Disraeli was startled to find that 'infanticide was practised as extensively and legally in England as it was on the banks of the Ganges.' It is the same to-day: occasional revelations lift the curtains; and show it active as ever; familiarity has led us to look upon it as inevitable; the question, what is to be done with the swarms of children multiplying in our towns, admitting, at present, of no moral solution.

With some elaboration, Disraeli describes the human creatures bred in such places which were growing up to take the place of the old English.

'Devilsdust'—so one of these children came to be called, for he had no legitimate name or parentage—having survived a baby-farm by toughness of constitution, and the weekly threepence ceasing on his mother's death, was turned out into the streets to starve or to be run over.

Even this expedient failed. The youngest and feeblest of the band of victims, Juggernaut spared him to Moloch. All his companions were disposed of. Three months' play in the streets got rid of this tender company, shoeless, half-naked, and uncombed, whose ages varied from two to five years. Some were crushed, some were lost; some taught cold and fever, crept back to their garrets or their cellars, were dosed with Godfrey's Elixir, and died in peace. The nameless one, Devilsdust, would not disappear: he always got out of the way of the carts and horses, and never lost his own. They gave him no food: he foraged for his own, and shared with the dogs the garbage of the streets. But still he lived: stunted and pale, he defied even the fatal fever which was the only habitant of his cellar that never quitted it, and slumbering at night on a bed of mouldering straw, his only protection against the plashy surface of his den, with a dung-heap at his head and a cesspool at his feet, he still clung to the only roof that sheltered him from the tempest. At length, when the nameless one had completed his fifth year, the pest which never quitted the nest of cellars of which he was a citizen raged in the quarter with such intensity that the extinction of its swarming population was menaced. The haunt of this child was peculiarly visited. All the children gradually sickened except himself: and one night when he returned home he found the old woman herself dead and surrounded only by corpses. The child before this had slept on the same bed of straw with a corpse; but then there were also breathing things for his companions. A night passed only with corpses seemed to him itself a kind of death. He stole out of the cellar, quitted the quarter of pestilence, and, after much wandering, lay down near the door of a factory.

The child is taken in, not out of charity, but because an imp of such a kind happens to be wanted, and Devilsdust grows up, naturally enough, a Chartist and a dangerous member of society. But was there ever a more horrible picture drawn? It is like a chapter of Isaiah in Cockney novelist dress. Such things, we are told, cannot happen now. Can they not? There was a recent revelation at Battersea not so unlike it. The East-end of London produces crimes which are not obliterated because they are forgotten; and rag bundles may be seen on frosty nights at London housedoors, which, if you unroll them, discover living things not so unlike poor Devilsdust. For the future, these waifs and strays are at least to be sent to school. The school will do something, especially if one full meal a day is added to the lessons; but what is the best of Board schools compared to the old apprenticeship? The apprentice had his three full meals a day, and decent clothes, and decent lodging, and was taught some trade or handicraft by which he could earn an honest living when his time was out. The school cannot reach the miserable home. The school teaches no useful occupation, and when school-time is over the child is again adrift upon the world. He is taught to read and write. His mind is opened. Yes. He is taught to read the newspapers, and the penny-dreadfuls, and his wits are sharpened for him. Whether this will make him a more useful or more contented member of society, time will show.

Devilsdust was but one of many products of the manufacturing system which Disraeli saw and meditated upon.

He found a hand-loom weaver starving with his children in a garret, looking back upon the time when his loom had given him a cottage and a garden in his native village. The new machinery had ruined him, and he did not complain of the inevitable. But, as it was too late for him to learn another trade, he argued that if a society which had been created by labour suddenly became independent of it, that society was bound to maintain those whose only property was labour, out of the profits of that other property which had not ceased to be productive.

He talks with a superior artisan, who says to him:

'There is more serfdom in England now than at any time since the Conquest. I speak of what passes under my daily eyes when I say that those who labour can as little change or choose their masters now as when they were born thralls. There are great bodies of the working classes of this country nearer the condition of brutes than they have been at any time since the Conquest. Indeed, I see nothing to distinguish them from brutes, except that their morals are inferior. Incest and infanticide are as common among them as among the lower animals. The domestic principle wanes weaker and weaker every year in England nor can we wonder at it when there is no comfort to cheer and no sentiment to hallow the home.

'I am told a working man has now a pair of cotton stockings, and that Henry VIII himself was not as well off ... I deny the premises. I deny that the condition of the main body is better now than at any other period of our history—that it is as good as it has been at several. The people were better clothed, better lodged, and better fed just before the Wars of the Roses than they are at this moment. The Acts of Parliament, from the Plantagenets to the Tudors, teach us alike the prices of provisions and the rate of wages.'

'And are these the people?' the hero of the story asks himself, after such conversations. 'If so, I would I lived more among them. Compared with this converse, the tattle of our saloons has in it something humiliating. It is not merely that it is deficient in warmth and depth and breadth; that it is always discussing persons instead of principles; choking its want of thought in mimetic dogmas, and its want of feeling in superficial raillery. It is not merely that it has neither imagination, nor fancy, nor sentiment, nor knowledge to recommend it, but it appears to me, even as regards manners and expressions, inferior in refinement and phraseology, trivial, uninteresting, stupid, really vulgar.'

The tattle of politics was no better than the tattle of the saloons. Disraeli's experience in the northern towns had shown him what a problem lay before any Government of England which deserved the name. The Reform Bill was now twelve years old, and political liberty, so far, had not touched the outside of the disease. London, with its cliques and parties, its balls and festivities, seemed but an iridescent scum over an abyss of seething wretchedness. Here was work for rulers, if ruling was ever again to mean more than intrigue for office and manipulation of votes. Devilsdusts by thousands were generating in the vapour of Free Trade industry, while the Tadpoles and the Tapers, the wire-pullers of the House of Commons, were in a fever of agitation whether the Great Bedchamber question was to bring back the Melbourne Ministry, or whether Peel was to have his way.

*Tadpole*: The malcontent Liberals who have turned them out are not going to bring them in again. That makes us equal. Then we have an important section to work upon, the Sneaks, the men who are afraid of a dissolution. I will be bound we make a good working Conservative majority of twenty-five out of the Sneaks.

*Taper:* With the Treasury patronage, fears and favours combined, and all the places we refuse our own men, we may count on the Sneaks.

*Tadpole*: There are several religious men who have wanted an excuse for a long time to rat. We must get Sir Robert to make some kind of a religious move, and that will secure Sir Litany Lax and young Mr Salem.

*Taper:* It will never do to throw over the Church Commission. Commissions and committees ought always to be supported.

*Tadpole*: Besides, it will frighten the saints. If we could get Sir Robert to speak at Exeter Hall, were it only a slavery meeting!—that would do.

*Taper:* It is difficult: he must be pledged to nothing, not even to the right of search. Yet if we could get up something with a good deal of sentiment and no principle involved, referring only to the past, but with his practical powers touching the present! What do you think of a monument to Wilberforce or a commemoration of Clarkson?

*Tadpole*: There is a good deal in that. At present go about and keep our fellows in good humour. Whisper nothings that sound like something. But be discreet. Do not let there be more than half-a-hundred fellows who believe they are going to be Under-Secretaries of State. And be cautious about titles. If they push you, give a wink and press your finger to your lips. I must call here on the Duke of FitzAquitaine. This gentleman is my particular charge. I have been cooking him these three years. I had two notes from him yesterday, and can delay no longer. The worst of it is he expects I shall bear him the non-official announcement of his being sent to Ireland, of which he has about as much chance as I have of being Governor-General of India. It must be confessed ours is critical work sometimes, friend Taper. But never mind: we have to do with individuals; Peel has to do with a nation; and therefore we ought not to complain.

Is this a libel, or is it a fair account of the formation and working of English governments? Let those answer who have read the memoirs of the leading statesmen of the present century. Is there anywhere to be found, in the records of the overthrow or building-up of Cabinets, any hint, even the slightest, of an insight into the condition of the country, or of a desire to mend it? Forces were at work shattering the bodily frames and destroying the souls of millions of those whom they were aspiring to guide. Do we find anything at all, save man for a new turn of the political kaleidoscope? Might not Sidonia, might not Disraeli himself, reasonably doubt whether such methods of selecting administrations would be of long continuance?

Enough of *Sybil*. Disraeli skilfully contrives to distribute poetical justice among his imaginary characters—to bring his unworthy peers to retribution, and to reward the honest and the generous. He could do it in a novel. Unfortunately, the reality is less tractable. 'A year ago,' he says, in concluding the story, 'I presumed to offer to the public some volumes (*Coningsby*) that aimed at calling their attention to the state of political parties, their origin, their history, their present position. In an age of mean passions and petty thoughts, I would have impressed upon the rising race not to despair, but to seek in a right understanding of the history of their country, and in the energies of heroic youths, the elements of national welfare. The present work advances a step in the same emprise. From the state of parties it would draw public thought to the state of the people whom those parties for two centuries have governed. The comprehension and the cure of this greater theme depend upon the same agencies as the first. It is the past alone that can explain the present, and it is youth alone that can mould the remedial future ... The written history of our country for the last ten years has been a mere phantasm ... Oligarchy has been called Liberty; an exclusive priesthood has been christened a National Church. Sovereignty has been the title of something that has had no dominion, while absolute power has been wielded by those who profess themselves the servants of the people. In the selfish strife of factions, two great existences have been blotted out of the history of England: the monarch and the multitude. As the power of the Crown has diminished, the privileges of the people have disappeared, till at length the sceptre has become a pageant, and the subject has degenerated again into a serf.

'That we may live to see England once more possess a free monarchy, and a privileged and prosperous people, is my prayer; that these great consequences can only be brought about by the energy and devotion of our youth, is my persuasion ... The claims of the future are represented by suffering millions, and the youth of a nation are the trustees of posterity.'

# IX

*The New Gospel—Effect on English character—The Manchester School—*
*Tendencies of Sir Robert Peel—The Corn Laws—Peel brought into office*
*as a Protectionist—Disraeli and Peel—Protracted duel—Effect of Disraeli's*
*speeches—Final declaration of Peel against the Corn Laws—Corn Laws*
*repealed—Lord George Bentinck—Irish Coercion Bill—The Canning*
*episode—Defeat and fall of Peel—Disraeli succeeds to the Leadership of the*
*Conservative Party*

WITH THE LIGHT WHICH IS thrown by *Sybil* on the workings of Disraeli's mind, it is easy to understand the feelings with which he regarded the words and actions of Sir Robert Peel. He had seen, or supposed himself to have seen, a poisonous fungus eating into the heart of English life. In town and country, among the factory operatives, and on the estates of the rich and the noble, there was one rapid process of degeneracy. The peasantry were serfs, without the redeeming features of serfdom; the town artisans were becoming little better than brutes. In the cities, family and the softer influences of home were ceasing to exist. Children were being dragged up in misery or were left to die, and life was turned into a flaring workshop in which the higher purposes of humanity were obliterated or forgotten. The cause was everywhere the same. The gospel of political economy had been substituted for the gospel of Christ. The new law was to make money; the new aim of all classes, high and low alike, was to better their condition, as it was called, and make the most of their opportunities. Each must look out for himself: one man was not an other's keeper; labour was an article of trade, which the employer was to buy as cheap as he could get it, and the workman was to sell for the most that he could get. There their duties to each other ended, and the results were the scenes which he had witnessed in Marley and Mowbray. The further trade was extended under the uncontrolled conditions demanded by the 'Manchester school,' the more these scenes would multiply.

With the powerful Protectionist majority returned by the elections of 1841, Peel, in Disraeli's opinion, had an opportunity of bringing these demoralising tendencies under the authority of reason and conscience. The Corn Laws were but one feature of the problem. The real question was whether England was to remain as she had been, the nursing mother of a noble breed of men, or whether the physical and moral qualities of a magnificent race were to be sacrificed to a rage for vulgar wealth. Disraeli had not flattered his party. In Trafford and in the elder Millbank, he had drawn manufacturers who were splendidly alive to their duties. The ennobled landowners he had left to be represented by such men as Lord Marley. He was a Radical of the Radicals, a Radical who went to the root of the mischief. Like Carlyle, he was telling his country that unless they brought authority to deal with it, the England which we were so proud of would speedily forfeit her place among the nations of the world. It is likely enough that Peel would have failed if he had tried. His own followers were thinking more of their rents than of the moral condition of the people. But at any rate he was not trying, and evidently had no thought of trying. He took the course which promised most immediate success. To restore authority required an aristocracy who could be trusted to use it, and there was none such ready to hand. Wages must be left to the market where he found them. All that he could do to help the people was to cheapen the food which was bought with them, to lay taxation on the shoulders best able to bear it, and by education and such other means as he could provide to enable the industrious and the thoughtful to raise themselves, since neither legislation nor administration could raise them. Cheap food and popular education was his highest ideal. Peel could see what was immediately before him clearer than any man. His practical sagacity forbade him to look farther or deeper.

But the difficulty of his position lay in his having been brought into power as a Protectionist. The constituencies had given him his majority in reply to his own Protectionist declarations. If Free Trade was to be made the law of the land was Peel to repeat the part which be had played in Catholic emancipation? All reasonable Conservatives knew that the corn laws must be modified; but the change, if inevitable, need not be precipitate. Peel's great defect, Disraeli said in his *Life of Lord George Bentinck*, was that he wanted imagination, and in wanting that he wanted prescience. No one was more sagacious when dealing with the circumstances before him. His judgment was faultless,

LORD BEACONSFIELD                                    101

provided that he had not to deal with the future. But insight into consequences is the test of a true statesman, and because Peel had it not Catholic
emancipation, Parliamentary Reform, and the abrogation of the commercial
system were carried in haste or in passion, and without conditions or mitiga-
tory arrangements. On Canning's death the Tories might have had the game
in their hands. A moderate reconstruction of the House of Commons, the
transfer of the franchises of a few corrupt boroughs to the great manufacturing towns, would have satisfied the country. Peel let the moment pass, and
the Birmingham Union and the Manchester Economic School naturally followed. His policy was to resist till resistance was ineffectual, and then to grant
wholesale concessions as a premium to political agitation. The same scene was
being enacted over again. Sir Robert had rejected Lord John Russell's eight-
shilling duty. It appeared now, from the course in which he was drifting, that
the duty would be swept away altogether.

    In whatever way Peel had acted it is not likely that the state of England at
present would have differed materially from what it is. The forces which were
producing either the decay or the renovation of the Constitution, whichever
it proves to be, were too powerful for the wisest statesman either to arrest or
materially direct. Plato thought that had he been born a generation sooner
he might have saved Greece. The Olympian gods themselves could not have
saved Greece. But when untoward events arrive they are always visited on the
immediate actors in them, and Disraeli visited on Peel the ruin of his own
party and the disappointment of his own hopes. Perhaps, as he was but half
an Englishman, his personal interest in the question at issue was not extreme.
It is possible that he had resented Peel's neglect of him. At any rate he saw
his opportunity and used it to make his name famous. Hitherto he had been
known in the House of Commons as a brilliant and amusing speaker, but of
such independent ways that even the Conservatives gave him but a limited
confidence. So little had he spared his own friends in vote, speech, or writing that he may be acquitted of having dreamt of becoming their immediate
leader. But Peel had laid himself open. The Premier's policy, supported as it
was by his political pupils and the Liberal Opposition, Disraeli knew to be
practically irresistible. He was therefore spared the necessity of moderating
his own language. At least he could avenge his party and punish what he
could not prevent. It was his pride when he made an attack to single out the
most dangerous antagonist. Sir Robert Peel was the most commanding member of the House of Commons, and the most powerful oratorical athlete.

    Disraeli's speeches during Peel's Ministry and the effects which they pro-
duced can be touched but superficially in a narrative so brief as this, but

they formed the turning-point of his public life. His assaults when he began were treated with petulant contempt, but his fierce counter-hits soon roused attention to them. The Liberals were entertained to see the Conservative chief dared and smitten by one of his own followers. The country members felt an indignant satisfaction at the deserved chastisement of their betrayer. The cheers in Parliament were echoed outside the walls and rang to the farthest corner of the Continent. With malicious skill Disraeli touched one after the other the weak points of a character essentially great but superficially vulnerable. Like Laertes he anointed his point, but the venom lay in the truth of what he said, and the suffering which he inflicted was the more poignant because administered by a hand which Peel had unfortunately despised. Disraeli was displaying for the first time the peculiar epigrammatic keenness which afterwards so much distinguished him, and the skill with which he could drive his arrows through the joints in the harness. Any subject gave him an opening. Peel supposed that he had rebuked and silenced him by quoting in a dignified tone Canning's lines upon 'A Candid Friend.' The allusion was dangerous, for Peel's conduct to Canning had not been above reproach. Disraeli took an occasion when the general policy of the Ministry was under discussion to deliver himself in his clear, cold, impassive manner of a few sentences which hit exactly the temper of the House. Peel was generally accused of having stolen the Liberal policy. The right honourable gentleman, he said, had caught the Whigs bathing and had walked away with their clothes. He had tamed the shrew of Liberalism by her own tactics. He was the 'political Petruchio who had outbid them all.' Then came the sting. Peel had a full memory, and was rather proud of the readiness with which he could introduce quotations. Disraeli first touched his vanity by complimenting him on the success with which he used such weapons, 'partly because he seldom quoted a passage which had not previously received the mead of Parliamentary approbation, partly because his quotations were so happy … We all admire Canning,' he said; 'we all, or at least most of us, deplore his untimely end. We sympathised with him in his fierce struggle with supreme prejudice and sublime mediocrity, with inveterate foes and with candid friends. Mr Canning! and quoted by the right honourable gentleman. The theme, the poet, the speaker!—what a felicitous combination!'

The shaft which Peel had lightly launched was returned into his own breast and quivered there. The House of Commons, bored with dullness, delights in an unusual stroke of artistic skill. The sarcasm was received with cheers the worse to bear because while the Radicals laughed loud Peel's own side did not repress an approving murmur. He was like the bull in the Spanish arena when the *chulos* plant their darts upon his shoulders. 'He hoped,' he said, 'that the honourable member, having discharged the accumulated virus of the last week, now felt more at his ease;' but the barb had gone to the quick, and Peel, however proudly he controlled himself, was the most sensitive of men.

The tormentor left him no rest. A few days later came Mr Miles's motion for the application of surplus revenue to the relief of agriculture. Peel, when in opposition, had argued for the justice of this proposal. In office he found objections to it; and Disraeli told his friends that they must not be impatient with Sir Robert Peel. 'There is no doubt,' he said, 'a difference in the right honourable gentleman's demeanour as leader of the Opposition and as Minister of the Crown. But that is the old story. You must not contrast too strongly the hours of courtship with the years of possession. I remember the right honourable gentleman's Protection speeches. They were the best speeches I ever heard. But we know in all these cases when the beloved object has ceased to charm it is vain to appeal to the feelings.'

Sidney Herbert had spoken of the agricultural members as whining to Parliament at every recurrence of temporary distress. Disraeli again struck at Peel, dealing Sidney Herbert an insolent cut by the way.

'The right honourable gentleman,' he continued, 'being compelled to interfere, sends down his valet, who says in the genteelest manner, "We can have no whining here." But, sir, that is exactly the case of the great agricultural interest, that beauty which everyone wooed and one deluded. Protection appears to me to be in the same condition that Protestantism was in 1828. For my part, if we are to have Free Trade, I, who honour genius, prefer that such measures should be proposed by the honourable member for Stockport [Mr Cobden] than by one who, though skilful in Parliamentary manoeuvres, has tampered with the generous confidence of a great people and a great party. For myself, I care not what may be the result. Dissolve, if you please, the Parliament, whom you have betrayed, and appeal to the people, who I believe mistrust you. For me there remains this at least, the opportunity for expressing thus publicly my belief that a Conservative Government is an organised hypocrisy.'

This speech became famous. O'Connell, who, like Disraeli himself, bore no malice, when asked his opinion of it said it was all excellent except the peroration, and that was matchless. Disraeli, who had calmly watched the effect of his assaults, told his sister that 'Peel was stunned and stupefied, lost his head, and vacillating between silence and spleen, spoke much and weakly, assuring me that I had not hurt his feelings, that he would never reciprocate personalities, having no venom, &c. &c.'

A wasp which you cannot kill buzzing round your face and stinging when it has a chance will try the patience of the wisest. The Maynooth grant might have been a safe subject, for no one had advocated justice to Ireland more strongly than Disraeli; but he chose to treat it as a bid for the Irish vote. He called Peel 'a great Parliamentary middleman,' swindling both the parties that he professed to serve, and with deadly ingenuity he advised the Roman Catholic members to distrust a man 'whose bleak shade had fallen on the sunshine of their hopes for a quarter of a century.'

Driven beside himself at last, either on this or on some similar occasion, I have been assured that Peel forgot his dignity and asked a distinguished friend to carry a challenge from him to his reviler. The friend, unwilling to give Disraeli such a triumph and more careful of Peel's reputation than Peel himself, did not merely refuse, but threatened, if the matter was pursued farther, to inform the police.[1]

Disraeli asked Lord John Russell if he was not weary of being dragged at the triumphal car of a conqueror who had not conquered him in fair fight. 'Habitual perfidy,' he said, 'was not high policy of state.' He invited the Whig leader to assist him 'in dethroning the dynasty of deception and putting an end to the intolerable yoke of official despotism and Parliamentary imposture.'

Though the Free-Traders were revolutionising the tariff old-fashioned statesmen on both sides still hesitated at the entire abolition of the Corn Laws. It had been long assumed that without some protection the soil of England must fall out of cultivation. The Corn Law Leaguers were prepared even for that consummation, although they denied the probability of it. Disraeli, laying aside his personalities, showed in a noble passage that when he chose he could rise to the level of a great subject. He said:

> The leading spirits on the benches I see before me have openly declared their opinion that if there were not an acre of land cultivated in England it would not be the worse for this country. You have all of you in open chorus announced your object to be the monopoly of the commerce of the universe, to make this country the workshop of the world. Your system and ours are exactly contrary. We invite union; we believe that national prosperity can only be produced by the prosperity of all classes. You prefer to remain in isolated splendour and solitary magnificence. But, believe me, I speak not as your enemy when I say it will be an exception to the principles which seem hitherto to have ruled society if you can maintain the success at which you aim without the possession of that permanence and stability which the territorial principle alone can afford. Although you may for a moment flourish after their destruction, although your

ports may be filled with shipping, your factories smoke on every plain, and
your forges flame in every city, I see no reason why you should form an exception to that which the page of history has mournfully recorded, that you should
not fade like Tyrian dye and moulder like the Venetian palaces.

The great Whig peers, who were the largest of the territorial magnates,
were not yet prepared to cut their own throats. Lord John was still for his
eight-shilling duty. Peel was for a sliding scale which would lower the duty
without extinguishing it. But, as Disraeli observed, 'there is nothing in which
the power of circumstance is more evident than in politics. They baffle the
forethought of statesmen and control even the apparently inflexible laws of
national development and decay.' In the midst of the debate on the customs
duties came the Irish famine, and the Corn Laws in any shape were doomed.
Protection might have been continued in a moderate form if this catastrophe
had not occurred, provided the lords of the soil could have reverted to the
practice of their forefathers and looked on their rents as the revenue of their
estates, to be expended on the welfare of their dependents. But it was not in
them and could not come out of them. On the top of distress in England
followed the destruction of the sole means of support which the recklessness
of the Irish proprietors had left to five millions of peasants. Sir Robert Peel
informed his Cabinet that the duties on grain must be suspended by order
of Council, and that if once removed they could never be re-imposed. The
Cabinet split; Lord Stanley left him. He felt himself that if the Corn Laws
were to be repealed he was not the statesman who ought to do it. He resigned,
but he could not escape his fate. Lord John Russell could not form a Ministry
and 'handed the poisoned chalice back to Peel,' who was forced to return and
fulfil his ungracious office. He announced at the opening of the session of
1846 that the debates had convinced him not only of the impolicy but of the
injustice of the Corn Laws, and he warned his followers that if they defeated
him on a question of their personal interests 'an ancient monarchy and a
proud aristocracy might not be found compatible with a reformed House of
Commons.' The intimation and the threat were received with silent dismay.
Disraeli alone was able to give voice to their indignation, and in the style of
which he had made himself such a master he said that he at least was not one
of the converts; he had been sent to the House to advocate protection, and
to protection he adhered. In bitter and memorable words he compared Peel
to the Turkish admiral who had been sent out to fight Mehemet Ali, and had
carried his fleet into the harbour at Alexandria, alleging as his excuse that he
had himself an objection to war, that the struggle was useless, and that he had

accepted the command only to betray his master. Up to this time the Tory party had but half liked Disraeli. Many of his utterances in the House and out of it had a communistic taint upon them. Now, forlorn and desperate, a helpless flock deserted by the guardian whom they trusted, they cheered him with an enthusiasm which is only given to an accepted chief. 'So keen was the feeling and so spurring the point of honour that a flock deserted by their shepherds should not be led, as was intended, to the slaughter-house with- out a struggle, that a stimulus to exertion was given which had been rarely equalled in the House of Commons.'

Lord George Bentinck sold his racehorses and converted himself into a politician with a vigour of which no one had suspected him of being the possessor. Bentinck in youth had been Canning's secretary. He was then a moderate Whig, but had deserted politics for the turf. He was roused out of his amusements by the menaced overthrow of the principles in which he had been bred. His sense of honour was outraged by this second instance of what he regarded as Peel's double-dealing, and the Tories, whose pride would have been wounded by submitting avowedly to be led by an adventurer, were reconciled to Disraeli as second in command while they had Bentinck for his coadjutor and nominal chief. After the Peelites had separated from them they were still a powerful minority. If parties could but be forced back into their natural positions 'they could still exercise the legitimate influence of an Opposition in criticising details and insisting on modifications.' Free trade 'could be better contended against when openly and completely avowed than when brought forward by one who had obtained power by professing his hostility to it.' They were betrayed and they had a right to be angry; for Peel only, as parties stood, could carry repeal complete, and it was they who had given Peel his power.

Complaint, resistance were equally vain. The Bill for the repeal of the Corn Laws went through its various stages. On the third reading on May 15, when the battle was practically over, Disraeli again delivered a speech in which, dis- pensing with his epigrams and sarcasms, he displayed the qualities of a great and far-seeing statesman.

'I know,' he said, 'that there are many who believe that the time has gone by when one can appeal to those high and honest impulses that were once the mainstay and the main element of the English character. I know, sir, that we appeal to a people debauched by public gambling, stimulated and encour- aged by an inefficient and short sighted Minister. I know that the public mind is polluted by economic fancies, a depraved desire that the rich may become richer without the interference of industry and toil. I know that all confidence in public men is lost. But, sir, I have faith in the primitive and enduring elements of the English character. It may be vain now in the midnight of their intoxication to tell them that there will be an awakening of bitterness. It may be idle now in the spring-tide of their economic frenzy to warn them that there may be an ebb of trouble. But the dark and inevitable hour will arrive. Then when their spirit is softened by misfortune they will recur to those principles which made England great, and which, in our belief, alone can keep England great. Then too, perhaps, they may remember, not with unkindness, those who, betrayed and deserted, were neither ashamed nor afraid to struggle for the good old cause, the cause with which are associated principles the most popular, sentiments the most entirely national, the cause of labour, the cause of the people, the cause of England.'

The Bill passed both Houses, the noble Lords preferring their coronets to their convictions. The Conservative defeat was complete and irreparable. 'Vengeance, therefore, had succeeded in most breasts to more sanguine sentiments; the field was lost, but at any rate there was retribution for those who betrayed it.' The desire of vengeance was human. Perhaps there was a feeling, more respectable, that if Peel was allowed to triumph some other institution might be attacked on similar lines; but it cannot be said that the occasion which the Conservatives used to punish him was particularly creditable to them. Ireland was starving, and Ireland was mutinous. Ordinary law proving, as usual, unequal to the demand upon it, Peel was obliged to bring in one of the too familiar Coercion Bills. Both parties when in office are driven to this expedient. The Liberals when in Opposition generally denounce it. The Conservatives, as believing in order and authority, are in the habit of supporting the Administration, even if it be the Administration of their rivals. However discontented Peel might know his followers to be, he had no reason to expect that they would desert him on such a ground as this. His Coercion Bill passed the Lords without difficulty. It was read a first time in the House of Commons in an interval in the Corn Laws debate. A Conservative Opposition at such a crisis was at least factious, for there was danger of actual rebellion in Ireland. It was factious and it was not easy to organise. The opportunity was not a good one, but if it was allowed to escape a second was not likely to offer. Disraeli was a freelance, and had opposed Coercion before. Lord George had committed himself by his vote on the first reading. But he had a private grudge of his own against Peel. They resolved to try what could be done, and called a meeting of the Conservative party. They found their friends cold. 'There is no saying how our men will go,' Lord George said to Disraeli. 'It may be perilous, but if we lose this chance the traitor will escape. I will make the plunge.'

Lord George's avowed ground was that he could no longer trust Peel and 'must therefore refuse to give him unconstitutional powers.' On the merits he would probably have been defeated; but the main point was lost sight of in the personal quarrel to which the debate gave rise. Peel's conduct on the Corn Laws had revived the recollection of his treatment of Catholic Emancipation; When Canning, in 1827, was proposing to deal with it Peel had refused to join his Ministry on this avowed ground, and Canning's death was popularly connected with his supposed mortification at his failure on that occasion. Disraeli, as we have seen, had given Peel one sharp wound by referring to this episode in his career. Lord George dealt him another and a worse. The object was to prove that Peel's treachery was an old habit with him. He insisted that while he had refused to support Emancipation if introduced by Canning in 1827 he had himself changed his opinion about it two years before, and that he had himself heard him avow the alteration of his sentiments.

'We are told now,' Lord George said, speaking on the Coercion Bill—'we hear it from the Minister himself—that he thinks there is nothing humiliating in the course which he has pursued, that it would have been base and dishonest in him, and inconsistent with his duty to his Sovereign, if he had concealed his opinions after he had changed them; but I have lived long enough, I am sorry to say, to remember the time when the right honourable Baronet chased and hunted an illustrious relative of mine to death, and when he stated that he could not support his Ministry because, as leading member of it, he was likely to forward the question of Catholic Emancipation. That was the conduct of the right honourable Baronet in 1827, but in 1829 he told the House he had changed his opinion on that subject in 1825 and had communicated that change of opinion to the Earl of Liverpool.' 'Peel,' he said, 'stood convicted by his own words of base and dishonest conduct, conduct inconsistent with the duty of a Minister to his Sovereign.' 'He'(Lord George) 'was satisfied that the country would not forgive twice the same crime in the same man. A second time had the right honourable Baronet insulted the honour of Parliament and of the country, and it was now time that atonement should be made to the betrayed constituencies of the Empire.'

This had nothing to do with the Coercion Bill, and the motive of a charge so vindictive could only have been to irritate passions which did not need any further stimulus. The manners of Parliament are not supposed to have improved in recent periods, but the worst scenes in our own day are tame reproductions of the violence of forty years ago. The House of Commons was then the real voice of the country, and the anger of the Conservatives was the anger of half a nation. Lord George's charge was based on a speech alleged to have been made in the House itself. It was therefore absurd to accuse Peel of secret treachery. Any treachery which there might have been was open and avowed. But did Peel ever make such a speech? He rose as if stunned by the noise, and said peremptorily that the accusation was destitute of foundation. 'It was as foul a calumny as a vindictive spirit ever directed against a public man.' The House adjourned in perplexity and astonishment. Lord George was positive; he had been himself present, he said, when the words were spoken. The question became more perplexed on reference to the reports in the newspapers. The incriminated passage was not in the report in Hansard, which had been revised by Sir Robert; but it was found in the *Mirror of Parliament,* and also in the *Times.* It was discovered also that Sir Edward Knatchbull had drawn attention to Peel's words at the time, and had enquired why he had not supported Canning if, as he alleged, he had changed his mind as early as 1825. This seemed decisive. Lord George could not speak again by the rules of the House, and handed his authorities to Disraeli to use for him when the debate was renewed. Disraeli was not likely to fail with such materials, and delivered an invective to which the fiercest of his previous onslaughts was like the cooing of a dove. He was speaking as an advocate. It does not follow that he believed all he said, but the object was to make Peel suffer, and in this he undoubtedly succeeded. Peel made a lame defence, and the matter was never completely cleared up. Sir Edward Knatchbull's speech could not be explained away. The House, however, was willing to be satisfied. Lord John Russell, winding up the discussion and speaking for the Opposition, accepted Peel's denial, declaring that both on Catholic Emancipation and on the Corn Laws he had done good service to his country, but agreed that on both occasions he had turned round upon his pledges and ought not to be surprised if his friends were angry with him. Disraeli, in telling the story afterwards in his Life of Lord George, said that the truth was probably this: 'that Peel's change on the Emancipation question had not been a sudden resolve—that he had probably weighed the arguments for and against for a considerable time, and that having to make a complicated and embarrassing statement when he announced that he had gone round, and to refer by dates to several periods as to his contingent conduct, had conveyed a meaning to the House different from what he had intended.' Thus looked at his conduct might be explained to his entire vindication. Disraeli, however, still insisted that both Bentinck and himself had been also right in bringing the charge. The point before the House was Peel's general conduct. He had twice betrayed the party who had trusted his promises. Lord George said that to denounce men who had broken their pledges was public duty. 'If the country could not place faith in the pledges of their representatives the authority of the House of Commons would fall.' However that might be the storm decided the wavering minds of the Tory army, and with it the fate of Sir Robert Peel. In voting against the Coercion Bill they would be voting against their own principles, and the utmost efforts were made to retain them in their allegiance. Persuasion and menace were alike unavailing. 'The gentlemen of England,' of whom it had once been Sir Robert's proudest boast to be the leader, declared against him. He was beaten by an overpowering majority, and his career as an English Minister was closed.

Disraeli's had been the hand which dethroned him, and to Disraeli himself, after three years of anarchy and uncertainty, descended the task of again building together the shattered ruins of the Conservative party. Very unwillingly they submitted to the unwelcome necessity. Canning and the elder Pitt had both been called adventurers, but they had birth and connection, and they were at least Englishmen. Disraeli had risen out of a despised race; he had never sued for their favours; he had voted and spoken as he pleased, whether they liked it or not. He had advocated in spite of them the admission of the Jews to Parliament, and many of them might think that in his novels he had held the Peerage up to hatred. He was without Court favour, and had hardly a powerful friend except Lord Lyndhurst; He had never been tried on the lower steps of the official ladder. He was young too—only forty-two—after all the stir that he had made. There was no example of a rise so sudden under such conditions. But the Tory party had accepted and cheered his services, and he stood alone among them as a debater of superior power. Their own trained men had all deserted them. Lord George remained for a year or two as nominal chief: but Lord George died; the Conservatives could only consolidate themselves under a real leader, and Disraeli was the single person that they had who was equal to the situation. Not a man on either side in the House was more than his match in single combat. He had overthrown Peel and succeeded to Peel's honours.

His situation was now changed. So far he had remained the Tory Radical which he had first professed himself. He had his own views, and he had freely enunciated them, whether they were practical or only theoretic. No doubt he had thought that use might have been made of the reaction of 1841 to show the working men of England that the Tories were their real friends. He knew that the gulf which was dividing the rich from the poor was a danger to the Constitution. But, instead of far-reaching social legislation, Parliament had decided for the immediate relief of cheap bread. The country was committed to *laissez-faire* and liberty, and no reversion to earlier principles was now possible until *laissez-faire* had been tried out and the consequences of it tasted and digested. As an outsider he would have been still free to express his own opinions; as the leader of a party he had now to consider the disposition of his followers and the practical exigencies of the situation. All that was for the present possible was to moderate the pace of what was called Progress, keep the brake upon the wheels, and prevent an overturn in the descent of the incline. In the life of nations the periods of change are brief; the normal condition of things is permanence and stability. The bottom would be reached at last, and the appetite for innovation would be satiated.

1. I do not mention this story without careful enquiry.

# X

*Disraeli as Leader of the Opposition—Effects of Free Trade—Scientific discoveries—Steam—Railroads—Commercial revolution—Unexampled prosperity—Twenty-five years of Liberal government—Disraeli's opinions and general attitude—Party government and the conditions of it—Power of an Opposition Leader—Never abused by Disraeli for party interests—Special instances—The* coup d'état—*The Crimean War—The Indian Mutiny—The Civil War in America—Remarkable warning against playing with the Constitution*

MR DISRAELI'S CAREER HAS BEEN traced in detail from his birth to the point which he had now reached. Henceforward it is neither necessary nor possible to follow his actions with the same minuteness. The outer side of them is within the memory of most of us. The inner side can only be known when his private papers are given to the world. For twenty-five years he led the Conservative Opposition in the House of Commons, varied with brief intervals of power. He was three times Chancellor of the Exchequer under Lord Derby—in 1852, in 1858–9, and again in 1867—but he was in office owing rather to Liberal dissensions than to recovered strength on his own side. Being in a minority he was unable to initiate any definite policy; nor if the opportunity had been offered him would he have attempted to reverse the commercial policy of Peel. The country had decided for Free Trade, and a long Trade Wind of commercial prosperity seemed to indicate that the Manchester school had been right after all. On this question the verdict had gone against him, and the opinion of the constituencies remained against him. More than all, what Cobden had prophesied came to pass. Science and skill came to the support of enterprise. Railroads cheapened transport and annihilated distance. The ocean lost its terrors and became an easy and secure highway, and England, with her boundless resources, became more than ever the ocean's lord. Exports and imports grew with fabulous rapidity, and the prosperity which Disraeli had not denied might be the immediate effect exceeded the wildest hopes of the Corn Law League. Duty after duty was abandoned, and still the revenue increased. The people multiplied like bees, and yet wages rose. New towns sprang out of the soil like mushrooms, and the happy owners of it found their incomes doubled without effort of their own. Even the farmers prospered, for time was necessary, before America, and Russia, and India could pull down the market price of corn. Meat rose, farm produce of all kinds rose, and rent rose along with it, and the price of land. The farm labourer had his advance of a weekly shilling or two, and the agricultural interest, which had been threatened with ruin, throve as it had never thriven before. Althea's horn was flowing over with an exuberance of plenty, and all classes adopted more expensive habits, believing that the supply was now inexhaustible. The lords of the land themselves shook off their panic, and were heard to say that 'Free Trade was no such a bad thing after all.'

When things are going well with Englishmen they never look beyond the moment.

Pride in their port, defiance in their eye,
We see the lords of human kind go by.

Our countrymen of the last generation had confidence in themselves. They were advancing by leaps and bounds, and the advance was to continue for ever. Carlyle told them that their 'unexampled prosperity' was in itself no such beautiful thing, and was perhaps due to special circumstances which would not continue. Carlyle was laughed at as a pessimist. Yet as time goes on a suspicion does begin to be felt that both he and Disraeli were not as wrong as was supposed. The anticipated fall in wheat, though long delayed, has come at last; at last the land is falling out of cultivation, and the rents go back once more, and the labourers have lost their extra shillings. The English farmer is swamped at last under the competition of the outer world, and the peasantry, who were the manhood of the country, are shrinking in numbers. The other nations, who were to have opened their ports after our example, have preferred to keep them closed to protect their own manufactures add supply their own necessities.

Chimneys still smoke and engines clank, and the volume of our foreign trade does not diminish, but if the volume is maintained the profits fall, and our articles must be produced cheaper and ever cheaper if we are to hold our ground. As employment fails in the country districts the people stream into the towns. This great London of ours annually stretches its borders. Five millions of men and women, more than the population of all England at the time of the Commonwealth, are now collected within the limits of the Bills of Mortality. Once our English artisans were famous throughout Europe. They were spread among the country villages. Each workman was complete of his kind, in his way an artist; his work was an education to him as a man. Now he is absorbed in the centres of industry and is part of a machine. In the division of labour a human being spends his life in making pins' heads or legs of chairs, or single watch wheels, or feeding engines which work instead of him. Such activities do not feed his mind or raise his character, and such mind as he has left he feeds at the beer shop and music hall. Nay, in the rage for cheapness his work demoralises him. He is taught to scamp his labour and pass off bad materials for good. The carpenter, the baker, the smith, the mason learns so to do his work that it may appear what it professes to be, while the appearance is delusive, In the shop and manufactory he finds adulteration regarded as a legitimate form of competition. The various occupations of the people have become a discipline of dishonesty, and the demand for cheapness is corroding the national character.

Disraeli as a cool looker-on foresaw how it would be, but it was his fate to steer the vessel in the stream when it was running with the impetuosity of self-confidence. He could not stem a torrent, and all that he could do was to moderate the extent of its action. Only he refused to call the tendency of things Progress. 'Progress whence and progress whither?' he would ask. The only human progress worth calling by the name is progress in virtue, justice, courage, uprightness, love of country beyond love of ourselves. True, as everyone was saying, it was impossible to go back; but why? To go back is easy if we have missed our way on the road upwards. It is impossible only when the road is downhill.

His function was to wait till the fruit had ripened which was to follow, on such brilliant blossom, and to learn what the event would teach him; to save what he could of the old institutions, to avoid unnecessary interference, and forward any useful measures of detail for which opportunity might offer: meantime to watch his opponents and take fair advantage of their mistakes provided he did not injure by embarrassing them the real interests of the country. Party government in England is the least promising in theory of all methods yet adopted for a reasonable management of human affairs. In form it is a disguised civil war, and a civil war which can never end, because the strength of the antagonists is periodically recruited at the enchanted fountain of a general election. Each section in the State affects to regard its rivals as public enemies, while it admits that their existence is essential to the Constitution; it misrepresents their actions, thwarts their proposals even if it may know them to be good, and by all means, fair or foul, endeavours to supplant them in the favour of the people. No nation could endure such a system if it was uncontrolled by modifying influences. The rule till lately has been to suspend the antagonism in matters of Imperial moment, and to abstain from factious resistance when resistance cannot be effectual in the transaction of ordinary business. But within these limits and independent of particular measures each party proceeds on the principle that the tenure of office by its opponents is an evil in itself, and that no legitimate opportunity of displacing them ought to be neglected. That both sides shall take their turn at the helm is essential if the system is to continue. If they are to share the powers of the State they must share its patronage, to draw talent into their ranks. The art of administration can be learnt only by practice; young Tories as well as young Whigs must have their chance of acquiring their lessons. No party can hold together unless encouraged by occasional victory. Thus the functions of an Opposition chief are at once delicate and difficult. He must be careful *ne quid detrimenti capiat Respublica* through hasty action of his own. He must consider, on the other hand, the legitimate interests of his friends. As a member of a short-lived administration once bluntly expressed to me, 'you must blood the noses of your hounds,' but you must not for a party advantage embarrass a Government to the general injury of the Empire.

Under such circumstances the details of past Parliamentary sessions are for the most part wearisome and unreal. The opposing squadrons are arranged as if for battle, exhorted night after night in eloquence so vivid that the nation's salvation might seem at stake. The leaders cross swords. The newspapers spread the blaze through town and country, and all on subjects of such trifling moment that they are forgotten when an engagement is over, the result of which is known and perhaps determined beforehand. When the division is taken, the rival champions consume their cigars together in the smoking-room and discuss the next Derby or the latest scandal. Questions are raised which wise men on both sides would willingly let alone, because neither party can allow its opponents an opportunity of gaining popular favour. The arguments are insincere. The adulterations of trade pass into Parliament and become adulterations of human speech. It is a price which we pay for political freedom, and a price which tends annually to rise. Thus it is rightly felt to be unfair to remember too closely the words or sentiments let fall in past debates.

The modern politician has often to oppose what in his heart he believes to be useful, and defend what he does not wholly approve. He has to affect to be in desperate earnest when he is talking of things which are not worth a second's serious thought. Everyone knows this and everyone allows for it. The gravest statesman of the century could be proved as uncertain as a weathercock, lightly to be moved as thistle-down, if every word which he utters in Parliament or on platform is recorded against him as seriously meant.

The greater part of our Parliamentary history during the twenty-five years of Disraeli's leadership of the Tory Opposition in the House of Commons is of this character. The nation was going its own way—multiplying its numbers, piling up its ingots, adding to its scientific knowledge, and spreading its commerce over the globe. Parliament was talking, since talk was its business, about subjects the very names of which are dead echoes of vanished unrealities. It may be claimed for Disraeli that he discharged his sad duties during all this time with as little insincerity as the circumstances allowed, that he was never wilfully obstructive, and that while he was dexterous as a party chief he conducted himself always with dignity and fairness. It cost him less than it would have cost most men, because being not deeply concerned he could judge the situation with coolness and impartiality. He knew that it was not the interest of the Conservative party to struggle prematurely for office, and he had a genuine and loyal concern for the honour and greatness of the country. Any proposals which he considered good he helped forward with earnestness and ability—proposals for shortening the hours of labour, for the protection of children in the factories, for the improvement of the dwelling-houses of the poor. He may be said to have brought the Jews into Parliament a quarter of a century before they would otherwise have been admitted there, for the Conservatives left to themselves would probably have opposed their admission to the end. He could accomplish little, but he prevented harm. The interesting intervals of the long dreary time were when the monotony was broken in upon by incidents from without—Continental revolutions, Crimean campaigns, Indian mutinies, civil wars in America, and such like, when false steps might have swept this country into the whirlpools, and there was need for care and foresight. On all or most of these occasions he signalised himself not only by refraining from taking advantage of them to embarrass the Government, but by a loftiness of thought and language unfortunately not too common in the House of Commons.

The coup d'état of Louis Napoleon did not deserve to be favourably received in England. The restoration of a military Government in France alarmed half of us by a fear of the revival of the Napoleonic traditions.

The overthrow of a Constitution exasperated the believers in liberty. All
alike were justly shocked by the treachery and violence with which the
Man of December had made his way to the throne. The newspapers and
popular orators, accustomed to canvass and criticise the actions of statesmen at home, forgot that prudence suggested reticence about the affairs
of others with whom we had no right to interfere. The army was master of
France, and to speak of its chief in such terms as those in which historians
describe a Sylla or a Marius was not the way to maintain peaceful relations
with dangerous neighbours. Neither the writers nor the speakers wished for
war with France. They wished only for popularity as the friends of justice
and humanity; but war might easily have been the consequence unless pen
and tongue could be taught caution. Disraeli applied the bit in a powerful
speech in the House. He had been acquainted with Louis Napoleon in the
old days at Lady Blessington's. He had no liking for him and no belief in
him; but he reminded the House and he reminded the nation that it was
not for us to dictate how France was to be governed, and that the language,
so freely used might provoke a formidable and even just resentment.

The Crimean war he was unable to prevent, but as good a judge as Cobden
believed that if Disraeli and Lord Derby had not been turned out of office in
1852 they would have prevented it, and a million lives and a hundred millions
of English money, which that business cost, need not have been sacrificed
over a struggle which events proved to be useless. Much was to be said for a
policy which would have frankly met and accepted the Emperor Nicholas's
overtures to Sir Hamilton Seymour. If a joint pressure of all the European
Powers had been brought to bear on Turkey, internal reforms could have
been forced upon her, and preparation could have been made peacefully for
the disappearance, ultimately inevitable, of the Turks out of Europe. If the
state of public opinion forbade this (and Disraeli himself would certainly
never have adopted such a course) something was to be said also for adher-
ing firmly from the first to the traditionary dogmas on the maintenance of
the integrity of the Turkish Empire, and this the Conservatives were prepared to do. Nothing at all was to be said for hesitation and waiting upon
events. The Tzar was deceived into supposing that while we talked we meant
nothing, and we drifted into a war of which the only direct result was a waste
of money which, if wisely used, might have drained the Bog of Allen, turned
the marshes of the Shannon into pasture ground, and have left in Ireland
some traces of English rule to which we could look with satisfaction.

The indirect consequences of fatuities are sometimes worse than their
immediate effects. It was known over the world that England, France, Turkey,

and Italy had combined to endeavour to crush Russia, and had succeeded only in capturing half of a single Russian city. The sepoy army heard of our failures, and the centenary of the battle of Plassy was signalised by the Great Mutiny. The rebellion was splendidly met. It was practically confined to the army itself; and over the largest part of the peninsula the general population remained loyal; but the murder of the officers, the cruelties to the women and children, and the detailed barbarities which were paraded in the newspapers, drove the English people into fury. Carried away by generous but unwise emotion, they clamoured for retaliatory seventies, which, if inflicted, would have been fatal to our reputation and eventually perhaps to the Indian Empire. Disraeli's passionless nature was moved to a warmth which was rare with him. Such feelings, he said, were no les than 'heinous.' We boasted that we ruled India in the interests of humanity; were we to stain our name by copying the ferocities of our revolted subjects?

His influence was no less fortunately exerted at the more dangerous crisis of the American civil war. On all occasions English instinct inclines to take the weaker side, but for many reasons there was in England a particular and wide-spread inclination for the South. There was a general feeling that the American colonies had revolted against ourselves; if they quarrelled, and a minority of them desired independence, the minority had as good a right to shake off the North as the thirteen original States to shake off the mother country. The North in trying to coerce the South was contradicting its own principle. Professional politicians even among the Liberals were of opinion that the transatlantic republic was dangerously strong, that it was disturbing the balance of power, and that a division on dissolution of it would be of general advantage. Those among us who disliked republican institutions, and did not wish them to succeed, rejoiced at their apparent failure, and would willingly have lent their help to make it complete.

The Northern Americans were distasteful to the English aristocracy. The Southern planters were supposed to be gentlemen with whom they had more natural affinity. The war was condemned by three-quarters of the London and provincial press, and when the Emperor Napoleon invited us to join with him in recognising the South and breaking the blockade it perhaps rested with Disraeli to determine how these overtures should be received. Lord Palmerston was notoriously willing. Of the Tory party the greater part would, if left to themselves, have acquiesced with enthusiasm. With a word of encouragement from their leader a great majority in Parliament would have given Palmerston a support which would have allowed him to disregard the objections of some of his colleagues. But that word was not spoken. Disraeli was as mistaken as most of us on the probable results of the conflict. He sup-posed, as the world generally supposed, that it must leave North America divided, like Europe, into two or more independent States; but he advised and he insisted that the Americans must be left to shape their fortunes in their own way. England had no right to interfere.

Events move fast. Mankind make light of perils escaped, and the questions which distracted the world a quarter of a century ago are buried under the anxieties and passions of later problems. Hereafter, when the changes and chances of the present reign are impartially reviewed, Disraeli will be held to have served his country well by his conduct at this critical contingency.

In domestic politics he was a partisan chief. His speeches in Parliament and out of it were dictated by the exigencies of the passing moment. We do not look for the real opinions of a leading counsel in his forensic orations. We need not expect to find Disraeli's personal convictions in what he occasion-ally found it necessary to say.

There did, however, break from him remarkable utterances on special occa-sions which deserve and will receive remembrance. Two extracts only can be introduced here, one on the state of the nation in 1849, when he spoke for the first time as the acknowledged Conservative leader, the other on Parliamentary Reform in 1865, the subject on which his own action two years later called out Carlyle's scornful comment. The first referred to the changed condition of things brought about by the adoption of Free Trade.

'In past times,' he said, 'every Englishman was taught to believe that he occupied a position better than the analogous position of individuals of his order in any other country in the world. The British merchant was looked on as the most creditable, the wealthiest, the most trustworthy merchant in the world. The English farmer ranked as the most skilful agriculturist ... The English manufacturer was acknowledged as the most skilful and successful, without a rival in ingenuity and enterprise. So with the British sailor; the name was a proverb. And chivalry was confessed to have found a last resort in the breast of a British officer. It was the same in the learned professions. Our physicians and lawyers held higher positions than those of any other countries ... In this manner English society was based upon the aristocratic principle in its complete and most magnificent development.

You set to work to change the basis on which this society was established. You disdain to attempt the accomplishment of the best, and what you want to achieve is the cheapest. The infallible consequence is to cause the impov-erishment and embarrassment of the people. But impoverishment is not the only ill consequence which the new system may produce. The wealth of England is not merely material wealth. It does not merely consist in the number of acres we have tilled and cultivated, nor in our havens filled with shipping, nor in our unrivalled factories, nor in the intrepid industry of our miners. Not these merely form the principal wealth of our country; we have a more precious treasure, and that is the character of the people. This is what you have injured. In destroying what you call class legislation you have destroyed the noble and indefatigable ambition which has been the source of all our greatness, of all our prosperity, of all our powers.

The noble ambition of which Disraeli was speaking was the ambition of men to do their work better and more honestly than others, and the rage for cheapness has indeed destroyed this, and destroyed with it English integrity. We are impatiently told that the schools will set it right again. Character, unfortunately, is not to be formed by passing standards, second or first. It is the most difficult of all attainments. It is, or ought to be, the single aim of every government deserving the name, and there is a curious remark of Aristotle that while aristocratic governments recognised the obligation and acted upon it democracies invariably forget that such an obligation exists. They assume that character will grow of itself. Of character ὁπόσον οὖν, ever so little would suffice, and so the old republic went to ruin, as they deserved to go. No subject deserves more anxious reflection. Yet Disraeli is the only modern English statesman who has given it a passing thought.

The second passage referred to the playing with the Constitution which had been going on ever since 1832. Lord Grey had dispossessed the gentry and given the power to the middle classes. The operatives, the numerical majority, were left unrepresented. Neither party wished to enfranchise them, for fear they might be tempted to inroads upon property. Each was afraid to confess the truth, and thus year after year the extension of the suffrage was proposed dishonestly and dropped with satisfaction. Lord John Russell made his last experiment in 1865, and Disraeli gave the House a remarkable warning, which, if he afterwards neglected it himself the statesmen who are now with light hearts proposing to break the Constitution to pieces may reflect upon with advantage.

There is no country at the present moment that exists under the same circumstances and under the same conditions as the people of this realm. You have an ancient, powerful, and richly endowed Church, and perfect religious liberty. You have unbroken order and complete freedom. You have landed estates as large as the Romans, combined with a commercial enterprise such as Carthage and Venice united never equalled. And you must remember that this peculiar country, with these strong contrasts, is not governed by force. It is governed by a most singular series of traditionary influences, which generation after generation cherishes and preserves because it knows that they embalm custom and represent law. And with this you have created the greatest empire of modern times. You have amassed a capital of fabulous amount. You have devised and sustained a system of credit still more marvellous, and you have established a scheme so vast and complicated of labour and industry that the history of the world affords no parallel to it. And these mighty creations are out of all proportion to the essential and indigenous elements and resources of the country. If you destroy that state of society remember this: *England cannot begin again.* There are countries which have gone through great suffering. You have had in the United States of America a protracted and fratricidal civil war, which has lasted for four years; but if it lasted for four years more, vast as would be the disaster and desolation, when ended, the United States might begin again, because the United States would then only be in the same condition that England was in at the end of the wars of the Roses, when probably she had not three millions of population, with vast tracts of virgin soil and mineral treasures not only undeveloped but undreamt of. Then you have France, France had a real revolution in this century, a real revolution, not merely a political but a social revolution. The institutions of the country were uprooted, the order of society abolished, even the landmarks and local names removed and erased. But France could begin again. France had the greatest spread of the most exuberant soil in Europe, and a climate not less genial. She had, and always had, comparatively a limited population, living in a most simple manner. France, therefore, could begin again, But England, the England we know, the England we live in, the England of which we are proud, could not begin again. I do not mean to say that after great trouble England would become a howling wilderness, or doubt that the good sense of the people would to some degree prevail, and some fragments of the national character survive; but it would not be the old England, the England of power and tradition and capital, that now exists. It is not in the nature of things. And, sir, under these circumstances I hope the House, when the question is one impeaching the character of our Constitution, will hesitate; that it will sanction no step that has a tendency to democracy, but that it will maintain the ordered state of free England in which we live.

# XI

*Literary work*—Tancred; or, the New Crusade—*Modern philosophy*—
*The* Vestiges of the Natural History of Creation—Life of Lord George
Bentinck—*Disraeli's religious views*—*Revelation as opposed to science*—
*Dislike and dread of Rationalism*—*Religion and statesmanship*—*The national
creed the supplement of the national law*—*Speech in the theatre at Oxford*—
*Disraeli on the side of the angels*

As Disraeli's public life grew more absorbing his literary work was
necessarily suspended. But before the weight of leadership was finally
laid upon him he had written two more books—*Tancred; or, the New
Crusade*, the third of the series of novels which he called a trilogy, and the
biography of his friend and comrade Lord George Bentinck.

*Tancred* of all his writings was that which he himself most esteemed.
When it was composed he was still under the illusion of a possible regenerated aristocracy. He saw that they had noble qualities, but they wanted the
inspiration of a genuine religious belief. Tancred, the only child and heir of
a ducal family, is an enthusiastic and thoughtful youth with high aspirations
after excellence. He is a descendant of the Crusaders, and his mind turns
back to the land which was the birthplace of his nominal creed. There alone
the Maker of the universe had held direct communication with man. There
alone, perhaps, it was likely that he would communicate with his creature
again. Christian Europe still regarded the Israelites as the chosen people. Half
of it still worshipped a Jew and the other half a Jewess. But between criticism
and science and materialism, and the enervating influence of modern habits,
the belief which lingered in form had lost its commanding power.

Before the diseases of society could be cured the creed must be restored to its authority. The Tractarians were saying the same thing in tones of serious conviction. Disraeli, the politician and the man of the world, was repeating it in a tone which wavered between mockery and earnestness, the mockery, perhaps, being used as a veil to cover feelings more real than they seemed.

Tancred, on leaving the University where he had brilliantly distinguished himself, is plunged into the London world. He meets attractive beings, whose souls, he imagines, must be as beautiful as their faces. One illusive charmer proves to be a gambler on the Stock Exchange; another has been studying the *Vestiges of the Natural History of Creation*, called here 'Revelations of Chaos,' and expounds the great mystery to him in a gilded drawing room.

"The subject is treated scientifically," said the Lady Constance. "Everything is explained by geology and astronomy, and in that way it shows you exactly how a star is formed. Nothing could be so pretty, a cluster of vapour, the cream of the Milky Way, a sort of celestial cheese churned into light. You must read it. 'Tis charming."

"Nobody ever saw a star formed," said Tancred.

"Perhaps not. You must read the 'Revelations;' it is all explained. But what is more interesting is the way in which man has been developed. You know all is development. The principle is perpetually going on. First there was nothing; then there was something; then—I forget the next. I think there were shells, then fishes. Then came—let me see—did we come next? Never mind that; we came at last, and at the next change there will be something very superior to us, something with wings. Ah, that is it! we were fishes. I believe we shall be crows; but you must read it."

"I do not believe I ever was a fish," said Tancred.

"Oh but it is all proved. Read the book. It is impossible to contradict anything in it; you understand it is all science. Everything is proved by geology, you know. You see exactly how everything is made, how many worlds there have been, how long they lasted, what went before, what comes next. We are a link in the chain as inferior animals were that preceded us. We in time shall be inferior. All that will remain of us will be some relics in a new Red Sandstone. This is development. We had fins; we may have wings."

The theory thus airily sketched has been established since, in a more completed argument, by Darwin. Such solid evidence as there is for it has been before mankind for thousands of years, and has not seemed unanswerable. The Jews and the Greeks knew as well as modern philosophers that human bodies are built on the same type, and are bred and supported by the same means as the bodies of animals; that the minds of animals are in 'the same way clumsy likenesses of ours. Compared to the real weight of these acknowledged facts the additions of Darwin, or of the author of the *Vestiges*, are relatively nothing. If the doctrine of development has passed into popular acceptance, if it has been received into Churches and adapted to Catholic theology, the explanation is not in the increased form of evidence but in a change in ourselves. Candid consideration of our natures, as we now find them makes it appear not so improbable that we are but animals after all. Tancred, fresh from Tractarian Oxford, is unconvinced. He hurries to Palestine, sees a vision of angels on Mount Sinai, falls in love with a Jewish maiden who is an embodied spirit of inspiration, and is interrupted at the moment of pouring out his homage by the arrival of 'the Duke and Duchess at Jerusalem.' Whether the coming of these illustrious persons was to end in a blessing on his enthusiasm or in recalling him to a better recognition of what was due to his station in society the story is silent.

The *Life of Lord George Bentinck* is an admirably written biography of the friend who had stood by Disraeli in his conflict with Peel, and who, after living long enough to show promise of eminence, had suddenly and prematurely died. To the student of the Parliamentary history of those times the book is of great value. To the general reader the most interesting parts of it are those which throw light on Disraeli's own mind.

The most important fact to every man is his religion. If we would know what a man is we ask what notions he has formed about his duty to man and God. The question is often more easily asked than answered, for ordinary persons repeat what they have learnt, and have formed no clear notions at all; and the few wise, though at bottom they may be as orthodox as a bishop, prefer usually to keep their thoughts to themselves. Disraeli, however, in this book invites attention to his own views. An insincere profession on such a subject forfeits the respect of everyone, and we are entitled to examine what he says and to enquire how far he means it.

Those who cannot bear suspense and feel the necessity of arriving at a positive conclusion, make their choice between two opinions—one, that God created the world and created man to serve Him, that He gave to man a revelation of His law and holds him answerable for disobedience to it: the other, that the world has been generated by the impersonal forces of nature; that all things in it, animate and inanimate, find their places and perform their functions according to their several powers and properties; that man having ampler faculties than other animals, discovers the rules which are good for him to follow, as he discovers other things, and that what he calls 'revelations' are no more than successive products of the genius of gifted members of his race thrown out in a series of ages. The second of these theories is what we generally call the 'creed of science;' the first is the religious and is represented by Judaism and Christianity. Disraeli, with a confessed pride in belonging himself to the favoured race, desires us to understand that he receives with full and entire conviction the fact that a revelation was really made to his fore fathers, and rejects the opposite speculation as unsupported by evidence and degrading to human nature. The subject is introduced in an argument for the admission of the Jews to Parliament. He does not plead for their admission on the principle of 'toleration,' which he rejects as indifferentism, but on the special merits of the Jews themselves, and on their services to mankind. He regards Christianity as simply completed Judaism. Those who profess to be Jews only he consider unfortunate in believing only the first part of their religion, but still as defending and asserting the spiritual view of man's nature in opposition to the scientific, and as holding a peculiar place in the providential dispensation. He speaks of the mysteries of Christianity in a tone which, if not sincere, is detestable. 'If,' he says, 'the Jews had not prevailed upon the Romans to crucify our Lord, what would have become of the atonement? But the human mind cannot contemplate the idea that the most important deed of time could depend upon human will. The immolator was preordained, like the Victim, and the holy race supplied both.' The most orthodox divine could not use severer words of censure than Disraeli used for the critical rationalism which treats the sacred history as a myth—for Bishop Colenso, for the Essayists and Reviewers. His words have not the ring of the genuine theological metal. Artificial and elaborate diction is not the form in which simple belief expresses itself. Yet the fault may not be entirely in Disraeli. Even when most in earnest he was inveterately affected. It is to be remembered also that in his real nature he remained a Jew, and his thoughts on these great subjects ran on Asiatic rather than on European lines. We imagine that the Scriptures must be read everywhere into the same meaning; we forget how much European thought has passed into them through the traditions of the Church and through the various translations. In the English version St. Paul reasons like an Englishman. A Jew reads in St. Paul's language allusions to oriental customs and beliefs of which Europeans know nothing; we have therefore no reason to suspect Disraeli of insincerity because he did not express himself as we do.

Perhaps he truth may be this: He was a Conservative English statesman he knew that the English Church was the most powerful Conservative institution still remaining. Criticism was eating into it on one side, and ritualism on the other, breaking through the old use and wont, the traditionary habits which were its strongest bulwarks. He wished well to the Church. He was himself a regular communicant, and he desired to keep it as it was. He believed in the religious principle as against the philosophic; and from the nature of his mind he must have known that national religions do not rest upon argument and evidence. When forms vary from age to age and country to country no one of them can be absolutely free from error. Plato, having drawn the model of a commonwealth with a code of laws as precise as positive enactment can prescribe, goes on to say that for conduct in ordinary life which law cannot reach there is the further rule of religion. Religion, however, is a thing which grows and cannot be made. The central idea that man is a responsible being is everywhere the same but the idea shapes various forms for itself into which legend, speculation, and prevailing opinions necessarily enter. As time goes on, therefore, questions rise concerning this or that fact and this or that ceremony, which if indulged will create general scepticism. Such enquiries must be sternly repressed. In religion lies the only guidance for human life. The wise legislator, therefore, will regard the Church of his country as the best support of the State. The subject will reflect that although observances may seem offensive and stories told about the gods may seem incredible; yet as a rule of action a system which has been the growth of ages is infinitely more precious than any theory which he could think out for himself. He will know that his own mind, that the mind of any single individual, is unequal to so vast a matter, that it is of such immeasurable consequence to him to have his conduct wisely directed that, although the body of his religion be mortal like his own, he must not allow it to be rudely meddled with. He may think as he likes about the legends of Zeus and Here, but he must keep his thoughts to himself: a man who brings into contempt the creed of his country is the deepest of criminals; he deserves death and nothing less. Θανάτῳ ζημιούσθω, 'Let him die for it'—a remarkable expression to have been used by the wisest and gentlest of human lawgivers.

Disraeli's opinions on these subjects were perhaps the same as Plato's. He too may have had his uncertainties about Zeus and Hero, and yet have had no uncertainty at all about the general truth of the teaching of the Church of England, while as a statesman he was absolutely convinced of the necessity of supporting and defending it, defending it alike from open enemies and from the foolish ecclesiastical revivalism into which Tractarianism had de generated. The strength of the Church lay in its hold upon the habits of the people, and whoever was breaking through the usages which time had made familiar and consecrated was equally dangerous and mischievous. The critics were bringing in reason to decide questions which belonged to conscience and imagination. The ritualists were bringing back pagan superstition in a pseudo-Christian dress. He despised the first. He did what he could to restrain the second with a Public Worship Bill as soon as he had power to interfere. Late in his career, when he was within view of the Premiership, he used an opportunity of expressing his feeling on the subject in his own characteristic manner.

Oxford having produced the High Churchmen, was now generating rationalists and philosophers. Intellectual society was divided into the followers of Strauss and Darwin and those who believed that the only alternative was the *Summa Theologiae*. Both streams were concentrated in support of the Liberal leader, who was Disraeli's political antagonist; one because he represented progress, the other because in matters spiritual he was supposed to hold the most advanced Catholic doctrines. In the year 1864 Disraeli happened to be on a visit at Cuddesdon, and it happened equally that a diocesan conference was to be held at Oxford at the time, with Bishop Wilberforce in the chair. The spiritual atmosphere was, as usual, disturbed. The clerical mind had been doubly exercised by the appearance of Colenso on the 'Pentateuch' and Darwin on the *Origin of Species*. Disraeli, to the surprise of everyone, presented himself in the theatre. He had long abandoned the satins and silks of his youth, but he was as careful of effect as he had ever been, and had prepared himself in a costume elaborately negligent. He lounged into the assembly in a black velvet shooting-coat and a wide-awake hat, as if he had been accidentally passing through the town. It was the fashion with University intellect to despise Disraeli as a man with neither sweetness nor light; but he was famous, or at least notorious, and when he rose to speak there was general curiosity. He began in his usual affected manner, slowly and rather pompously, as if he had nothing to say beyond perfunctory platitudes.

The Oxford wits began to compare themselves favourably with the dullness of Parliamentary orators, when first one sentence and then another startled them into attention. They were told that the Church was not likely to be disestablished. It would remain, but would remain subject to a Parliament which would not allow an *imperium in imperio*. It must exert itself and reassert its authority, but within the limits which the law laid down. The interest grew deeper when he came to touch on the parties to one or other of which all his listeners belonged. High Church and Low Church were historical and intelligible, but there had arisen lately, the speaker said, a party called the Broad, never before heard of. He went on to explain what Broad Churchmen were.

'It would not be wise to treat the existence and influence of this new party with contempt … It is founded on the principle of criticism. Now doubt is an element of criticism, and the tendency of criticism is necessarily sceptical.

It is quite possible that such a party may arrive at conclusions which we may deem monstrous. They may reject inspiration as a principle and miracles as a practice. That is possible: and I think it quite logical that having arrived at such conclusions they should repudiate creeds and reject articles of faith, because creeds and articles of faith cannot exist or be sustained without acknowledging the principle of inspiration and the practice of miracles. All that I admit. But what I do not understand, and what I wish to draw the attention of this assembly and of this country generally to, is this: that, having arrived at these conclusions, having arrived conscientiously at the result that with their opinions they must repudiate creeds and reject articles, they should not carry their principles to their legitimate end, but are still sworn supporters of ecclesiastical establishments, fervent upholders of or dignitaries of the Church … If it be true, as I am often told it is, that the age of faith has passed, then the fact of having an opulent hierarchy, supported by men of high cultivation, brilliant talents and eloquence, and perhaps some ambition, with no distinctive opinions, might be a very harmless state of affairs, and it would certainly not be a very permanent one. But, my Lord, instead of believing that the age of faith has passed when I observe what is passing round us, what is taking place in this country, and not only in this country, but in other countries and other hemispheres, instead of believing that the age of faith has passed I hold that the characteristic of the present age is a craving credulity. My Lord, man is a being born to believe, and if no Church comes forward with its title-deeds of truth sustained by the traditions of sacred ages, and by the convictions of countless generations to guide him, he will find altars and idols in his own heart, in his own imagination. And what must be the relations of a powerful Church without distinctive creeds with a being of such a nature? Before long we shall be living in a flitting scene of spiritual phantasmagoria. There are no tenets, however extravagant, and no practices, however objectionable, which will not in time develop under such a state of affairs, opinions the most absurd and ceremonies the most revolting.

'Consider the country in which all this may take place. Dangerous in all countries, it would be yet more dangerous in England. Our empire is now unrivalled for its extent; but the base, the material base of that empire is by no means equal to the colossal superstructure. It is not our iron ships, it is not our celebrated regiments, it is not these things which have created or indeed really maintain an empire. It is the character of the people. I want to know where that famous character of the English people will be if they are to be influenced and guided by a Church of immense talent, opulence, and power without any distinctive creed. You have in this country accumulated wealth that has never been equalled, and probably it will still increase. You have a luxury that will some day peradventure rival even your wealth; and the union of such circumstances with a Church without a distinctive creed will lead, I believe, to a dissolution of manners and morals, which prepares the tomb of empires.

'The opinions of the new school are paralysing the efforts of many who ought to be our friends. Will these opinions succeed? My conviction is that they will fail ... Having examined all their writings, I believe without exception, whether they consist of fascinating eloquence, diversified learning, or picturesque sensibility exercised by our honoured in this University [Dean Stanley], and whom to know is to admire and regard; or whether you find them in the cruder conclusions of prelates who appear to have commenced their theological studies after they have grasped the crozier [Bishop Colenso]; or whether I read the lucubrations of nebulous professors [Frederick Maurice] who, if they could persuade the public to read their writings, would go far to realise that eternal punishment which they deny; or, lastly, whether it be the provincial arrogance and precipitate self-complacency which flash and flare in an essay or review—I find the common characteristic of their writings is this that their learning is always second-hand ... When I examine the writings of their masters, the great scholars of Germany, I find that in their labours [also] there is nothing new. All that inexorable logic, irresistible rhetoric, bewildering wit could avail to popularise these views was set in motion to impress the new learning on the minds of the two leading nations of Europe [by the English and French deistical writers of the last century], and they produced their effect [in the French Revolution]. When the turbulence was over, when the waters had subsided, the sacred heights of Sinai and of Calvary were again revealed, and amidst the wreck of thrones, extinct nations, and abolished laws mankind, tried by so many sorrows, purified by so much suffering, and wise with such unprecedented experience, bowed again before the Divine truths that Omnipotence had entrusted to the custody and promulgation of a chosen people ...

'The discoveries of science are not, we are told, consistent with the teachings of the Church ... It is of great importance when this tattle about science is mentioned that we should attach to the phrase precise ideas. The function of science is the interpretation of nature, and the interpretation of the highest nature is the highest science. What is the highest nature? Man is the highest nature. But I must say that when I compare the interpretation of the highest nature by the most advanced, the most fashionable school of modern science with some other teaching with which we are familiar. I am not prepared to admit that the lecture-room is more scientific than the Church. What is the question now placed before society with a glib assurance the most astounding? The question is this: Is man an ape or an angel? I, my Lord, I am on the side of the angels. I repudiate with indignation and abhorrence the contrary view, which I believe foreign to the conscience of humanity. More than that, from the intellectual point of view the severest metaphysical analysis is opposed to such a conclusion ... What does the Church teach us? That man is made in the image of his Maker. Between these two contending interpretations of the nature of man and their consequences society will have to decide. This rivalry is at the bottom of all human affairs. Upon an acceptance of that Divine interpretation for which we are indebted to the Church, and of which the Church is the guardian, all sound and salutary legislation depends. That truth is the only security for civilisation and the only guarantee of real progress.'

Mr Disraeli is on the side of the angels. Pit and gallery echoed with laughter. Fellows and tutors repeated the phrase over their port in the common room with shaking sides. The newspapers carried the announcement the next morning over the length and breadth of the island, and the leading article writers struggled in their comments to maintain a decent gravity. Did Disraeli mean it, or was it but an idle jest? and what must a man be who could exercise his wit on such a subject? Disraeli was at least as much in earnest as his audience.

The phrase answered its purpose. It has lived and become historical when the decorous protests of professional divines have been forgotten with the breath which uttered them. The note of scorn with which it rings has preserved it better than any affectation of pious horror, which indeed would have been out of place in the presence of such an assembly.

# XII

*Indifference to money—Death of Isaac Disraeli—Purchase of Hughenden—*
*Mrs Brydges Willyams of Torquay—An assignation with unexpected results—*
*Intimate acquaintance with Mrs Willyams—Correspondence—Views on many*
*subjects—The Crown of Greece —Louis Napoleon—Spanish pedigree of Mrs*
*Willyams*

'ADVENTURES ARE TO THE ADVENTUROUS:' so Ixion had written in Athene's album. Nothing is more commonplace than an ordinary parliamentary career. Disraeli's life was a romance. Starting with the least promising beginning, with a self which seemed like madness to everyone but himself, his origin a reproach to him and his inherited connections the least able to help him forward on the course which he had chosen, he had become, at a comparatively early age, by the mere force of his personal genius, the political chief of the proudest aristocracy in the world. His marriage had given him independence for the time, but his wife's income depended on her life, and a large part of it had long to be expended in paying the interest of his debts. Like his own Endymion he had no root in the country. The talents which he had displayed in Parliament would have given him wealth in any other profession. But he had neglected fortune for fame and power, and was not clear of his early embarrassments even when first Chancellor of the Exchequer. Being the leader of the country gentlemen, he aspired to be a country gentleman himself, to be a magistrate, to sit in top boots at quarter sessions and manage local business. Part of his ambition he attained. In 1847 he became member for his own county, and was so popular that he kept his seat without a contest as long as he remained in the House of

Commons; but for several years after he represented Buckinghamshire his connection with the soil was no more than nominal. Fortune, however, was again to stand his friend in a strange manner. He received a large sum from a private hand for his *Life of Lord George Bentinck*, while a Conservative millionaire took upon himself in addition the debts to the usurers, the three per cent with which he was content being exchanged for the ten per cent. under which Disraeli had so long been staggering. Isaac Disraeli lived long enough to see his son realise the dreams which he had himself long regarded with indifference or provocation. Dying in 1848, he left the remainder of the family fortune to be divided among his children. Benjamin Disraeli discharged his last filial duties in re-editing his father's works and prefixing to them an interesting biography of him. The portion which came to him was not considerable, but it was sufficient to enable him to purchase the manor of Hughenden, in the immediate neighbourhood of Bradenham, and Mrs Disraeli raised in the park a handsome monument to the old man, as if to fasten the name and fame of the Disraelis upon the ground. Neither, however, would the estate have been bought or the monument erected upon it but for another singular accident, as romantic as the rest of his history.

At Mount Braddon, at Torquay, there resided an elderly widowed lady named Mrs Brydges Willyams. She was of Jewish birth, daughter and heiress of a certain Mender da Costa, who traced his origin, like Disraeli, to a great family in Spain. Her husband, one of the Willyamses of Cornwall, who was a man of some note there, had died in 1820. His wife was left without children; she had no near relations, and with a large fortune at her own disposal. She was reputed, because perhaps she lived much in retirement, to be of eccentric habits. Being vain of her race, she was attracted by Disraeli's career, and she was interested in his writings. A Spanish Jewish origin was common to herself and to him, and some remote connection could, I have heard, be traced between the House of Lara, from which Disraeli descended, and her own, Mendez da Costa. At last, at the beginning of 1851, she wrote to him, professing general admiration and asking for his advice on some matter of business.

Men whose names are before the world often receive letters of this kind from unknown correspondents. Disraeli knew nothing of Mrs Willyams, and had no friends at Torquay whom he could ask about her. He threw the letter in the fire and thought no more of it. The lady persevered. Disraeli happened about the same time to be on a visit to Monckton Mimes at Frystone; one of the party was a Devonshire man, and Disraeli asked him if he knew anything of a mad woman living in Torquay named Willyams. The gentleman, though not personally acquainted with Mrs Willyams, was able to assure him that, though eccentric, she certainly was not mad. The lady, when the first Great Exhibition was opened, wrote again, pressing for an interview, and appointing as a place of meeting the fountain in the Exhibition building. The Disraeli of practical life was as unlike as possible to the heroes of his own novels. His mysterious correspondent might be young and beautiful or old and ugly. In either case the proposal could have no attraction for him. His person was well known, and an assignation at so public a place could not pass unnoticed. In his most foolish years he had kept clear of entanglements with women, and did not mean to begin. He was out of town when the letter arrived. He found it when he returned, but again left it unnoticed. A third time, however, the lady wrote, and in more pressing terms appointed another hour at the same place. The perseverance struck him as singular. He showed the note to two intimate friends, who both advised him not to neglect a request which might have meaning in it. He went. By the side of the fountain he found sitting an old woman, very small in person, strangely dressed, and peculiar in manner; such a figure as might be drawn in an illustrated story for a fairy godmother. She told him a long story of which he could make nothing. Seeing that he was impatient she placed an envelope in his hands, which, she said, contained the statement of a case on which she desired a high legal opinion. She begged him to examine it at his leisure. He thrust the envelope carelessly in his pocket, and supposing that she was not in her right mind thought no more about the matter. The coat which he was wearing was laid aside, and weeks passed before he happened to put it on again. When he did put it on the packet was still where it had been left. He tore it open, and found a bank note for a thousand pounds as a humble contribution to his election expenses, with the case for the lawyers, which was less absurd than he had expected. This was, of course, submitted to a superior counsel, whose advice was sent at once to Torquay with acknowledgments and apologies for the delay. I do not know what became of the thousand pounds. It was probably returned. But this was the beginning of an acquaintance which ripened into a close and affectionate friendship. The Disraelis visited Mount Braddon at the close of the London season year after year. The old lady was keen, clever, and devoted. A correspondence began, which grew more and more intimate till at last Disraeli communicated freely to her the best of his thoughts and feelings. Presents were exchanged weekly. Disraeli's writing-table was adorned regularly with roses from Torquay, and his dinners enriched with soles and turbot from the Brixham trawlers. He in turn provided Mrs Willyams with trout and partridges from Hughenden, and passed on to her the venison and the grouse which his friends sent him from the Highlands. The letters which they exchanged have been happily preserved on both sides. Disraeli himself when he had leisure; when he had none Mrs Disraeli wrote instead of him. The curious and delicate idyll was prolonged for twelve years, at the end of which Mrs Willyams died, bequeathing to him her whole fortune, and expressing a wish, which of course was complied with, that she might be buried at Hughenden, near the spot where Disraeli was himself to lie. The correspondence may hereafter be published, when a fit time arrives, with the more secret papers which have been bequeathed to the charge of the executors. I have been permitted a hasty perusal of these letters. Disraeli tells Mrs Willyams of his work in Parliament, of the great people that he falls in with, of pomp and ceremonies, grand entertainments, palaces of peers and princes, such things as all women, old or young, delight to hear of. More charming are pictures of his life at Hughenden, his chalk stream and his fish, his swans and his owls, and his garden, which he had made a Paradise of birds. Now and then his inner emotions break out with vehemence. The Indian Mutiny and the passions called out by it shocked him into indigna-tion; although in his allusions to persons with whom he was either in contact or in collision there is not a single malicious expression. A few extracts follow, gathered at random:

'What wondrous times are these,' he writes in 1861. 'Who could have supposed that the United States of America would have been the scene of a mighty revo-lution? No one can foresee its results. They must, however, tell immensely in favour of an aristocracy.'

In 1862 came the second exhibition at South Kensington.

'This,' he wrote, 'is not so fascinating a one as that you remember, when you made me an assignation by the crystal fountain, which I was ungallant enough not to keep, being far away when it arrived at Grosvenor Gate. But though not so charming it is even more wonderful. One was a woman—this is a man.'

In the session of the same year he had been overworked, and Mrs Willyams had prescribed for him.

*Hughenden: September* 2, 1862.—I am quite myself again; and as I have been drink-ing your magic beverage for a week, and intend to pursue it, you may fairly claim all the glory of my recovery, as a fairy cures a knight after a tournament or a battle. I have a great weakness for mutton broth, especially with that magical sprinkle which you did not forget. I shall call you in future after an old legend and a modern poem "the Lady of Shalot." I think the water of which it was made would have satisfied even you, for it was taken every day from our stream, which rises among the chalk hills, glitters in the sun over a very pretty cascade, then spreads and sparkles into a little lake in which is a natural island. Since I wrote to you last we have launched in the lake two most beautiful cygnets, to whom we have given the names of Hero and Leander. They are a source to us of unceasing interest and amusement. They are very handsome and very large, but as yet dove-coloured. I can no longer write to you of Cabinet Councils or Parliamentary struggles. Here I see nothing but trees or books, so you must not despise the news of my swans.

Here follows an historical incident not generally known:—

*December* 9, 1862.—They say the Greeks, resolved to have an English king, in consequence of the refusal of Prince Alfred to be their monarch, intend to elect Lord Stanley. If he accepts the charge I shall lose a powerful friend and colleague. It is a dazzling adventure for the House of Stanley, but they are not an imaginative race, and I fancy they will prefer Knowsley to the Parthenon, and Lancashire to the Attic plains. It is a privilege to live in this age of rapid and brilliant events. What an error to consider it a utilitarian age. It is one of infinite romance. Thrones tumble down, and crowns are offered like a fairy tale; and the most powerful people in the world, male and female, a few years back were adventurers, exiles, and demireps. *Vive la bagatelle!* Adieu.

*February* 7, 1863.—The Greeks really want to make my friend Lord Stanley their king. This beats any novel. I think he ought to take the crown; but he will not. Had I his youth I would not hesitate even with the earldom of Derby in the distance.

*March* 21, 1863.—The wedding [of the Prince of Wales] was a fine affair, a thing to remember. After the ceremony there was a splendid *déjeuner* at Windsor. The Queen was very anxious that an old shoe should be thrown at the royal pair on their departure, and the Lord Chamberlain showed me in confidence the weapon with which he had furnished himself. He took out of his pocket a beautiful white satin slipper which had been given him for the occasion by the Duchess of Brabant. Alas! when the hour arrived his courage failed him. This is a genuine anecdote which you will not find in the "Illustrated London News."

In 1863 Poland revolted, encouraged by the results of the Crimean war, which had enfeebled Russia, by the French campaign for the liberation of

Italy, and by the supposed sympathy of England with oppressed nationali-
ties. Louis Napoleon knew that his own throne was undermined, and was
looking for safety in some fresh successful adventure. England had refused
to join him in the recognition of Southern independence in America.
Poland was another opportunity. The two extracts which follow deserve
particular attention. Disraeli had known the French Emperor in London
and did not trust him.

*October* 17, 1863.—The troubles and designs of the French Emperor are aggravated and disturbed by the death of Billault, his only Parliamentary orator and
a first-rate one. With, for the first time, a real Opposition to encounter, and
formed of the old trained speakers of Louis Philippe's reign, in addition to
the young democracy of oratory which the last revolution has itself produced,
the inconveniences, perhaps the injuries, of this untimely decease are incalculable. It may even force by way of distraction the Emperor into war. Our
own Ministry have managed their affairs very badly, according to their friends.
The Polish question is a diplomatic Frankenstein, created out of cadaverous
remnants by the mystic blundering of Lord Russell. At present the peace of the
world has been preserved not by statesmen, but by capitalists. For the last three
months it has been a struggle between the secret societies and the Emperor's
millionaires. Rothschild hitherto has won, but the death of Billault may be as
fatal to him as the *poignard* of a Polish patriot, for I believe in that part of the
world they are called "patriots," though in Naples only "brigands."

*November* 5, 1863.—The great Imperial sphinx, is at this moment speaking. I
shall not know the mysterious utterances until to-morrow, and shall judge of
his conduct as much by his silence as by his words. The world is very alarmed
and very restless. Although England appears to have backed out of this possible
war there are fears that the French ruler has outwitted us, and that by an alliance with Austria and the aid of the Italian armies he may cure the partition
of Poland by a partition of Prussia; Austria in that case to regain Silesia, which
Frederick the Great won a century ago from Maria Theresa, France to have
the Rhine, and Galicia and Posen to be restored to Poland. If this happens it
will give altogether a new form and colour to European politics. The Queen
is much alarmed for the future throne of her daughter; but as the war will be
waged for the relief of Poland, of which England has unwisely approved, and
to which in theory she is pledged, we shall really be checkmated and scarcely
could find an excuse to interfere even if the nation wished.

Disraeli's arms and motto have been a subject of some speculation. The motto, '*Forti nihil difficile*,' has been supposed to have been originated by himself, as an expression of his personal experience. The vanity, if vanity there was in the assumption, of such a bearing, was the vanity of ancestry, not the vanity of a self-made man. When he told the electors at Aylesbury that his descent was as pure as that of the Cavendishes, he was not alluding to Abraham, but to his Castilian progenitors. While leading the aristocracy of England he claimed a place among them in right of blood. Mrs Willyams descended from a similar stock. She desired to quarter her coat with the bearings of the Mendez da Costas, and Disraeli undertook to manage it for her. He had to use the help of 'ambassadors and Ministers of State.' He laid under contribution the private cabinet of the Queen of Spain, and gave himself infinite trouble that the poor old lady might have the panels of her carriage painted to her satisfaction. Among the many letters on the subject there is one which explains the arms of Beaconsfield.

*July* 23, 1859.—The Spanish families never had supporters, crests, or mottoes. The tower of Castile, which I use as a crest, and which was taken from one of the quarters of my shield, was adopted by a Lara in the sixteenth century in Italy, where crests were the custom—at least in the north of Italy—copied from the German heraldry. This also applies to my motto. None of the southern races, I believe, have supporters or crests. This is Teutonic. With regard to the coronet, in old days, especially in the south, all coronets were the same, and the distinction of classes from the ducal strawberry leaf to the baron's balls is of comparatively modern introduction.

When the harlequin's wand of Pitt converted Warren, the club waiter, into an earl, the Heralds' College traced his descent for him to the Norman Fitzwarren. Robert Burns was content to take his patent of nobility from a more immediate source. Disraeli doubtless had a right to use the bearings of the Laras if he cared about such things. But a Spanish pedigree at best was a shadowy sort of business, and one could rather wish that he had let it alone.

# XIII

SOMETHING ELSE TOO AS WELL as the Castilian pedigree Disraeli might
have done better to leave to others. In 1865 he had uttered his memorable warning in the House of Commons against playing tricks with the
Constitution. Other countries might emerge out of a revolution and 'begin
again.' England could not begin again. Lord John Russell's Reform Bill was
thrown out. The Whig Ministry fell in 1867, and Lord Derby came a third
time to the helm with Disraeli for his Chancellor of the Exchequer. They at
least, it might have been thought, would have let alone a subject on which the
latter had pronounced so recently so emphatic an opinion. But they were still
a Ministry on sufferance, and how to turn a minority into a majority was still
an unsolved problem. The spectre of Reform was unexorcised. Both parties
had evoked it at intervals, when they wished ultimately to pose before the
world as the people's friends. Yet no experienced statesman, Whig or Tory,
unless from unworthy jealousy, would have opened his lips to recommend
a change from which he could not honestly expect improvement. Even the
working classes themselves, who were to be admitted to the suffrage, were
not actively demanding it. No good had come to them from the great Bill
of 1832. 'I don't care who is in or who is out,' said a rough artisan to me. 'I

could never see that any of them cared for us.' They had been told that they were living in a world where everyone was to look out for himself; that their interests would never be attended to till they had representatives who would force attention to them. But their general sense was that the ills which they complained of were out of reach of Parliament, and they were looking for a remedy in combination among themselves which would take the place of the old Guilds. The ancient organisation of labour had been destroyed in the name of Liberty. Their employers had piled up fortunes. They had been left 'free,' as it was called, with their families to multiply as they would, and to gather their living under the hoofs of the horses of a civilisation which had become an aggregate of self-seeking units. To this they had been brought by a Parliamentary government, which, as far as they were concerned, was no government at all; and they were incredulous of any benefit that was to arrive to them from improvements in a machine so barren. Thus they were looking rather with amused indifference than active concern while the parties in the House of Commons were fencing for the honour of being their champion.

And yet Reform was in the air. The educated mind of England had been filled to saturation with the new Liberal philosophy. In the old days a 'freeman' was a master of his craft, and not till he had learnt to do, and do well, some work which was useful to society did he enter upon his privileges as a citizen. The situation was now reversed. To be 'free' was to have a voice in making the laws of the country. Those who had no votes were still in bondage, and bondage was a moral degradation. Freedom was no longer a consequence and a reward, but the fountain of all virtue; a baptismal sacrament in which alone human nature could be regenerated. In Great Britain and Ireland there were some thirty millions of inhabitants. Of these, under the Reform Bill of 1832, three hundred thousand only were in possession of their birthright. What claim, it was asked, had a mere fraction to monopolise a privilege which was not only a power in the State but the indispensable condition of spiritual growth and progress? We heard much about generous confidence in the people, about the political stability to be expected from broadening the base of the pyramid, about the elevating consciousness of responsibility which would rise out of the possession of a vote—beautiful visions of the return of Astraea, the millennium made into a fact by the establishment of universal liberty. Of all this Disraeli believed nothing. No one hated empty verbiage more than he. His dislike of cant was the most genuine part of him. But he too had once imagined that the working-men were safer depositaries of power than the ten-pound householders; and even old Tories, though they thought an extension of the franchise foolish and needless, did not suppose it would be necessarily dangerous unless accompanied with a vast redistribution of seats. Thus, although the mass of the existing voters were content with their privileges, and were not eager to share them, the House of Commons had already committed itself by second readings to the principle of Reform. The question would return upon them again and again till it was settled, and as things stood either party had a Parliamentary right to deal with it.

What were Lord Derby and Disraeli to do? Accident had brought them into power, and accident or some adverse resolution of the House might at any time displace them. Experienced Parliamentary politicians had observed that the shake of the Constitution from the Act of 1832 had arisen more from the manner in which it was carried than from the measure in itself. A second Radical Reform Bill, which might be passed in a similar manner, was evidently imminent; the multitude, who were so far quiet, might again be stirred; and if once the classes and the masses were pitted against one another the breaking loose of a torrent might sweep away Church, House of Lords, landed estates, and all that was left of the old institutions of England. Such were the arguments on public grounds; to which, though it was unavowed, might be added the pleasure of 'dishing the Whigs.'

But if Disraeli had looked back upon his own past career he might have remembered to have once said that there were considerations higher than any of these—that public men ought to be true to their real convictions. The Liberals had professed to believe in Reform. The Tories had never looked on it as more than an unwelcome and a useless necessity. Lord Derby had been a member of Lord Grey's first Reform Cabinet. Disraeli in his enthusiastic youth had called himself a Radical. But Lord Derby had been cured of his illusions; and Disraeli had learnt the difference between realities and dreams. They might think that the danger of concession was less than the danger of resistance, but that was all. There were persons credulous enough to hope that there might be found men at last among their Parliamentary leaders who would adhere in office to what they had said in Opposition. In the opinion of the Conservatives, the need of England was wise government, not political revolution. They might have said. That if the experiment of Democracy was to be tried it should be tried by those who were in favour of the change on their own responsibility. They themselves would have no hand in it. They might be turned out of office, but the country would know that they had been faithful to their word, and could be relied upon when there was need of them again. Tories of the old school would have said so and dared the consequences, which might not have been very terrible after all, and Parliamentary government would have escaped the contempt into which it is now so rapidly falling.

Unfortunately political leaders have ceased to think of what is good for the nation, or of their own consistency, or even of what in the long run may be best for themselves. Their business is the immediate campaign, in which they are to outmanoeuvre and defeat their enemies. On this condition only they can keep their party together. The Conservatives had been out of office, with but short-lived intervals, for thirty-five years. Peel's Government had been, as Disraeli said, not Conservative at all, but an organised hypocrisy. If they were to regard themselves as condemned to be in a perpetual minority, with no inducement to offer to tempt ability or ambition into their ranks, they would inevitably become disheartened and indifferent. The Parliamentary Constitution depended on the continuance of two parties, and if one of these disappeared the constitution would itself cease to exist.

Disraeli's notion that the aristocracy were to recover their power by an alteration of their ways had proved 'a devout imagination.' The ancient organisation was visibly crumbling, and progress, whether it was upwards or was the rule of the hour. Lord Derby was old and out of health, and Disraeli himself was the ruling spirit of the Cabinet. Though born an Englishman, and proud of the position which he had won, he had not an English temperament, and he was unembarrassed by English prejudices. He surveyed the situation with the coolness of a general and the impartiality of a friend who had no personal interests at stake. He prided himself on his knowledge of the English character; and to some extent he did know it, though he mistook the surface for the substance. He believed—and the event a few years later seemed to show that he was right—in the essential Conservatism of the great mass of the people, and he resolved upon a 'leap into the dark.' He regretted the necessity. He did not hide from himself that he too was 'stealing the Whigs' clothes while they were bathing.' History was repeating itself. His situation too much resembled that of his old leader whom he had overthrown. His own language could be retorted upon him, and the more violent he had been at Peel the more severe would be his condemnation. But a strategist must be governed by circumstances, and he could plead that the position was not entirely the same. Peel had been pledged to Protection, and was at the head of an unbroken majority returned in the Protectionist interest. In going over to Free Trade he had made a social revolution and destroyed his party. Disraeli could say that he had never opposed the principle of an extension of the suffrage, that he had more than once openly advocated it. He had always protested against the assumption that the Liberals had a monopoly of the question.

All agreed that reform was inevitable; if conducted by the Conservatives with a drag upon the wheel, it might be harmless, and might add to their strength. To persuade himself was more easy than to convince his party. Old-fashioned Toryism was stubborn and distrustful—distrustful of the measure in itself, and distrustful of the leader whom, for want of ability in themselves, they were compelled to follow. He found it necessary to 'educate' them, as he scornfully said. He told them that they could not hold together on the principle of mere resistance to the spirit of the age. Change was the order of the day. To cease to change would be to cease to live. They must accept the conditions. Party government is perhaps an accident of a peculiar period. To divide the intellect of the country into hostile camps, each struggling to outwit or outbid the other, is not a promising, and may not be a permanent, method of conducting the affairs of a great country. But it is a present fact, theoretically admired and practically accepted and acted on, and while it continues, the opposing chiefs have to disregard the reproaches of inconsistency. They have to do what occasion requires—attack, defend, snatch advantages, and improve opportunities.

In earlier years, Disraeli, by speech and writing, had tried for a nobler policy. He had hoped for a real government again, to be brought about by an aristocratic regeneration. But the aristocracy had not regenerated themselves. The American war, which was to have shown the superiority of aristocracies to democratic republics, had had precisely the opposite effect. He was carrying on the administration with a minority. His business now as a general was to go with the times, and if possible change his minority into a majority. Tory principles were dead. His best chance was in the daring stroke, on which Carlyle so scornfully commented, and in throwing himself boldly upon the masses of the people.

All admit Disraeli's dexterity as a Parliamentary commander. To succeed, he knew that he must outbid the highest offers of his opponents. He shook his Cabinet in the process. Three of his most distinguished supporters—Lord Salisbury, Lord Carnarvon, and General Peel—threw up their offices and left him. But the body of his army consented to go with him. He could be confident in the general support of the Opposition. Their consent could not be refused. For form's sake, and to satisfy his followers, he introduced a few limitations of which he must have foreseen that the Liberals would demand the surrender, and to which his easy sacrifice of them showed that he attached no importance. He carried a bill which in its inevitable developments must give the franchise to every householder in the United Kingdom; and he gained for his party the credit, if credit it was, of having passed a more completely democratic measure than the most Radical responsible statesman had as yet dared to propose. The reproaches which were heaped upon him are fresh in the memories of many of us. Carlyle roused himself out of the sorrows into which he had been plunged by his wife's death to write his *Shooting Niagara*. In Carlyle's opinion, the English people had gone down the cataract at last, and nothing was left to them but to continue their voyage to the ocean on such shattered fragments of their old greatness as they could seize and cling to. A quarter of a century has gone by and the Constitution still holds together. The prophet of Chelsea may yet prove to have been clear-sighted. There are sounds in the air of cracking timbers, and signs of rending and disruption. But a powerfully organised framework does not break with a single shock, and Disraeli scored a victory. Enemies said that he had covered himself with ignominy; but the disgrace sat light upon him, and by his manoeuvres he had secured for his party at least one more year of office. Time must pass before the newly enfranchised voters could be placed upon the register. If the Liberals forced a dissolution before the process was completed, a new Parliament would have to be chosen by the old constituencies, and they would gain nothing even if they were again in a majority, for there would be an appeal to the fresh electors, whose votes no one could count upon. Two general elections close one upon another would be so inconvenient that the country would resent it upon them. They had therefore to wait and digest their spleen, while new honours descended upon the triumphant Disraeli. Lord Derby's health broke down; he was no longer equal to the work of office. He retired, and the author of *Vivian Grey* became Prime Minister. The post which in the extravagance of youthful ambition he had told Lord Melbourne could alone satisfy his ambition was actually his own, and had been won by courage, skill, and determination and only these. He *libertino patre natus*, a *libertinus* himself—without wealth, without connection, for the peers and gentlemen of England resented his supremacy while they used his services—had made himself the ruler of the British Empire. He had not stooped to the common arts of flattery. He had achieved no marked successes in the service of the country. It was supposed, perhaps without ground, that he was not even a *grata persona* to the highest person in the realm, till Her Majesty was compelled to accept his supremacy. He had won his way by parliamentary ability and by resolution to succeed. Whether it be for the interest of the nation in the long run to commit its destinies to men of such qualifications is a question which it will by-and-by consider. If a time comes when party becomes faction, and the interests of the empire are sacrificed visibly in contention for office, when the wise and the honest hold aloof from politics as a game in which they can no longer take part, Parliamentary government will fall into the contempt which Disraeli himself already secretly felt for it. The system will collapse, and other methods will be tried. Disraeli, however, had risen by the regular process, and according to the representative principle was the chosen of the country. Among rival politicians his elevation created irritation more than surprise, for it had been long regarded as inevitable. Outside Parliamentary circles there was no irritation at all, but rather pride and pleasure. Englishmen like those who have made a position for themselves by their own force of character. Disraeli's public life was before the world. He had made innumerable enemies. A thousand calumnies had pursued him. His actions, good, bad, and indifferent, had been coloured to his least advantage. He had been described as an adventurer and a charlatan, without honesty, without sincerity, without patriotism; a mercenary, a gladiator; the Red Indian of debate.

If this was the true account of him, one has to ask oneself in wonder what kind of place the House of Commons must be, when such a man can be selected by it as its foremost statesman. There he had sat for thirty years, session after session, ever foremost in the fight, face to face with antagonists who were reputed the ablest speakers, the most powerful thinkers whom the country could produce. Had his enemies' account of him been true, why had they not exposed and made an end of him? The English people had too much respect for their institutions to believe in so incredible a story. The violence of the attacks recoiled upon their authors. With his accession to the Premiership he became an object of marked and general regard. When he went down to Parliament for the first time in his new capacity, he was wildly cheered by the crowds in Palace Yard. The shouts were echoed along Westminster Hall and through the lobbies, and were taken up again warmly and heartily in the House itself, which had been the scene of so many conflicts—the same House in which he had been hooted down when he first rose to speak there.

And the tribute was to himself personally. He was not the representative of any great or popular cause. Even in carrying his Reform Bill he had not stooped to inflated rhetoric, or held out promises of visionary millenniums. He was regarded merely as a man of courage and genius, not-less honest than other politicians because his professions were few.

# XIV

DISRAELI, IN APPROPRIATING PARLIAMENTARY REFORM, obliged the Liberals to look about them for another battle-cry at the next election—something popular and plausible which would touch the passions of the constituencies. The old subjects were worn out or disposed of. It had become necessary to start a new game. The genuine Radical desires to make a new world by a reconstruction of society. He has his eye always on one other of the old institutions, which he regards as an obstacle to progress. There are, therefore, at all times, a number of questions which are gradually 'ripening,' as it is called, but which wait to be practically dealt with till the opportunity presents itself. Among these the Liberal leader had now to make his choice. A small advance would not answer. Disraeli had ventured a long and audacious step. The other side must reply in a second and a longer if the imagination was to be effectively awakened.

The Established Church of England, the Land Laws, the House of Lords, perhaps the Crown, were eventually to be thrown into the crucible; but the nation was not yet prepared for an assault on either of these. The weak point was found in Ireland, which at all times had been the favourite plaything of

English faction. Three millions of Irish had fled across the Atlantic to escape
from famine since the failure of the potato. Some had gone of their own wills,
some had been roughly expelled from their homes. With few exceptions, they
had borne the cost of their own exportation. Those who went first sent home
money to bring out their families and friends, and the economists had congratulated themselves that the Irish difficulty was at last disposed of, at no expense
to the British taxpayer. A few insignificant persons, who understood the Irish
character, knew too well that the congratulations were premature. If the poor
Irish were really our fellow-subjects, these persons thought that some effort
should have been made to soften their expulsion, and to provide or at least to
offer them homes in the vast colonial territories which then belonged to us.
Past efforts in that direction, indeed, had not been encouraging. For several
generations we had poured shiploads of Irish into the West Indies. Scarcely
a survivor of Celtic blood is now to be found in those islands. It would have
been something, however, to have shown that we were generously anxious
to bear our share in the undeserved calamity which had fallen on an ill-used
people, and to try to repair the efforts of centuries of negligence. If we left
them to their own resources without regret, with an avowed confession that
we were glad to be rid of them, Irish disaffection would become more intense
than ever. We did so leave them. They streamed across to the United States,
carrying hatred of England along with them, while the walls of the deserted
villages in Connaught preached revenge to those who were left at home. The
exiles throve in their new land—a fresh evidence, if they needed more, that
English domination had been the cause of their miseries. They multiplied,
and became a factor in American political life. They fought, and fought well,
in the American Civil War. When the Civil War was over, they hoped for a
war with England, and tried to kindle it in Canada. The 'Alabama' question
having been settled peacefully, they failed in their immediate purpose; but
none the less they were animated with an all-pervading purpose of revenge;
and there were many thousands of them who had escaped the Southern bul-
lets who were ready for any desperate adventure. An invading force was to
cross the Atlantic, while Ireland organised itself in secret societies to receive
them as it did to receive the French in 1797. Chester Castle and the Fenian
rebellion of 1867 are not yet forgotten even in these days of short memories
and excited hopes. The rising was abortive. It failed, as Irish rebellions have so
often failed, because the Irish people trusted in their numbers and neglected
to make serious preparations. The American general who came over to take
the command had been told that he would find ten thousand men drilled
and armed. He did not find five hundred, and he left the enterprise in con-

tempt. The scattered risings which followed were easily suppressed, and were suppressed with gentleness. The exhortation of a leading Liberal journal to make an example of the rebels in the field, because executions afterwards were inconvenient, was happily not attended to. But the leniency with which the leading insurgents were treated was construed into a confession of weakness. The rebellious spirit was fed from America, and detached acts of violence, attempted rescues of prisoners, and blowing up of gaols showed that Ireland was as unsubdued as ever. The great Liberal champion saw the occasion which he required. The Clerkenwell explosion, he explained afterwards, had brought the Irish question within the range of practical politics, and in this extraordinary acknowledgment invited an inflammable people to persevere in outrage if they desired to secure their rights. He declared in a memorable speech that the cause of Irish wretchedness had been Protestant Ascendency. Protestant Ascendency was the Irish upas tree, with its three branches, the Church, the land, and the education. The deadly growth once cut down, the animosity would end, and the English lion and the Irish lamb would lie down together: in peace. That to disarm the garrison was a likely mode of reconciling an unwilling people to a connection which they detest, was an expectation not in accordance with general human experience; still less when it was confessedly recommended as a reward of insurrection. But the Irish question was ingeniously selected as a counterstroke to Disraeli's Reform Bill. Had Disraeli but left Reform to its owners the Liberals would have been provided with work a home and have left Ireland alone. But the deed was done, and many circumstances combined to suggest to the eminent statesman who had discovered the secret of Irish disaffection that here was the proper field for his genius, and that he was peculiarly the person to put his hand to the plough. The Irish Church had long been a scandal to Liberal sentiment, and Disraeli himself had denounced it. The land was the favourite subject of Radical declamation. Land-owning in Ireland showed under its least favourable aspect, and could there be assaulted at best advantage. It was true that the control of Ireland was vital to the safety of Great Britain, and that the Protestants there were the only part of the population whose loyalty could be depended on. Until recent years the Protestant feeling in England and Scotland would have forbidden a revolutionary change avowedly intended to weaken the Protestant settlement; but the extended franchise, either already conceded or made inevitable by Disraeli's Bill, would throw four-fifths of the representation of Ireland into Nationalist hands, and the adhesion of such a phalanx would give the party which could secure it an overwhelming preponderance, while the Protestant prejudices which had served hitherto as a check were wearing away.

Sixty years ago the British nation adhered almost unanimously to the traditions of the Reformation. It had grown to its present greatness as a Protestant power. The Pope was still the Man of Sin. Roman doctrine, either pure or modified into Anglicanism, was regarded with suspicion, aversion, or contempt. Conversions were unheard of, and the few surviving hereditary Catholics were unobtrusive and politically ciphers. Catholic Emancipation in restoring them to power restored them at the same time to social consequence. The Liberals who had advocated that great measure, historians, statesmen, and philosophers, broke with the principles of which their predecessors had once been the staunchest advocates, changed front, and traduced the Reformation itself, to which Liberalism owed its existence. While Macaulay and Buckle were cursing Cranmer, the Oxford Movement made its way among the clergy, was welcomed largely by the upper classes, whose nerves were offended by Puritan vulgarities, and leavened gradually the whole organisation of the Church of England. Men of intellect who would once have interfered had ceased to care for such things, and allowed them to go their own way. The Rationalists and critics, whom Disraeli so sagaciously disliked, worked havoc in a party whose whole belief was in their Bible. The Evangelicals, who had been narrow and tyrannical in the days of their power, found themselves fading into impotence; while in the mass of the people a doctrinal faith was superseded by a vague religiosity which saw no particular difference between one creed and another.

The High Churchmen, who grew strong as their rivals declined, called themselves Catholics again, and abjured the name of Protestant. To unprotestantise the Church of England had been the confessed purpose of the first Tractarians, and the work had been effectively done. Mr Gladstone was the most distinguished of their lay adherents. The purity of his life, the loftiness of his principles, his well-known because slightly ostentatious piety commended him generally to the national confidence, English statesmen with strong religious convictions having been recently uncommon articles. Thus, in addition to the ordinary Radical forces, Mr Gladstone had the support of a great body of influential clergy, who, although tried at times by his questionable associations, continued to believe in him and uphold him—to uphold him especially in his onslaught upon their unfortunate Irish sister. The Irish Church had refused to follow in the new counter-Reformation. The Irish Church was Evangelical to the heart—actively, vigorously, healthily Evangelical—a Church militant in Luther's spirit. 'We have no Tractarians here,' said the Bishop of Cashel to me. 'We have the real thing, and know too much about it.' The life which was showing was of late growth too, and was therefore likely to continue. The Church of Ireland as a missionary institution had not been a success. Established by Elizabeth for political reasons, it had existed for two centuries and a half; making no impression on the mass of the population. Such Protestant spirituality as remained was confined to the Presbyterians of Ulster and the few Southern Nonconformists who were descended from the Cromwellian colonists. The bishops, secured after the Revolution by the Penal Laws, had received their large incomes and consumed them with dignity; but when they exerted themselves it was to persecute Protestant dissenters and drive them out of Ireland. The ancient churches fell to ruins. Incumbents ceased to reside where they had no congregations, left their parishes to underpaid curates, or more commonly to the tithe proctor. So things went on till the long negligence had borne its inevitable fruit. The Nonconformists were then let alone. The rebellion of 1798, the rapid growth of the Catholic population, the immediate contact with the Catholic system in an aggressive form, and the relaxation of the Penal Code gradually roused the clergy to exertion. The ruined churches were repaired or others provided, and before the middle of the present century the Protestant ministers in Ireland were showing a sincerity, a piety, a devotion to the work of their calling of exceptional and peculiar interest. I was myself at that time brought in contact with many of the Established clergy in the southern provinces. They had more of the saintly character of the early Christians than any clergy of any denomination that I had ever fallen in with.

After the tithe question had been settled they had no quarrels with the Catholic peasantry. They were poor, but they were charitable beyond their means. They were beloved, respected, trusted by all classes of the population. In every parish there was a resident educated gentleman, whose help in the most miserable times was never asked in vain if the occasion was not beyond the resources of those to whom the appeal was made. They made some few proselytes, and this was treated as a crime in them, while their rivals thought it no crime to convert a heretic. The Evangelical Calvinism which they generally professed was more attractive to the Celtic peasantry than the Episcopal *Via Media*. The Irish nature is impressible by a real belief, and the old creed which roused half Europe to fight for spiritual liberty in the sixteenth century in this one corner of the globe remained alive and active. The differences which had separated the Establishment from the Ulster Presbyterians had practically disappeared. For the first time since the Reformation the Protestants of Ireland were of one heart and one mind.

The time had been when such a disposition would have had the warm sympathies of the sister island. But the Protestant fire on this side of the

Channel had sunk to ashes, and the ashes themselves were cooling. Even among the Scotch and the Dissenters the creed of Knox and Cromwell had subsided into opinion flavoured with a vague Liberalism. While the English Church parties were drifting Romeward with an eagerness which to some persons appeared like the descent over a steep place of certain foolish animals, their poor Irish brethren who adhered to the faith of their fathers had lost their sympathy, and when the statesman whom they regarded with so much admiration proposed to disable and disendow the Irish branch of the Establishment, they looked on with indifference and did not withdraw their confidence in him. They did not actively approve. Even Mr Gladstone himself professed to feel some qualms of conscience. 'We do it wrong,' he said, 'being so majestical, to offer it the show of violence.' But by their silence they gave him their tacit sanction, and lent an air of respectability to a proceeding which without it he might have failed to go through with. They allowed the Irish Church to be dealt with politically, as a branch of his Protestant Ascendency which had been called an upas tree.

As a Churchman Mr Gladstone was a Tractarian as a statesman, he had become an advanced Radical. From neither point of view was the Irish Church to his liking. Yet as English statesman he was taking a bold, perhaps a rash step in endeavouring to weaken English authority in a country so ill-affected to us, when it had been built up with so many centuries of effort. Geographical position compels us to keep Ireland subject to the British Crown. That is the first fact of the situation—a situation which cannot be changed till we have lost our place as a great European power. The Irish, perhaps as much for this reason as for any other, have resisted and still resist. They might have been reconciled to their fate in return for other advantages if their own wills had been consulted; but they have resented the claim of necessity. Difference of religion has not been the cause of the hostility. Before the Reformation as much as after it they never missed an opportunity of injuring or attempting to break from us. The Reformation appeared to sanctify their quarrel, and caused a century of civil war and desolation; and the English Parliament, after all other means had been tried in vain to bring them to obedience, had determined to colonise the island with Scotch and English Protestants whose loyalty could be depended on. The land was taken forcibly away from the native owners, and was given to adventurers or to Cromwell's soldiers who would undertake to defend it. It was a violent measure; but to hold a country in subjection against its will is itself an act of violence which entails others. The Irish people had shown in five centuries of resistance that they could only be held to us by force. The colonists were the English garrison, and however grave their faults and miserable their deficiencies, the result was that Ireland had a century of peace. Twice during that period there was a civil war in Great Britain, and Ireland remained quiet. When the American colonies revolted, the Irish Catholics offered their swords and their services to 'the best of kings,' and only when the Penal Laws were relaxed and they were allowed an instalment of liberty did they again attempt insurrection. The Penal Laws are considered an atrocity. They were borrowed from the terms of the Revocation of the Edict of Nantes, and Voltaire, an impartial witness on such a subject, was able to use language about Ireland during the time when they were in force which deserves more attention than it has met with. '*Ce pays est toujours resté sous la domination de l'Angleterre, mais inculte, pauvre et inutile jusqu'à ce qu'enfin dans le dix-huitième siècle l'agriculture, les manufactures, les arts, les sciences, tout s'y est perfectionné, et l'Irlande, quoique subjuguée, est devenue une des plus florissantes provinces de l'Europe.*' (*Essai sur les Moeurs,* chap. 50). So Ireland appeared to the keenest eye in Europe at the time when it is the fashion to say that she was groaning under the hatefullest tyranny. The description was too favourable, yet it was relatively correct. The Irish are a military people. They are admirable as soldiers and police. They obey authority and prosper under it. They run wild when left to their own wills. An industrious people thrive best when free. A fighting people require to be officered, and when authority is firm and just are uniformly loyal. In Ireland, unfortunately, authority was not firm and was not just. The trade laws were iniquitous. The Protestant gentry were forced into idleness. They became a garrison without wholesome occupation; yet at worst such advance as Ireland did make was wholly due to them, and every step which was taken to reduce their power brought back the old symptoms. It cannot be said that the system was satisfactory; yet to abolish it altogether, to declare it to be a poisonous plant which required to be uprooted, was an adventure which ought not to have been entered upon without maturer consideration than it received. The injustice (such as there was) lay in the original sin of forcing an unwilling people into a connection which they detest. Protestant ascendency was the instrument by which the connection was maintained, and the only one which had even partially succeeded. If it was swept away, what was to take its place? Conciliation, we are told. But what had conciliation effected hitherto? The abolition of the Penal Laws was to have brought peace. It brought only a sword. The admission of the Catholics to the franchise was to have brought peace. It was followed instantly by rebellion. Parliament was opened to them, and tithe riots broke out, and midnight murdering. On the heel of each concession came a Coercion Act, because Ireland could not be governed otherwise. The eager Celt has regarded each step gained as the conquest of an outwork of English dominion which has served but to whet the appetite for attack and to weaken the defence. What reason was there to suppose that when they heard Church and landlords denounced, when they were told by a great English statesman that their grievances would only be attended to when they made themselves dangerous, the result would be different? The great grievance of all, the English sovereignty, would be left. If that too was to be sacrificed—if after the internal administration of their country was made over to themselves they showed that nothing would satisfy them except national independence—were the advocates of a trusting policy prepared to concede this point also? They might answer 'Yes' perhaps. Better Ireland should be free altogether than chained to England against her will. This might be their own opinion, but they could not answer for the English nation; and if the English nation refused, there would be nothing for it but civil war and a fresh conquest.

Before letting loose an agitation so far-reaching and of such uncertain consequence, Mr Gladstone ought to have laid out the whole problem for consideration in all its possible issues; not partially and crudely for an immediate election cry, but in a form in which it could be maturely discussed and paused over for years. To reverse and undo the policy of centuries was a step which ought not to have been ventured without the national consent. The electors knew less of Ireland even than Mr Gladstone himself, who ought to have made them first understand what it was which they were called on to sanction.

But these are not times for long reflection. A Parliamentary leader sees an opportunity. His followers echo him. Sentiment displaces reason, and a majority is the most conclusive of arguments.

Mr Gladstone brought forward his famous resolutions, carried them against Mr Disraeli's Government, and at the dissolution was rewarded by a majority so sweeping that resistance was impossible. Disraeli resigned without waiting for the meeting of Parliament—a sensible example which has been since followed. With his usual calmness he rallied his distracted followers and waited patiently while the two great branches of the upas tree were being hacked off, well aware that the hot stage would be followed by a cold one when the effects of this new departure began to show themselves. The Irish Church was reduced to a voluntary communion. Tenants and landlords were made joint owners of their lands—ill-mated companions set to sleep in a single bed, from which one or other before long was likely to be ejected. Ireland made its usual response; and within two years the state of Westmeath became so serious that the Cabinet which was to have won the Irish heart was obliged to move for a secret committee to consider how the administration was to be carried on. Disraeli on leaving office might if he had chosen have retired to the Upper House. He pleased himself better by prevailing on the Queen to confer a coronet on his faithful companion, and no act of his life gave him greater pride or pleasure. Mrs Disraeli[1] became Viscountess Beaconsfield, and he himself remained in the House of Commons, where he could watch and criticise.

A secret committee is only moved for on grave occasions. An evidence so rapid and so palpable of the results of Mr Gladstone's operations was an opportunity for the exercise of Mr Disraeli's peculiar powers. Of late years he had been sparing in his sarcasms. His speeches had been serious and argumentative, and the rapier and the whiplash had been laid aside. But they were lying ready for him, and he had not forgotten his old art. He did not again object as he had objected in Peel's case to granting extraordinary powers to a Government which he distrusted. He was willing to assist the Cabinet, since they needed assistance, in maintaining order in Ireland; Lord Hartington had reminded him that he had himself made a similar application in another Parliament. But he confessed his astonishment that such an application should be necessary. 'The noble lord,' he said, 'has made some reference, from that richness of precedent with which he has been crammed on this occasion, to what occurred in 1852; and in the midst of the distress of this regenerating Government of Ireland supported by a hundred legions and elected by an enthusiastic people in order to terminate the grievances of that country and secure its contentment and tranquillity, he must needs dig up our poor weak Government of 1852 and say, "There was Mr Napier, your attorney-general: he moved for a committee, and you were a member of his Cabinet." If I had had a majority of a hundred behind my back I would not have moved for that committee. I did the best I could. But was the situation in which I was placed similar to the situation of her Majesty's present Ministers? Look for a moment to the relations which this Government bears to the House of Commons with regard to the administration of Ireland. The right hon. gentleman opposite (Mr Gladstone) was elected for a specific purpose. He was the Minister who alone was able to cope with these long-enduring and mysterious evils that had tortured and tormented the civilisation of England. The right hon. gentleman persuaded the people of England that with regard to Irish politics he was in possession of the philosopher's stone. Well, sir, he has been returned to this House with an immense majority, with the object of securing the tranquillity and content of Ireland. Has anything been grudged him—time, labour, devotion? Whatever has been proposed has been carried. Under his influence, and at his instance, we have legalised confiscation, we have conse-crated sacrilege, we have condoned treason, we have destroyed Churches, we have shaken property to its foundations, and we have emptied gaols; and now he cannot govern one county without coming to a Parliamentary committee. The right hon. gentleman, after all his heroic exploits, and at the head of his great majority, is making government ridiculous.'

'We have legalised confiscation, we have consecrated sacrilege, we have condoned treason,' pronounced with drawling alliteration, was worth a whole Parliamentary campaign. Everyone recollected the words from the neatness of the combination; everyone felt and acknowledged their biting justice. Noone was a match for Disraeli in the use of the rapier. The composition of such sentences was an intellectual pleasure to him. A few years later, when the Prince Imperial was killed in South Africa, he observed, on hearing of it, 'A very remarkable people the Zulus: they defeat our generals, they convert our bishops, they have settled the fate of a great European dynasty.'

No Government was ever started on an ambitious career with louder pre-tensions or brighter promises than Mr Gladstone's Cabinet in 1868. In less than three years their glory was gone, the aureole had faded from their brows. The bubble of oratory, which had glowed with all the colours of the rainbow, had burst when in contact with fact, and the poor English people had awoke to the dreary conviction that it was but vapour after all. In April, 1872, the end was visibly coming, and Disraeli could indulge again, at their expense, in his malicious mockery. In a speech at Manchester he said:

> The stimulus is subsiding. The paroxysms ended in prostration. Some took ref-uge in melancholy, and their eminent chief alternated between a menace and a sigh. As I sat opposite the Treasury bench, the Ministers reminded me of those marine landscapes not unusual on the coasts of South America. You behold a range of exhausted volcanoes. Not a flame flickers on a single pallid crest. But the situation is still dangerous. There are occasional earthquakes, and ever and anon the dark rumbling of the sea.

1.  Lady Beaconsfield enjoyed her honours only for four years. She died December 15, 1872.

# XV

Once again in Opposition, Disraeli found leisure to return to his early occupations. As a politician, and at the head of a minority for the time hopelessly weak, he had, merely to look on and assist, by opportune sarcasms, the ebb of Liberal popularity.

In this comparative calm he resumed his profession as a novelist, which he had laid aside for more than twenty years, and delivered himself of a work immeasurably superior to anything of the kind which he had hitherto produced. *Vivian Grey* and *Contarini Fleming* were portraits of himself, drawn at an age of vanity and self consciousness. *Henrietta Temple* and *Venetia* were clever stories—written, probably, because he wanted money—but without the merit or the interest which would have given them a permanent place in English literature. The famous trilogy, *Coningsby, Sybil,* and *Tancred,* though of far greater value, have the fatal defect, as works of art, that they were avowedly written for a purpose. *Lothair* has none of these faults—Disraeli himself is imperceptible; the inner meaning of the book does not lie upon the surface. It was supposed, on its first appearance, to be a vulgar glorification of the splendours of the great English nobles into whose society he had been admitted as a *parvenu*, and whose condescension he rewarded by painting them in their indolent magnificence. The glitter and tinsel was ascribed to a Jewish taste for tawdry decoration, while he, individually, was thought to be glutted to satiation in the social Paradise, like 'Ixion at the feasts of the gods.' The divinities themselves were amused and forgiving. They did not resent—perhaps they secretly liked—the coloured photographs in which they saw themselves depicted. The life which Disraeli described was really their own, drawn naturally, without envy or malice; a life in which they enjoyed every pleasure which art could invent or fortune bestow, where they could discharge their duties to society by simply existing, and where they had the satisfaction of knowing that, by the mere gratification of their wishes, they were providing employment for multitudes of dependents. They had cultivated the graces of perfected humanity in these splendid surroundings, and *Lothair* was accepted as a voluntary offering of not undeserved homage.

In all Disraeli's writings, from his earliest age, there is traceable a conviction that no country could prosper under a free Constitution, without an aristocracy with great duties and great privileges; an aristocracy who, as leaders of the people, should be their examples also of manliness and nobility of character. He had observed how, as political power had passed away from the English peers, while their wealth remained, and increased, their habits had become more self-indulgent—they had become a superior but socially exclusive caste. They were still an estate of the realm, but they had become, like the gods of Epicurus, lifted above the toils and troubles of this mortal world, still feeding on the offerings which continued to smoke upon the altars, but of no definite use, and likely, it might be, to lose their celestial thrones, should mankind cease to believe in them. The occupation of the Elysians in the 'Infernal Marriage' was to go to operas and plays and balls, to wander in the green shades of the forest, to canter in light-hearted cavalcades over breezy downs, to banquet with the beautiful and the witty, to send care to the devil, and indulge the whim of the moment. It was easy to see who were meant by the Elysians. Privileged mortals they might be, but mortals out of whom, unless they roused themselves, no future rulers would ever rise to govern again the English nation. The Emperor Julian imagined that he could galvanise the dead gods of Paganism; Disraeli, believing that an aristocracy of some kind was a political necessity, had dreamt of an awakening of the young generation of English nobles to the heroic virtues of the age of the Plantagenets.

A quarter of a century had gone by since he had sent Tancred for inspiration to Mount Sinai. During all that time he had lived himself within the privileged circle. He had not over-estimated the high native qualities of the patrician lords and dames, but he had recognised the futility of his imaginations. They were as little capable of change as Venus and Apollo, and in his enforced leisure he drew their likenesses, with a light satire—so light that they failed to perceive it. The students of English history in time to come, who would know what the nobles of England were like in the days of Queen Victoria, will read *Lothair* with the same interest with which they read 'Horace' and 'Juvenal.' When Disraeli wrote, they were in the zenith of their magnificence. The industrial energy of the age had doubled their already princely revenues without effort of their own. They were the objects of universal homage—partly a vulgar adulation of rank, partly the traditionary reverence for their order, which had not yet begun to wane. Though idleness and flattery had done their work to spoil them, they retained much of the characteristics of a high-born race. Even Carlyle thought that they were the best surviving specimens of the ancient English. But their self-indulgence had expanded with their incomes. Compared with the manners of the modern palace or castle, the habits of their grandfathers and grandmothers had been frugality and simplicity and they had no duties—or none which they had been taught to understand. So they stand before us in *Lothair*. Those whom Elysian pleasures could not satisfy were weary of the rolling hours, and for want of occupation are seen drifting among the seductions of the Roman harlot; while from below the surface is heard the deep ground-tone of the European revolution, which may sweep them all away. We have no longer the bombast and unreality of the revolutionary epic. Disraeli has still the same subject before him, but he treats it with the mellow calmness of matured experience. He writes as a man of the world, with perfect mastery of his material, without a taint of ill-nature—with a frank perception of the many and great excellences of the patrician families, of the charm and spirit of the high-born matrons and girls, of the noble capabilities of their fathers and brothers, paralysed by the enchantment which condemns them to uselessness. They stand on the canvas like the heroes and heroines of Vandyck; yet the sense never leaves us that they are but flowers of the hothouse, artificially forced into splendour, with no root in outer nature, and therefore of no continuance.

The period of the story was the immediate year in which Disraeli was writing. The characters, though in but few instances portraits of living men and women, were exactly, even ludicrously, true to the prevailing type. We are introduced on the first page into a dukery the grandest of its kind; the owner of it, *the* duke, being too great to require a name, while minor dukes move like secondary planets in the surrounding ether. The duke has but one sorrow—that he has no home, his many palaces requiring a periodic residence at each. He is consoled each morning in his dressing-room, when he reviews his faultless person, by the reflection that his family were worthy of him. The hero is an ingenuous, pure-minded youth, still underage, though fast approaching his majority, the heir of enormous possessions, which, great as they descended from his father, have been increased to fabulous proportions by the progress of the country. His expectations rather oppress than give him pleasure, for he is full of generous aspirations, to which he knows not how to give effect. He feels only that his wealth will give him boundless powers for good or evil, and all that his natural piety and simplicity can tell him is that he ought to do something good with it. In an ordinary novel, a youth so furnished would be the natural prey of scheming mothers. Disraeli makes him the intended victim of a far more subtle conspiracy. His rank is vaguely indicated as only second to that of the duke himself. An absurd and unnatural consequence attaches to him in society, and he is marked as a prey by the power which aims at recovering England to the Church of Rome by the conversion of lords and ladies. He Is exposed to temptation through the innocence of his nature. Of his guardians, one is a Scotch Presbyterian earl, narrow, rugged, and honest; the other, a distinguished clergyman of the Anglican Church, an early friend of his father, who has 'gone over' to Rome, risen to high rank, and is at the head of the English Mission. The personality of this eminent man is visibly composed of the late Cardinal Wiseman and his successor, who is still present among us, and is so favourably known by his exertions for the improvement of the people. The function of Cardinal Grandison, as Disraeli represents him, is the propagation of Catholic truth among patrician circles. He has operated successfully on young and beautiful countesses, who, in turn, have worked upon their husbands.

The first converts of the apostles were the poor and the unknown. The Cardinal's superficial, but not altogether groundless, calculation, was that if he could convert earls and count the social influence of those great persons would carry the nation after them. Lothair, with his enormous fortune, would be a precious acquisition. His boyhood had been spent in Scotland, and, through his guardians' precautions, the Cardinal has no opportunities of influencing him—indeed, had scarcely seen him. They meet when he enters the world. Their connection places them on terms of immediate intimacy, and the web is spun round the fly with exquisite skill. Lothair is naturally religious, and no direct attempts are made upon his faith. Theological differences are treated with offhand ease; but he finds himself imperceptibly drawn into Catholic society. Accomplished Monsignori are ever at his side. Great ladies treat him with affectionate confidence, and he is delighted with an element where the highest, breeding is sanctified by spiritual devotion.

More delicate attractions are brought to bear—a lovely girl, so angelic that she is intended for a convent, lets him see that her destiny may, perhaps, be changed if she can find a husband with a spirit like her own. Lothair sinks rapidly under the combination of enchantments. An immense balance lies at his bankers, the accumulations of his minority. His conversations with Miss Arundel convince him that he must build a cathedral in London with it. It never occurred to him—nobody had even suggested to him—that his rent-roll entailed responsibilities towards the thousands of working families who were his own dependents, and by whose toil that wealth had been created. To build a cathedral, at any rate, would be a precious achievement—whether Catholic or Protestant might be decided when it was completed. He was, himself the only person who seemed ignorant which it was to be.

The spell which was cast by a lady, could be broken only by another lady's hand. Before Lothair is finally subdued, accident brings him in contact with Theodora, the wife of a rich American, dazzlingly beautiful, the incarnation of the Genius of the European revolution, to which her devotion is as intense as that of Miss Arundel to the Catholic Church. Two emotional impulses divide at present the minds of the passionate and the restless. The timid see salvation only in the reunion of Christendom and the returning protection of the Virgin. The bold and generous, weary of the cants, the conventionalisms, and unrealities of modern life, fling themselves into the revolutionary torrent, which threatens the foundations of existing civilisation.

In the convulsions of 1848, the revolutionary societies had shaken half the thrones in Europe. Disraeli, whose vision, unlike that of most contemporary statesmen, was not limited to the coming session, but looked before and after, had watched these two tendencies all through his life, well aware that they would have more to do with the future of mankind than the most ingenious Parliamentary manoeuvrings. While Premier he had learnt much of the working of the republican propaganda in France, Germany, and Russia. In the Irish Conspiracy, Catholic priests had been found, curiously, co-operating with American Fenians. Particular persons had fallen under his notice who were unknown to the outside world. At the moment when Lothair's future is hanging in the balance, he is led into relation with the fascinating representative of the revolutionary spirit. Theodora, whom Disraeli evidently likes better than any one else in the book, had been devoted from childhood to the cause of liberty. Her father and brothers had been killed in the fights of 1848. She herself, an orphan and an exile, had wandered to Paris, had sung in the streets, had been received into the secret associations, where, for her beauty and her genius, she had been regarded as a tutelary saint.

Pure as snow, Theodora had no thought but for the cause. The women worshipped her, the men idolised her. Like Rachel, she had electrified the Paris mob by starting forward at a great moment, and singing the 'Marseillaise.' She was the Mary Anne of the universal conspiracy against the existing tyranny which was called order, and a word from her at any moment could kindle the fire into a blaze. At the moment when this lady, an idealised Margaret Fuller, is introduced upon the scene, her thoughts are concentrated on the delivery of Rome from the Papacy. Thus simultaneously the two enthusiasms were centred on the same spot. The Catholic devotees were dreaming of the reunion of Christendom. Pio Nono was to summon an Ecumenical Council which was to be the greatest event of the century. To the revolutionists Rome was the mystic centre of European liberty. Rome being once free, and the detested priests made an end of, the Genius of Evil would spread its wings and depart, and mankind would at last be happy. Louis Napoleon was the uncertain element in the situation. Would he continue to support the Pope, or leave him to his fate?

The two parties watched each other, waiting the decision, and Theodora and her husband are in England, living at Belmont, a villa on the edge of Wimbledon, with an artistic and intellectual circle of friends. Here Lothair is introduced. He finds himself in an atmosphere delightful, yet entirely strange to him, presided over by a divine being. The lady is ten years older than himself, on the best terms with her American, and without further room in her heart for any but ideal objects. Disraeli contrives, with extraordinary skill, to let the fascination exercise its full power without degenerating into a vulgar intrigue. All is airy and spiritual. Lothair was on the edge of becoming a Catholic, because 'society ought to be religious.' Theodora is as 'religious' as Miss Arundel, but with a religion independent of dogma. He confides in her, tells her of his struggles, confesses his devotion to herself. When his passion takes too warm a tone, she gently waives it aside with a grace which intensifies the affection without allowing it to degrade itself.

Cardinal Grandison and his countesses are watching for their council, which is to be the 'event of the century.' To Lothair 'the great event' is his own coming of age, and the celebration of it at his magnificent castle. Dukes and earls, bishops and cardinals, Monsignori and English clergy, sheriffs and county magistrates, gather at Muriel for the occasion, and Theodora and her husband are specially-invited guests. All that is loyallest and brightest in the English nation is brought out in Lothair's welcome to his inheritance. The object is to show the unadulterated respect which still remains for our great nobles, the future which is still within their reach if they know how to seize it—a respect, however, tinged slightly with artificiality and unreality in the exaggeration of the outward splendour. As a by-play, the chiefs of the two Churches continue their struggle for Lothair's soul. The 'Bishop,' a well-known prelate of those days, and a college friend of Cardinal Grandison before their creed had divided them, now meet in the lists, followed by their respective acolytes. The Bishop and the Anglican countesses arrange an early 'celebration' in the chapel, where Lothair is to renew his vows to the Church of his fathers. The Catholics look at it as a magical rite, which may spoil the work which they are hoping to accomplish. The sureness of foot with which Disraeli moves in these intricate labyrinths, the easy grace with which the various actors play their parts, might tempt one to forget what a piece of gilded tinsel it all is, but for the disbelieving interjections of common sense from less devout spectators. St. Aldegonde, the most attractive of all the male characters in the book, a patrician of the patricians and the heir of a dukedom, affects Radicalism of the reddest kind. Bored with the emptiness of an existence which he knows not how to amend, a man who in other times might have ridden beside King Richard at Ascalon, or charged with the Black Prince at Poitiers, lounges through life in good-humoured weariness of amusements which will not amuse, and outrages conventionalism by his frank contempt for humbug. Him they had not dared to invite to be present at the 'celebration.' On a Sunday morning, when the party generally were observing the ordinary proprieties, he appears in the breakfast-room in rough and loose week day costume, pushes his hands through his dishevelled locks, and exclaims, as he stands before the fire, regardless of the Bishop's presence, 'How I hate Sundays!' The Bishop makes a dignified retreat. When St. Aldegonde's wife gently reproves him, he adds impenitently to his sins, saying, 'I don't like bishops, I don't see the use of them; but I have no objection to him personally. I think him an agreeable man, not at all a bore. Just put it right, Bertha,' &c. St. Aldegonde is a perfect specimen of a young English noble, who will not cant or lie; the wisest and truest when counsel or action is needed of him, yet with his fine qualities all running to waste in a world where there is no employment for them.

Neither Bishop nor Cardinal secure their prey. Theodora carries the day. The French withdraw from Rome; she has secret information that they are not to return, and that the secret societies are ready to move. The opportunity has arrived. Nothing is wanted but arms and money. The cathedral is abandoned, the accumulations of Lothair's minority are thrown into Theodora's hands, and he himself enters into the campaign for the liberation of Rome.

A republican general, who has been incidentally seen before, a friend of Mazzini and Garibaldi, now appears on the scene. From Muriel we pass to an Italian valley on the Roman frontier, where a force is collecting to join Garibaldi and advance on the Holy City. Theodora is in the camp. Rome itself is ready to rise on the first glinting of their lances. The General moves forward, and fights and wins a battle at Viterbo; but in the moment of victory all is lost. Louis Napoleon has changed his mind, and the French return; a stray shot strikes Theodora, and mortally wounds her. The sound of the guns at Civita Vecchia saluting the arrival of the French ships reaches her ears as she hangs between life and death. Her heart breaks; her last words are to tell Lothair that 'another and a more powerful attempt will be made to gain him to the Church of Rome,' and she demands and obtains a promise from him that 'he will never enter that communion.'

When he wrote *Coningsby* and *Sybil*, Disraeli regretted the Reformation. The most ardent admirer of the Middle Ages did not regard the overthrow of the ecclesiastical rule, and the suppression of the religious houses, with more displeasure, or believed more devotedly in the virtues of the abbots and the beneficent working of the monastic system. In his *Life of Lord George Bentinck* he had so far changed his mind that he refuses to *Roman Catholic* the dignity of capital letters. Twenty additional years of experience had taught him that the modern Roman hierarchy was as unscrupulous as the Reformers had described their predecessors, and that, of the many dangers which threatened England, there was none more insidious than the intrigues of ultramontane proselytisers.

The battle of Mentana follows, and Garibaldi's defeat by the French. Lothair is shot down at the General's side, and is left for dead on the field. Being found breathing, he is taken up with the other wounded. His English Catholic friends are in Rome for the winter, and devote themselves to the care of the hospitals. An Italian woman brings word to Miss Arundel that one of her countrymen is lying at the point of death, who may be recovered if she takes charge of him. He is found to be Lothair, and the opportunity is seized for a thaumaturgical performance as remarkable as the miracle-working at Lourdes. The woman who brought the account is discovered, by a halo round her head, to have been the Virgin in person; Lothair, unknown to himself; to have fallen not as a Garibaldian but as a volunteer in the Papal army. He is carried, unconscious, to the enchanter's cave, in the shape of a room in the Agostini Palace. He is watched over while in danger by a beautiful veiled figure. He is surrounded in convalescence by adroit Monsignori, and prevailed on to assist in a ceremony which is represented to him as a mere thanksgiving for his recovery, but in which he finds himself walking first in a procession, candle in hand, at Miss Arundel's side, she and he the special objects of the

Virgin's care. The next morning the whole performance is published in full in the *Papal Gazette*, and his Cardinal guardian then appears on the stage, to tell him that he is 'the most favoured of men,' and that the Holy Father in person will immediately receive him into the Church.

Too weak from illness to express his indignation in more than words, he protests against the insolent deceit. No where in English fiction is there any passage where the satire is more delicate than in the Cardinal's rejoinder. Lothair opens a window into Disraeli's mind, revealing the inner workings of it more completely than anything else which he wrote or said. For this reason I have given so many pages to the analysis of it, and must give one or two more.

"I know there are two narratives of your relations with. the battle of Mentana," observed the Cardinal, quietly. "The one accepted as authentic is that which appears in this Journal; the other account, which can only be traced to yourself, has, no doubt, a somewhat different character. But considering that it is in the highest degree improbable, and that there is not a tittle of collateral or confirmatory evidence to extenuate its absolute unlikelihood, I hardly think you are justified in using, with reference to the statements in this article, the harsh expressions which I am persuaded on reflection you will feel you have hastily used."

"I think," said Lothair, with a kindling eye and a burning cheek, "that I am the best judge of what I did at Mentana."

"Well, well," said the Cardinal, with dulcet calmness, "you naturally think so; but you must remember you have been very ill, my dear young friend, and labouring under much excitement. If I was you—and I speak as your friend—I would not dwell too much on this fancy of yours about the battle of Mentana. I would, myself, always deal tenderly with a fixed idea. Nevertheless, in the case of a public event, a matter of fact, if a man finds that he is of one opinion, and all orders of society of another, he should not be encouraged to dwell on a perverted creed. Your case is by no means an uncommon one. It will wear off with returning health. King George IV believed he commanded at the battle of Waterloo, and his friends were at one time a little alarmed; but Knighton, who was a sensible man, said, 'His Majesty has only to leave off Curaçoa, and, rest assured, he will gain no more victories.' Remember, sir, where you are. You are in the centre of Christendom, where truth, and alone truth, resides. Divine authority has perused this paper, and approved it. It is published for the joy and satisfaction of two hundred millions of Christians, and for the salvation of all those who, unhappily for themselves, are not yet converted to the faith. It records the most memorable event of this century. Our Blessed Lady has personally appeared to her votaries before during that period, but never at Rome;

wisely and well she has worked in villages, as did her Divine Son. But the time
is now ripe for terminating the infidelity of the world. In the Eternal City, amid
all its matchless learning and profound theology, in the sight of thousands, this
great act has been accomplished in a manner which can admit of no doubt
and lead to no controversy. Some of the most notorious atheists of Rome have
already solicited to be admitted to the offices of the Church. The secret societies
have received their death-blow. I look to the alienation of England as virtually
over. I am panting to see you return to the home of your fathers, and recover
it for the Church in the name of the Lord God of Sabaoth. Never was a man
in a greater position since Godfrey or Ignatius. The eyes of all Christendom are
upon you, as the most favoured of men, and you stand there like St. Thomas."

"Perhaps he was bewildered, as I am," said Lothair.

"Well, his bewilderment ended in his becoming an apostle, as yours will. I
am glad we have had this conversation, and that we agree. I knew we should.
To-morrow the Holy Father will himself receive you into the bosom of the
Church. Christendom will then hail you as its champion and regenerator."

Conscious that he was the victim of a lying conspiracy, yet as if his will
was magnetised, he finds himself driven to the slaughter, 'a renegade without conviction.' He is virtually a prisoner, but he contrives at night to pass
the Palace gate, wander about the ghostly city, and at last into the Coliseum,
where Benvenuto Cellini had seen a vision of devils, and Lothair imagines
that he sees Theodora, who reminds him of her warning. He is brought
back, senseless, by a spiritual sleuth-hound who had been sent after him;
and the result was, that on the morning which was to have made the unfortunate Lord of Muriel a Papist against his will, he is visited by an English
doctor, 'who abhorred priests, and did not particularly admire ladies.' He is
ordered instant change of scene, and is sent to Sicily—still in the custody of
'familiars'; but he evades their vigilance, embarks in a fishing-boat, reaches
Malta and an English yacht—and thenceforward his fortunes brighten
again. He visits the Greek islands. Of course he must go to Jerusalem—all
Disraeli's heroes who want spiritual comfort are sent to Jerusalem—not,
however, any longer to see visions of angels, but to find a 'Paraclete' in a
Syrian Christian from the Lake of Gennesaret, an Ebionite of the primitive
type, whose religion was a simple following of Christ.

In recovered health of mind and body, Lothair returns to England, where
he finds the world as he had left it. He supposes his adventures would be on
everyone's lips. His acquaintances ask him, coolly, what he has been doing
with himself, and how long he has been in town. The Cardinal is again glid-

ing through the gilded drawing rooms, but ignores the Roman incident as if it had never been. Miss Arundel subsides into her sacred vocation. The hero, freed from further persecution, marries the beautiful daughter of the duke, who had been the object of his boyish affection—a lady, needless to say, of staunchest Protestant integrity.

Such is *Lothair*, perhaps the first novel ever written by a man who had previously been Prime Minister of England. Every page glitters with wit or shines with humour. Special scenes and sentences are never to be forgotten: the Tournament of Doves at the Putney Villa, where the ladies gather to see their lords at their favourite summer amusement; the wounded blue rock, which was contented to die by the hand of a duke, but rose and fluttered over a paling, disdaining to be worried by a terrier; the artist who hesitates over a mission to Egypt, but reflects that no one has ever drawn a camel, and that, if he went, a camel would at last be drawn; the definition of critics—as those who had failed in literature and art. But the true value of the book is the perfect representation of patrician society in England in the year which was then passing over; the full appreciation of all that was good and noble in it; yet the recognition, also, that it was a society without a purpose, and with no claim to endurance. It was then in its most brilliant period, like the full bloom of a flower which opens fully only to fade.

# XVI

*The exhausted volcanoes—Mr Gladstone's failure and unpopularity—Ireland*
*worse than before—Loss of influence in Europe—The election of 1874—*
*Great Conservative majority—Disraeli again Prime Minister with real*
*power—His general position as a politician—Problems waiting to be dealt*
*with—The relations between the Colonies and the Empire—The restoration*
*of the authority of the law in Ireland—Disraeli's strength and Disraeli's*
*weakness—Prefers an ambitious foreign policy—Russia and Turkey—The*
*Eastern Question—Two possible policies and the effects of each—Disraeli's*
*choice— Threatened war with Russia—The Berlin Conference—Peace with*
*honour—Jingoism and fall of the Conservative party—Other features of his*
*administration—Goes to the House of Lords as Earl of Beaconsfield and receives*
*the Garter—Public Worship Act—Admirable distribution of patronage—*
*Disraeli and Carlyle—Judgment of a conductor of an omnibus*

THE DESTINIES WERE FIGHTING FOR Disraeli. The exhausted volcanoes continued on the Treasury bench; but England had grown tired of them. They had been active when their activity had been mischievous. In quiescence they had allowed the country to become contemptible. The defeat of France and the establishment of a great German empire had changed the balance of power in Europe. England had not been consulted, and had no voice in the new arrangements. Russia took advantage of the confusion to tear up the Black Sea Treaty, and throw the fragments in our faces. The warmest Radical enthusiast could not defend the imbecility with which the outrage was submitted to. A Minister was sent to Paris to inform Prince Bismarck that, if Russia persisted, we should go to war. When Russia refused to be frightened, the uncertain Premier said in Parliament that the Minister had exceeded his instructions. It appeared, on inquiry, that the instructions had not been exceeded, but that nothing had been meant but an idle menace, which had failed of its effect. The English people, peculiarly sensitive about the respect paid to their country abroad, because they feel that it is declining, resented the insult from the Russians upon the Cabinet, which was charged with pusillanimity. The settlement of the Alabama claims, though prudent and right, was no less humiliating. The generous policy which was to have won the Irish heart had exasperated one party without satisfying the other. The third branch of the upas tree still waited for the axe. The minds even of Radicals could not yet reconcile themselves to the terms of a concordat which would alone satisfy the Catholic hierarchy. The Premier, deceived by the majority which still appeared to support him, disregarded the rising murmurs. He had irritated powerful interests on all sides, from the army to the licensed victuallers; while of work achieved he had nothing to show but revolutionary measures in Ireland, which had hitherto been unattended with success. The bye-elections showed with increasing distinctness the backward swing of the political pendulum, and very marked indeed at this time was the growth of the personal popularity of Disraeli. At least, he had made no professions, and had ventured no extravagant prophecies. He had always stood up staunchly, for the honour of his country. Brief as had been his opportunities of office, he had accomplished, after all, more positive practical good than his rivals who boasted so loudly. Their function had been to abolish old-established institutions, and the effect had been but a turn of the kaleidoscope—a new pattern, and nobody much the better for it. Disraeli had been contented with a 'policy of sewage,' as it was disdainfully called. He had helped to drain London; he had helped to shorten the hours of children's labour. His larger exploit had been to bring the Jews into Parliament, and to bring under the crown the government of India. Sensible people might question the wisdom of his Reform Bill, but he had shown, at any rate, that he was not afraid of the people; and the people, on their side, were proud of a man who had raised himself to so high a place in the face of thirty years of insult and obloquy. His position was the triumph of the most respectable of Radical principles—the rule to him that deserve to rule. They came to call him Dizzy; and there is no surer sign that a man is liked in England than the adoption of a pet name for him. His pungent sayings were repeated from lip to lip. He never courted popular demonstrations, but if he was seen in the streets he was followed by cheering crowds. At public meetings which had no party character he was the favourite of the hour. At a decorous and dignified assembly where royalties were present, and the chiefs of both political parties, I recollect a burst of emotion when Disraeli rose which, for several minutes, prevented him from speaking, the display of feeling being the more intense the lower the strata which it penetrated, the very waiters whirling their napkins with a passion which I never on any such occasion saw exceeded or equalled.

Mr Gladstone was inattentive to the symptoms of the temper of the people, and proceeded with his Irish Education Bill. The secularist Radicals were dissatisfied with a proposal which gave too much power to the Catholic priests. The Court of Rome and the Irish bishops were dissatisfied because it did not give enough. Impatient of opposition, Mr Gladstone punished Parliament with a dissolution, and was astonished at the completeness of his overthrow.

For the first time since 1841 a strong Conservative majority was returned, independent of Irish support—a majority large and harmonious enough to discourage a hope of reducing it either by intrigue or by bye-elections. England, it really seemed, had recovered from her revolutionary fever-fit, and desired to be left in quiet after half-a-century of political dissipation. Seven or six years of Conservative administration were now secured. There were those who shook their heads, disbelieved in any genuine reaction till lower depths had been reached, and declared that 'it was only the licensed victuallers.' Mr Gladstone's long Parliamentary experience led him to think that, at any rate, it would last out the remainder of his own working life, and that his political reign was over. Disraeli had taken Fortune's buffets and Fortune's favours with equal composure, and had remained calm under the severest discomfitures. Mr Gladstone retired from the leadership of the Liberal party, and left Lord Hartington to repair the consequences of his own precipitancy. 'Power,' the Greek proverb says, 'will show what a man is.' Till this time, Disraeli had held office but on sufferance. He was now trusted by the country with absolute authority, and it remained to be seen what he would make of it. He could do what he pleased. He could dictate the foreign and colonial policy. He was master of the fleet and the army. He had made himself sovereign of England, so long as his party were true to him; and the long eclipse through which he had conducted them to eventual triumph guaranteed their fidelity. He had won his authority, not by the favour of a sovereign, not by having been the champion of any powerful interest, but by the personal confidence in himself which was felt by the body of the people.

He was now to show whether he was or was not a really great man. In his early career he had not concealed that his chief motive was ambition. He had started as a soldier of fortune, and he had taken service with the party among whom, perhaps, he felt that he would have the best chance of rising to eminence. Young men of talent were chiefly in the other camp—among the Conservatives he might expect fewer rivals. But the side which he had chosen undoubtedly best suited the character of his own mind; under no circumstances could Disraeli have been a popular apostle of progress, or have taught with a grave face the doctrines of visionary freedom. He regarded all that as nonsense, even as insincere nonsense, not believed in even by its advocates. On all occasions he had spoken his mind freely, careless what prejudice he might offend. Even on the abolition of slavery, on which English self-applause was innocently sensitive, he alone of public men had dared to speak without enthusiasm. The emancipation of the negroes, he said in a debate upon the sugar trade, 'was virtuous but was not wise.' Politics was his profession, and as a young barrister aspires to be Lord Chancellor Disraeli aspired to rise in the State. He had done the Conservatives' work, and the Conservatives had made him Prime Minister; but he had committed himself to few definite opinions, and, unlike most other great men who had attained the same position, he was left with a comparatively free hand. Lord Burghley was called to the helm to do a definite thing; to steer his country through the rocks and shoals of the Reformation. His course was marked out for him, and the alternatives were success or the scaffold. Disraeli had the whole ocean open, to take such course as might seem prudent or attractive. There was no special measure which he had received a mandate to carry through, no detailed policy which he had advocated which the country was enabling him to execute. He was sincerely and loyally anxious to serve the interests of the British Empire and, restore its diminished influence, but in deciding what was to be done it was natural that he would continue to be guided by an ambition to make his Ministry memorable, and by the cosmopolitan and oriental temperament of his own mind.

Two unsettled problems lay before him after his Cabinet was formed, both of which he knew to be of supreme importance. Ireland, he was well aware, could not remain in the condition in which it had been left by his predecessors. The Land Act of 1870 had cut the sinews of the organisation under which Ireland had been ruled since the Act of Settlement. The rights of owners were complicated with the rights of tenants, and the tenants had been taught that by persevering in insubordination they might themselves become the owners altogether. The passions of the Irish nation had been excited; they had been led to believe that the late measures were a first step towards the recovery of their independence. Seeds of distraction had been sown broadcast, which would inevitably sprout at the first favourable season. A purely English Minister with no thought but for English interests, and put in possession of sufficient power to make himself obeyed, would, I think, have seized the opportunity to reorganise the internal government of Ireland. The land question might have been adjusted on clear and equitable lines, the just rights secured of owners and occupiers alike. The authority of the law could have been restored, nationalist visions extinguished, and a permanent settlement arrived at which might have lasted for another century. No one had said more emphatically than Disraeli that the whole system of Irish administration demanded a revolutionary change. He was himself at last in a position to give effect to his own words. This was one great subject. The other was the relation of the colonies to the mother country. In the heyday of Free Trade, when England was to be made the workshop of the world, the British Empire had been looked on as an expensive illusion. The colonies and India were supposed to contribute nothing to our wealth which they would not contribute equally if they were independent, while both entailed dangers and responsibilities, and in time of war embarrassment and weakness. A distinguished Liberal statesman had said that the only objection to parting with the colonies was that without them England would be so strong that she would be dangerous to the rest of the world. These doctrines, half avowed, half disguised under specious pleas for self-government, had been acted on for a number of years by the Liberal authorities at the Colonial Office. The troops were recalled from New Zealand, Canada, and Australia. Constitutions were granted so unconditional, so completely unaccompanied with provisions for the future relations with the mother country, that the connection was obviously intended to have an early end. These very serious steps were taken by a few philosophical statesmen who happened to be in power without that consultation with the nation which ought to have preceded an action of such large con sequence. The nation allowed them to go on in unsuspicious confidence, and only woke to know what had been done when the dismemberment of the Empire came to be discussed as a probable event. One is tempted to regret that the old forms of ministerial responsibility have gone out of fashion. They might have served as a check on the precipitancy of such over-eager theorists. The country, when made aware of what had been designed, spoke with a voice so unanimous that they disclaimed their intentions, sheltered themselves behind the necessity of leaving the colonies to manage their own affairs, and assured the world that they desired nothing but to secure colonial loyalty; but these hasty measures had brought about a form of relation which, not being designed for continuance, had no element of continuance in it; and the ablest men who desire the maintenance of the Empire are now speculating how to supply the absence of conditions which might have been insisted on at the concession of the colonial constitutions, but which it is now too late to suggest.

Disraeli's attention had been strongly drawn to this question. He was imperialist in the sense that he thought the English the greatest nation in the world and wished to keep them so. At the Crystal Palace in 1872 he had spoken with contempt and indignation of the policy which had been followed, and had indicated that it would be the duty of the Conservatives as far as possible to remedy the effects of it. His words show that he thought a remedy not impossible, and it is worth while to quote them.

'Gentlemen,' he said, 'if you look to the history of this country since the advent of Liberalism forty years ago you will find there has been no effort so continuous, so subtle, supported by so much energy, and carried on with so much ability and acumen as the attempts of Liberalism to effect the disintegration of the Empire of England. And, gentlemen, of all its efforts this is the one which has been the nearest to success. Statesmen of the highest character, writers of the most distinguished ability, the most organised and efficient means have been employed in this endeavour. 'It has been proved to all of us that we have lost money by our colonies. It has been shown with precise, with mathematical demonstration that there never was a jewel in the crown of England that was so truly costly as the possession of India. How often has it been suggested that we should at once emancipate ourselves from this incubus? Well, that result was nearly accomplished. When those subtle views were adopted by the country under the plausible plea of granting self-government to the colonies I confess that I myself thought that the tie was broken. Not that I, for one, object to self-government. I cannot conceive how our distant colonies can have their affairs administered except by self-government. But self-government, in my opinion, when it was conceded ought to have been conceded as part of a great policy of imperial consolidation. It ought to have been accompanied with an imperial tariff; by securities for the people of England for the enjoyment of the unappropriated lands which belonged to the sovereign as their trustee, and by a military code which should have precisely defined the means and the responsibilities by which the colonies should be defended, and by which, if necessary, this country should call for aid from the colonies themselves. It ought, further, to have been accompanied by some representative council in the metropolis which would have brought the colonies into constant and continuous relations with the home Government. All this, however, was omitted because those who advised that policy—and I believe their convictions were sincere—looked upon the colonies of England, looked even upon our connection with India, as a burden on this country, viewing everything in a financial aspect, and totally passing by those moral and political considerations which make nations great and by the influence of which alone men are distinguished from animals.

'Well, what has been the result of this attempt during the reign of Liberalism for the disintegration of the Empire? It has entirely failed. But how has it failed? Through the sympathy of the colonies with the mother country. They have decided that the Empire shall not be destroyed; and in my opinion no Minister in this country will do his duty who neglects any opportunity of reconstructing as much as possible our colonial empire and of responding to those distant sympathies which may become the source of incalculable strength and happiness to this land.'

A few persons, perhaps many, had hoped from these words that Disraeli, when he came into power again, would distinguish his term of rule by an effort which, even if it failed by immediate result, would have strengthened the bonds of good feeling, and if it succeeded, as it might have done, would have given him a name in the world's history as great as Washington's. Difficult such a task would have been, for the political and practical ties had been too completely severed; but the greatness of a statesman is measured by the difficulties which he overcomes. Whether it was that Disraeli felt that he was growing old, and that he wished to signalise his reign by more dazzling exploits which would promise immediate results; whether it was that he saw the English nation impatient of the lower rank in the counsels of Europe to which it had been reduced by the foreign policy of his predecessors, that he conceived that the people would respond to his call and would repay a Tory Government which was maintaining the honour of the country by a confirmed allegiance; whether there was something in his own character which led him, when circumstances gave him an opening, to prefer another course to that which he had sketched in the words which I have quoted; or whether—but it is idle to speculate upon motives. He is said to have believed that there was a Conservative Trade Wind which would blow for many years; he may have thought that Ireland and the colonies might lie over to be dealt with at leisure. '*Ceux qui gouvernent,*' says Voltaire, '*sont rarement touches d'une utilité éloignée, tout sensible qu'elle est, surtout quand cet avantage futur est balancé par les difficultés présentes.*' The two great problems which he could have, if not settled, yet placed on the road to settlement, he decided to pass by. He left Ireland to simmer in confusion. His zeal for the consolidation of the Empire was satisfied by the new title with which he decorated his sovereign. And his Administration will be remembered by the part which he played in the Eastern question, and by the judgment which was passed upon him by the constituencies. Disraeli particularly prided himself on his knowledge of the English character. He had seen that no Ministers were ever more popular in England than the two Pitts; and they were popular because they maintained

in arms the greatness of their country. He had seen Lord Palmerston borne triumphantly into power to fight Russia, and rewarded for the imperfect results
of the Crimean war with a confidence which was continued till his death. But
in these instances there had been, or had seemed to be, a real cause which the
nation understood and approved. Lord Chatham was winning America for
the Anglo-Saxon race. His son was defending the independence and commerce of England against the power of Bonaparte. And Lord Palmerston had
persuaded the country that its safety was really threatened by Russian preponderance. Disraeli strangely failed to perceive that times were changed, that
the recollections of the Crimean war no longer excited enthusiasm, that it
was no longer possible to speak of Turkey with a serious face as the 'bulwark
of civilisation against barbarism.' He was right in supposing that his party
would go along with him, and that of the rest the scum and froth would be on
his side. The multitude would shout for war out of excitement, and for war
with Russia because Russia was a Power with which they supposed we could
fight with a chance of success. But the serious thought of the nation, which
always prevails in the end, was against him and he could not perceive it. The
English bishops persuaded Henry V to pursue his title to the crown of France
to detach him from schemes of Church reform. Louis Napoleon attacked
Germany to save his own shaking throne. Disraeli hoped to cool the Radical
effusiveness by rousing the national pride. The barren conquests of Henry
prepared the way for the wars of the Roses. Louis Napoleon brought only
ruin upon himself. Disraeli failed, as he deserved to fail. He thought that he
was reviving patriotic enthusiasm, and all that he did was to create jingoism.

Of the tens of thousands who gathered in Hyde Park to shout for war how
many had considered what a war with Russia might involve? Bismarck could
not understand Disraeli's attitude. 'Why cannot you be friends with Russia
and settle your differences peacefully?' he said to him at the beginning of
the dispute. 'Why not put an end once for all to this miserable Turkish business, which threatens Europe every year or two with war?' Why not, indeed?
Russian interests and English interests divide the continent of Asia. These
two Powers between them are engaged in the same purpose of bringing the
Eastern nations under the influence of Western civilisation. It would be a
misfortune to humanity if either they or we should cease our efforts. The
world smiles when we complain of Russian aggression. The Asiatic subjects
of the Queen of England are two hundred millions. The Asiatic subjects of
Russia are forty millions. The right on both sides is the right of conquest.

They have annexed territories and we have annexed territories. Annexations
are the necessary results of the contact of order with anarchy. If we work

together the regeneration of Asia may proceed peacefully and beneficently. If we quarrel in earnest, as things now stand, the whole enormous continent will be split into factions, nation against nation, tribe against tribe, family against family. From the Bosphorus to the Wall of China, and perhaps inside it, there will be an enormous faction-fight, with an amount of misery to mankind of which no recorded war has produced the like. It will be a war, too, which can lead to no atoning results. England staggers already under the vastness of her responsibilities, and even if she conquers can undertake no more. That we might not conquer is an eventuality which our pride may refuse to entertain; yet such a thing might happen, and if we are defeated we are a lost nation. Russia might recover, but we could not; a disaster on the Dardanelles or the Afghan frontier would cost us our Indian Empire.

In such a war we stand to lose all and to gain nothing, while in itself it would be nothing less than a crime against mankind. We are told that a cordial co-operation with Russia is impossible. It will not be made more possible by a quarrel over Turkey. Yet to a peaceful arrangement we must come at last if the quarrel is not to be pursued till one or other of us is destroyed. These are the broad facts of the situation, to which the fate of the Principalities or of the Bosphorus itself are as feathers in the balance. Disraeli, in whose hands for the moment the tremendous decision rested, chose to overlook them. He persevered in the policy of upholding the Turkish Empire. It was the traditional policy of England, and, as he professed to consider, the most consistent with English interests. It may be that he remembered also that the Turks had befriended his own race when the Russians had been their bitterest enemies. It may be that something of his early vanity still lingered in him, and that he was tempted by the proud position of being the arbiter of Europe. But fact was against him. Turkish rule in Europe is an anachronism, and neither force nor diplomacy can prevent the final emancipation of Christian nations from Mahometan dominion. He chose a course which gave him for a moment an ephemeral glory, but it was at the cost of undoing the effects of his whole political life, wrecking again the party which he had reorganised and giving a fresh lease of power to the revolutionary tendencies which threatened the dismemberment of the Empire.

The Eastern question was beginning to simmer when Disraeli came into power, but the symptoms had not yet become acute and he had leisure for internal politics. He desired to strengthen Conservative institutions. Of these the Church of England ought to have been the strongest, but it was distracted by internal disorders. The Romanising party was the counterpart of Radicalism. The original Tractarians had imagined themselves to be champions of old Tory principles, but revolutionary movements draw instinctively together. Romanisers and Radicals had the common belief that they were wiser than their fathers, that they must have something 'deeper and truer than satisfied the last century.' The reformers of the State wished to remodel the Constitution, the Ritualists to restore Church principles and bring back the Mass. The Radical chief sympathised with both of them. They returned his regard; and vast numbers of the clergy fell off from their old allegiance.

Disraeli, keenly as he observed the outer features of the situation, was not entirely at home in such subjects. He did not see that the lay members of the Church, who had once been earnest Protestants, had now grown indifferent about it. If the clergy liked to amuse themselves with altars and vestments and elaborate services the clergy might have their way for all that the laity cared about the matter. Old Tory families still hated Puritans and Puritanism, and had not realised the change of front which made Protestants Conservatives and Radicals into allies of the Papacy. Disraeli believed that an Act of Parliament could check a tendency which ran in a current where legislation could not reach. He passed a Public Worship Act to put down ritualism,[1] and it has been scarcely more effective than Lord John Russell's demonstration against Papal aggression. This disease has not been checked; acrimonious lawsuits promoted by a few antediluvian Protestant parishioners have failed, and will continue to fail, because public opinion refuses to support the promoters. Suffering priests and bishops pose as martyrs, and there is unwillingness to punish them. By the Constitution the Church of England rests on an Act of Parliament, but sooner than effectively use its controlling power Parliament will consent to disestablishment. The Public Worship Act exasperated the enthusiastic clergy and their friends. It secretly offended not a few of Disraeli's aristocratic followers. For the purpose for which it was passed it was as ineffectual as, to use President Lincoln's simile, 'a Pope's Bull against a comet,' and demonstrations which are not followed by action do not add to a statesman's influence.

This, however, and all other internal subjects lost their interest when Servia rose against the Turks, when the Servian defeat brought the Russians across the Danube, and the passions, the alarms, the panics of the Crimean episode revived in all their frenzy. Circumstances had altered. England had no longer France for an ally. Turkey had then been saved, and allowed a fresh lease of life on condition of mending her administration and behaving better to her Christian subjects. Turkey had amended nothing, and could amend nothing. So far as Turkey was concerned, the only result had been a Turkish loan, and on this the interest had ceased to be paid. Nevertheless the familiar cries rose again. Our old ally was in danger. The Dardanelles were the keys of India. We were threatened on the Indus, we were threatened in the Mediterranean. Quiet voices could get no hearing, and eloquence could be only met by eloquence. Mr Gladstone, if by his Irish action he had let loose the winds at home, did a service then which must be remembered to his honour. He forced the country to observe what the rule of Turkey meant. He insisted, not entirely in vain, on the indignity, the shame, the dishonour which we should bring on ourselves, by taking the side of the Bulgarian assassins. He succeeded in making Disraeli pause at a critical time and preventing measures which might have led to an immediate conflict, and the Turkish successes at Plevna and in Armenia seemed for a time to dispense with the necessity of armed interference. The Turk, it was hoped, would be able to defend his provinces with his own hand. But, as Disraeli said truly, the English are the most enthusiastic people in the world. They have an especial love for courage, and the bravery of the Turks in the field made them forget or disbelieve in the 'atrocities.' When Kars fell and Plevna fell, when the Russian armies forced the Balkans in the dead of winter, and the Ottoman resistance collapsed, the storm rose again into a hurricane. Mr Gladstone and the *Daily News* stood their ground. Disraeli waived aside the horrible story of Turkish cruelties, as, if not false, yet as enormously exaggerated. Such as it was the ferocity had not after all cut deep into Bulgarian memories. If the dead have any knowledge of what is passing upon earth he must laugh in his grave when the Bulgarian survivors of these horrors are now inviting the Turks into an alliance, with them against their Russian deliverers. Deeds of violence have been too common in some countries to make a deep impression. The fugitive Macdonalds from Glencoe were lost in astonishment at the interest which political passion had created in the murder of their kinsmen. Public opinion, so far as it expressed itself in words, continued strongly in Disraeli's favour. He said amidst general applause that he would not allow Turkey to be crushed. He did not desire war, but he was prepared for war if the Russians entered Constantinople, and on two occasions peace hung upon a thread. A plan of campaign was formed, not for local resistance but for war on an universal scale. The British fleet went up within sight of the Golden Horn to cover the Turkish capital. Gallipoli was to be occupied. Turkestan was to be set on fire through the Afghan country; and, I believe, so ambitious was the scheme, another force was to have advanced from the Persian Gulf into Armenia. Not all the Cabinet were prepared for these adventures. Lord Carnarvon and Lord Derby resigned, and caused some passing hesitation, and as the Russians left Constantinople unentered that particular crisis passed away. But the Russian conquerors had dictated their own terms of peace, and when Disraeli insisted that the terms should not stand till they had been revised at a European Conference England again applauded and admired. He determined to attend the Conference in person, and the remarkable impression which he produced there was the culminating point of his singular career. On Prince Bismarck, who respects firmness more than eloquence, it was an impression eminently favourable. French is the language generally used at the meetings of European plenipotentiaries. Disraeli spoke French tolerably, and had prepared a French address. It was represented to him, however, that his peculiar power of creating an effect would be impaired by his accent, and he spoke actually in English. There were two points, I believe, on which the peace of Europe hung in the balance, one referring to Batoum, which was not to be fortified; the other to the division of the two Bulgarias, which the treaty of San Stefano had joined. Heavy guns are now mounted at Batoum, and we are none the worse for it. The large Bulgaria, so much dreaded, has become a fact again, with the warm approbation of the anti-Russian Powers. Yet on threads so slight as these the lives or deaths, perhaps, of millions of men at that moment depended. After a stormy debate on the Balkan question Disraeli broke up the Conference and announced that he should return home and take other measures. Russia, at Bismarck's entreaty, yielded a point which had no substantial significance. Disraeli had the glory of extorting a concession by a menace. We imagine that the days are past when nations can go to war for a point of honour, but we are no wiser than our fathers after all.

War, however, was avoided, and Disraeli had won his diplomatic victory. He returned to London in a blaze of glory, bringing peace with honour, and all the world sang the praises of the patriot Minister. He thought himself that he had secured the ascendency of the Conservatives for a quarter of a century at least. In 1876 he had passed from the leadership of the House of Commons to the House of Lords, reviving in an earldom the title which he had given to his wife, and which had died with her. He now received the Garter, the most coveted of all English decorations, because bestowed usually of free grace and not for merit, but for him the reward of his unequalled services. Yet it was all hollow. The public welfare, the public security of the Empire had not been advanced a step. Before the shouts had died away we were astonished by a secret treaty with Turkey, by which we had bound ourselves to the future defence of her Asiatic dominions, an obligation which we shall fulfil as much and as little as we fulfilled a similar obligation to Denmark. We had bound ourselves to secure a better administration of the Turkish provinces, an undertaking which we cannot fulfil; and we had acquired an addition to our Empire in Cyprus, a possession of which we can make no use. The country was surprised, and not particularly pleased, but on the whole it was still proud and gratified, and if Disraeli had dissolved Parliament when he returned from Berlin there is little doubt what its verdict would then have been. But he waited, believing himself secure in his achievements, and Fortune, which had stood his friend so long, now turned upon him. The spirit of a great nation called into energy on a grand occasion is the noblest of human phenomena. The pseudo-national spirit of jingoism is the meanest and the most dangerous. A war had been lighted in Afghanistan as part of the Eastern policy. It was easier to kindle than to extinguish. Sir Bartle Frere in South Africa imagined that he too could have an Imperial policy. He went to war with the Kaffirs. He went to war with the Zulus, whom, if he had been wise, he would have helped and favoured as a check upon the ambition of the Boers. A British regiment was cut to pieces. The Zulus in expiation were shot down in thousands and their nationality extinguished. Frere's policy was his own; Lord Beaconsfield was not responsible for it, and did not approve of it. Yet the war went on.

The Transvaal had been annexed against the will of the people. Disraeli had fallen before that measure had borne its fruits, but he lived to hear of Majuba Hill and the ignominious capitulation in which, in that part of the world also, jingoism came to its miserable end.

The grand chance had been given to English Conservatism, and had been lost in a too ambitious dream. Like drunkards recovering from a debauch and revolting at their own orgies, the constituencies once more recalled the Radicals to power with a fresh impulse to the revolutionary movement, and Disraeli may have reflected too late on the uselessness of embarking on 'spirited policies,' which the next swing of the democratic pendulum may reduce to impotence.

His administration was not useless. Unambitious home measures were passed for the comfort or benefit of the people, which may be remembered gratefully when the Berlin Conference is forgotten. His patronage, and especially his literary and art patronage, was generously and admirably exercised. John Leech had for twenty years made him ridiculous in the cartoons in *Punch*. Leech had a pension which would have died with him. Disraeli continued it to his widow and his children. Most notable was his recognition of the duty of the country to bestow some public honour on Thomas Carlyle. For half a century Carlyle had worked his way in disregarded poverty. The wise throughout Europe had long acknowledged in him the most remarkable writer of his age. He had been admired for his genius and reverenced for his stern integrity; the German Empire had bestowed upon him its most distinguished decoration; but in England it is held that the position which an eminent man of letters makes for himself can receive no added lustre from the notice of the Government; and Carlyle had been left severely alone in his modest home at Chelsea under all the changes of Administration, while peerages and titles were scattered among the brewers and the City million-aires. Disraeli, who was a man of intellect as well as a politician, perceived the disgrace which would attach to all parties if such a man as this was allowed to pass away as one of the common herd. Carlyle, indeed, had never spoken of him except with contempt, but it was Disraeli's special credit that while he never forgot a friend he never remembered a personal affront. He saw at once that no common pension or decoration at so late an hour could atone for the long neglect. In a letter as modest as it was dignified he implied that he did not offer Carlyle a peerage because a hereditary honour would be a mockery to a childless old man; but he did offer in the Queen's name, and pressed him to accept, the Grand Cross of the Bath, a distinction never before conferred upon any English author, with a life income corresponding to such a rank. Carlyle in his poorest days would never have accepted a pension. Stars and ribands had no attraction for him at any time, and less than none when he had one foot in the grave. He declined, but he was sensible of the compli-ment, and was touched at the quarter from which it came.

'Very proper of the Queen to offer it,' said the conductor of a Chelsea omnibus to me, 'and more proper of he to say that he would have nothing to do with it. 'Tisn't they who can do honour to the likes of he.' But Disraeli saved his country from the reproach of coming centuries, when Carlyle will stand among his contemporaries as Socrates stands among the Athenians, the one pre-eminently wise man to whom all the rest are as nothing.

---

1. It should be said that the Bill, though supported by Disraeli, was introduced by the Primate, and was not a Cabinet measure.

# XVII

*Retirement from office—Dignity in retreat—Hughenden—Lord Beaconsfield as a landlord—Fondness for country life—'Endymion'—Illness and death—Attempted estimate of Lord Beaconsfield—A great man? or not a great man?—Those only great who can forget themselves—Never completely an Englishman—Relatively great, not absolutely—Gulliver among Lilliputians— Signs in 'Sybil' of a higher purpose, but a purpose incapable of realisation— Simplicity and blamelessness in private life—Indifference to fortune—Integrity as a statesman and administrator*

'Was man in der Jugend wünscht, davon hat man im Alter die Fülle' (What one desires in one's youth one has enough of in one's age).

DISRAELI HAD WON IT ALL, all that to his young ambition had seemed the only object for which it was worthwhile to live. Yet he had gained the slippery height only, perhaps, to form a truer estimate of the value of a personal triumph. It was his to hold but for a moment, and then he fell, too late in life to retrieve another defeat. When the shadows lengthen and the sun is going down, earthly greatness fades to tinsel, and nothing is any longer beautiful to look back upon but the disinterested actions, many or few, which are scattered over the chequered career. Disraeli, like many other distinguished men, had to pay the penalty of his character. A fool may have his vanity satisfied with garters and peerages. Disraeli must have been conscious of their emptiness.

When the result of the elections of 1880 was known he again accepted his fate, as Mr Gladstone had done six years before, without waiting for the meeting of Parliament. He submitted with dignity, though with the fatal consciousness that at his age he could not hope to witness a reversal of the judgment upon him. He did not talk petulantly of retiring from politics. He took his place again as leader of the Opposition in the House of Lords, and showed no signs of weakened power. But he had always been impatient of the details of business, and his chief pleasure was now to retire to Hughenden, with or without companions, most frequently alone. For a fortnight together he would remain there in solitude, wandering through the park or through the Bradenham woods, which in his youth had been the scene of so many ambitions or moody meditations. His trees, his peacocks, his swans, his lake and chalk stream were sadly associated with the memories of his married life. He was so fond of his trees that he directed in his will that none of them should be cut down. He was on pleasant terms with his tenants and labourers; he visited them in their cottages, and was specially kind to old people and to little children. The 'policy of sewage,' with which he had been taunted as a Minister, was his practice as a landlord. No dust-heaps, or cesspools, or choked drains, or damp floors were to be seen among the Hughenden tenements. To such things he looked with his own eyes, and he said he never was so happy as when left to himself in these occupations.

Of his reflections at this period some may be found hereafter in the papers which he bequeathed to Lord Rowton. No particular traces appear in the last literary work which in his final leisure he contrived to accomplish. He had left *Endymion* half-finished when he took office in 1874; he went on with it when office had left him, perhaps. because he had thought himself obliged to buy a house in London on retiring from Downing Street and wanted money.

There is nothing remarkable in *Endymion* except the intellectual vivacity, which shows no abatement. It is in the style of his earlier novels, and has little of the serious thought which is so striking in *Sybil* and *Lothair*. There are the same pictures of London fashionable life and fashionable people, in the midst of them a struggling youth pushing his way in the great world, and lifted out of his difficulties, as he himself had been, by a marriage with a wealthy widow. As before many of the figures are portraits. Myra, the heroine, impatient, restless, ambitious, resolute to raise herself and her brother above the injuries of fortune, is perhaps a likeness of himself in a woman's dress. But the calm mastery of modern life, the survey, wide as the world, of the forces working in English society, the mellow and impartial wisdom which raises *Lothair* from an ephemeral novel into a work of enduring value, all this is absent. It is as if disappointment had again clouded his superior qualities and had brought back something of his original deficiencies. The most interesting feature in *Endymion* is the exact photograph of the old manor house at Bradenham, and the description of the feelings with which a fallen and neglected statesman of once brilliant promise retired there into unwelcome poverty. Except for this the book might have been unwritten and nothing would have been lost of Disraeli's fame. It throws no fresh light upon his own character. He wanted money and it brought him ten thousand pounds.

The sand ran rapidly out. Lord Beaconsfield was in his place at the opening of the session of 1881. The effects of the return of the Liberal party were already visible in all parts of the Empire. He spoke with something of his old force on the state of things which was to be expected in Ireland. He spoke on India and foreign politics. He could not foresee the bombardment of the Alexandrian forts, the conquest of Egypt, to be followed by the disgrace of Khartoum. He escaped the mortification of the surrender to Russia on the Afghan frontier. But he lived to hear of the conclusion of the annexation of the Transvaal. He saw the enemies of England again at their work across St. George's Channel, and a Government again in power whose rule was to purchase peace by concession. His own part was played out. He had not succeeded, and it was time for him to be gone. In the middle of March he had an attack of gout, which was aggravated by a cold. At first no danger was anticipated, but he grew worse day after day, and on the 19th of April Benjamin Disraeli had taken his last leave of a scene in which he had so long been so brilliant an actor. When an English statesman dies, complimentary funeral orations are spoken over him in Parliament as part of the ordinary course; but Disraeli had been so uncommon a man that the displays on this occasion had more in them than they often have of genuine sincerity. He had been so long among us that his name had become a household word. The whole nation, of all shades of politics, felt that a man was gone whose place could not be filled, who in a long and chequered career had not only won his honours fairly but deserved affectionate remembrance.

He was infinitely clever. In public or private he had never done a dishonourable action; he had disarmed hatred and never lost a personal friend. The greatest of his antagonists admitted that when he struck hardest he had not struck in malice. A still higher praise belongs to himself alone—that he never struck a small man.

The Abbey was offered, and a public funeral; and if honour there be in such interments he had an ample right to it. By his own desire he was buried at Hughenden, by the side of his wife and the romantic friend who had conceived so singular an attachment to him. There those three rest side by side, Disraeli and his faithful companion disguised as Earl and Viscountess, but thought of only by the present generation under their own familiar name, and the eccentric and passionate widow who had devoted her fortune to him. In life there had been a peculiar bond between these three. Disraeli had innumerable admirers, but there were not many to whom he trusted his inmost confidence. Gratitude was stronger in him even than ambition, and as to his wife and to Mrs Willyams he owed the most, to them, perhaps, he was most completely attached. It was a strange union, but they had strange natures, and they lie fitly and well together—far away from the world, for which neither of them cared, in a quiet parish church in Buckinghamshire.

A biography, however brief, must close with a general estimate. What estimate is to be formed of Disraeli? We have a standard by which to measure the bodily stature of a man; we have none by which to measure his character; neither need we at any time ask how great any man is, or whether great at all, but rather what he is. Those whom the world agrees to call great are those who have done or produced something of permanent value to humanity. We call Hipparchus great, or Newton, or Kepler, because we owe to them our knowledge of the motion of the earth and the stars. Poets and artists have been great men; philosophers have been great men. The mind of Socrates governs our minds at the present day. Founders of religion have been great men; reformers have been great men: we measure their worth by the work which they achieved. So in society and politics we call those great who have devoted their energies to some noble cause, or have influenced the course of things in some extraordinary way. But in every instance, whether in art, science, religion, or public life, there is an universal condition, that a man shall have forgotten himself in his work. If any fraction of his attention is given to the honours or rewards which success will bring him there will be a taint of weakness in what he does. He cannot produce a great poem, he cannot paint a great picture, he cannot discover secrets of science, because these achievements require a whole mind and not a divided mind. The prophet will be a prophet of half-truths, because the whole truth will not be popular. The statesman who has not purified himself of personal motives will never purify a disordered Constitution. Even kings and conquerors who are credited with nothing but ambition—the Alexanders and the Caesars, the Cromwells and Napoleons— have been a cause in themselves, have been the representatives of some principle or idea. Their force, when they have succeeded, has been an impulse from within. They have aimed at power to impress their own personality outside them, but their operations are like the operations of the forces of nature, working from within outwards rather than towards an end of which they have been conscious. A man whose object is to gain something for himself often attains it, but when his personal life is over his work and his reputation perish along with him.

In this high sense of the word Lord Beaconsfield cannot be called great, either as a man of letters or as a statesman. *Vivian Grey* is nothing but a loud demand on his contemporaries to recognise how clever a man has appeared among them. In every one of his writings there is the same defect, except in *Sybil* and in *Lothair*. It is absent in *Sybil* because he had been deeply and sincerely affected by what he had witnessed in the great towns in the North of England; it is absent in *Lothair* because when he wrote that book his personal ambition had for the time been satisfied, and he could look round him with the *siccum lumen* of his intellect. He had then reached the highest point of his political aspiration, and money he did not care for unless required for pressing necessities. It is clear from *Sybil* that there had been a time when he could have taken up as a statesman, with all his heart, the cause of labour. He had suffered himself in the suffering and demoralisation which he had witnessed, and if the 'young generation' to whom he appealed would have gone along with him he might have led a nobler crusade than Coeur de Lion. But it was not in him to tread a thorny road with insufficient companionship. He had wished, but had not wished sufficiently, to undertake a doubtful enterprise. He was contented to leave things as he found them, instead of reconstructing society to make himself Prime Minister.

Thus it was that perhaps no public man in England ever rose so high and acquired power so great, so little of whose work has survived him. Not one of the great measures which he once insisted on did he carry or attempt to carry. The great industrial problems are still left to be solved by the workmen in their own unions. Ireland is still in the throes of disintegration. If the colonies have refused to be cast loose from us their continued allegiance is not due to any effort of his. From Berlin he brought back peace with honour, but if peace remains the honour was soon clouded. The concessions which he prided himself on having extorted are evaded or ignored, and the imperial spirit which he imagined that he had awakened sleeps in indifference. The voices which then shouted so loudly for him shout now for another, and of all those great achievements there remain only to the nation the Suez Canal shares and the possession of Cyprus, and to his Queen the gaudy title of Empress of India. What is there besides? Yet there is a relative greatness as well as an absolute greatness, and Lemuel Gulliver was a giant among the Lilliputians. Disraeli said of Peel that he was the greatest member of Parliament that there had ever been. He was himself the *strongest* member of Parliament in his own day, and it was Parliament which took him as its foremost man and made him what he was. No one fought more stoutly when there was fighting to be done; no one knew better when to yield, or how to encourage his followers. He was a master of debate. He had perfect command of his temper, and while he ran an adversary through the body he charmed even his enemies by the skill with which he did it. He made no lofty pretensions, and his aims were always perhaps something higher than he professed. If to raise himself to the summit of the eminence was what he most cared for, he had a genuine anxiety to serve his party, and in serving his party to serve his country; and possibly if among his other gifts he had inherited an English character he might have devoted himself more completely to great national questions; he might have even inscribed his name in the great roll of English worthies. But he was English only by adoption, and he never completely identified himself with the Country which he ruled. At heart he was a Hebrew to the end, and of all his triumphs perhaps the most satisfying was the sense that a member of that despised race had made himself the master of the fleets and armies of the proudest of Christian nations.

But though Lord Beaconsfield was not all which he might have been he will be honourably and affectionately remembered. If he was ambitious his ambition was a noble one. It was for fame and not for fortune. To money he was always indifferent. He was even ostentatious in his neglect of his own interests. Though he left no debts behind him, in his life he was always embarrassed. He had no vices, and his habits were simple; but he was generous and careless, and his mind was occupied with other things. He had opportunities of enriching himself if he had been unprincipled enough to use them. There were times when he could set all the stock exchanges of Europe vibrating like electric wires in a thunderstorm. A secret word from him would have enabled speculating capitalists to realise millions, with no trace left how those millions were acquired or how disposed of. It is said that something of the kind was once hinted to him—once, but never again. Disraeli's worst enemy never suspected him of avarice or dishonour. As a statesman there was none like him before, and will be none hereafter. His career was the result of a combination of a peculiar character with peculiar circumstances, which is not likely to recur. The aim with which he started in life was to distinguish himself above all his contemporaries, and wild as such an ambition must have appeared, he at least won the stake for which he played so bravely.